THIS IS GALEN DRAKE

THIS IS GALEN DRAKE

by Galen Drake

introduction by Joseph Auslander

DOUBLEDAY & COMPANY, INC., GARDEN CITY, NEW YORK, 1949

Galen Drake is heard regularly over the Columbia Broadcasting System's station WCBS, New York, under the auspices of the Housewives' Protective League.

TO FLETCHER WILEY,
my friend and colleague, without whose counsel and
encouragement this book would not have been possible

CONTENTS

INTRODUCTION

To millions of radio listeners there is a voice named Galen Drake. It is the coziest, coaxingest, convincingest voice on the air. It has been voted the most microgenic personality in radio today. It is an uncanny mixture of Kin Hubbard, Will Rogers, and just plain natural American schmalz. It has all the salty, offhand, elbows-on-the-table, down-to-earth sincerity of a Hoosier philosopher. It is wit in overalls and wisdom in levis.

If a man is known by the books he reads or the company he keeps, then Galen Drake is a pretty tough knot to untangle. He reads everything. He knows everybody. To Galen Drake the proper—and far the most exciting—study of mankind is man—and woman, to be sure—and he never stops studying both. He has a passion for people. One way or another, he is always engaged in trying to find out what makes us tick, in trying to track down the squeaks and unkink the kinks. He is always taking people apart and putting them together again like fine watches. It is, of course, an infinitely complex, delicate, dangerous, and fascinating adventure; next to books, perhaps even more than books (Galen Drake's first and fiercest love), the greatest and most fruitful adventure of all.

Here is a grab bag of good tangy talk, but with a difference. It is the talk of a singular man with a singular gusto for all the colorful and kaleidoscopic pageantry of life, all the sparkling and sprightly curiosities and oddities of knowledge from aardvark to zygote, from cabbages to kings. In addition to a memory with all the tenacious and elastic properties of bubble gum, Galen Drake possesses, to an uncommon degree, the power of selection, the sense of taste which can discriminate, in a flash, between the true and the false, the mica and the gold.

Personally, Galen Drake is an affable, easygoing fellow, of a profound and unaffected humility, who is at home anywhere, though you could hardly call him the backslapping bucko. In voice and manner he is gentle and courteous at all times; but that deceptively mild blue eye of his can flash fire and that tongue unleash lightning and thunder at any instance of injustice or act of cruelty. He is always and instinctively the infracaninophile—the defender of the underdog. Perhaps he reserves his special vials of scorn for the smug, self-righteous, sanctimonious breed of cat whose exaggerated ancestor worship—with its inevitable mumbo jumbo of racial and religious prejudice—is merely a cloak for his own glaring inadequacies.

Once, when we were discussing death and taxes and the high cost of tombstones, I ventured to inquire of Galen what he would like in the way of an epitaph—when the time came. He said, "You remember that wonderful prayer the Indians used to say when they went out into the forest to beg the Great Spirit for guidance. 'O Great Spirit, Maker of Men, forbid that I judge any man until I have walked for two moons in his moccasins.' Well, I don't know whether I deserve it, but I'd be mighty proud of an epitaph like that."

We recall how Sherlock Holmes once shocked the amiable, long-suffering Dr. Watson by his bland admission that he was not aware the earth traveled round the sun; and added insult to injury by remarking, "Now that I do know it I shall do my best to forget it." The good doctor's wry, comical expression of dismay and horror goads Sherlock to explain. "You see, I consider that a man's brain originally is like an empty attic, and you have to stock it with such furniture as you choose. A fool takes in all the lumber of every sort that he comes across, so that the knowledge which might be useful to him gets crowded out, or at best is jumbled up with a lot of other things, so that he has a difficulty in laying his hands upon it. . . . It is a mistake to think that that little room has elastic walls and can distend to any extent. . . . "

Now, this side idolatry, Galen Drake is an incorrigible Holmesian; nevertheless, his piety in this particular will not permit him to go along with his formidable hero. In fact, it is at this very point that the master sleuth and he part company. For Galen's mental housekeeper is pure pack rat; and his memory, monumental in disorder, is an infinitely expanding arsenal of apt illustration, pertinent anecdote, and bull's-eye caption. He is the robust refutation of Sherlock's thesis.

This is Galen Drake. His mind is always on the prowl in the jungles of human experience, always hunting down some hidden morsel of wisdom. He has a reporter's nose for the truth: even an unconsidered trifle may provide a feast.

This is Galen Drake. He loves a good story. He is himself a born storyteller, one of the best. He is also—which is not a negligible virtue —an excellent listener.

This is Galen Drake. He has a child's insatiable eagerness for knowing, a child's insatiable capacity for enthusiasm and wonder (plus the rare ability to communicate and kindle that knowledge, that enthusiasm, that wonder in the mind and heart of the listener). He has the honesty, the simplicity, the horizontal gaze of a child, steadfast and searching and utterly intolerant of buncombe. He has the mischievous and disturbing candor of a child.

This is Galen Drake. He loves to read. He would rather read than eat—and he loves to eat. But he would much rather talk than anything else—and he can talk about anything. He has a talent for talk that amounts to positive genius. Maybe it's in his blood and he can't help it. After all, his great-uncle was Stephen A. Douglas, who engaged in some plain and fancy debates with another talking man by the name of Abe Lincoln, and pretty near talked himself into the White House.

Endowed with the pertinacious curiosity of a child and the perpetual appetite of an encyclopedia, Galen Drake ranges the entire gamut of human knowledge and human experience. But he does not go around staggering under knowledge like a load on his back; he wears it like a flower in his lapel. He has nimble and capering graces of mind and spirit which leaven his learning and make him a robustious and rare companion. He has done more to rescue wisdom and truth from the jealous and exclusive clutches of the scholar than any man I know. He has performed a real public service in blowing the acrid archive dust off the thoughts and dreams and discoveries of the ages.

Incidentally, he is acknowledged to be one of the best salesmen on the air. He sells not only the products of his sponsors; he refuses to sell anything he isn't sold on first himself. He sells also such commodities as courage, faith, common sense, self-reliance, humility, tolerance, and truth—seasoned with a few warm chuckles and a considerable sprinkling of smiles.

They tell me that Galen Drake employs a variety of subtle and sometimes desperate devices to escape the consequences of success. This book, I believe, will not make his lot any easier. As F. Hopkinson Smith —or was it James Thurber?—long ago pointed out, the claw of the sea puss gets us all in the end.

Joseph Auslander

THIS IS GALEN DRAKE

WHAT THE BOYS WANT

Seems like somebody is always taking a poll on something. So, for the millionth time, some of the boys took a poll on what kind of a gal they'd most like to marry. Of course, they've only been doing that since the days of Helen of Troy, but that's all right. Here's one more. And the findings are kind of surprising; at least they surprised me.

Young fellows of college age put intelligence before beauty. And they list good health and love of children and neatness and good morals away ahead of sex appeal, and they want their gals to have some kind of religious training. Here's the way the college boys stack up the qualities they're looking for in wives: intelligence, beauty of form and figure, good health, congenial companionship, love for children, neatness, character, smart clothes, good sportsmanship, modesty, good morals, sincerity, wit, sense of humor, honesty, truthfulness, sex appeal, and friendliness.

But when you get to the older guys, it's all different. They want the good-lookers. The majority of mature men will state that a guy wants just two things in his woman: looks and personality. The most desirable, and remember, this is the gal the majority of men picked out, is just a little younger than her man, she's dark, reasonably slender, intelligent, has a fairly good figure, is taller than average, and is extremely affectionate in disposition. Now remember, I didn't figure out these things; the rest of the boys did. The emphasis on physical attractiveness is pronounced among the older fellows, but only ten per cent insisted that a wife has to be really pretty. The other ninety per cent settled for smart-looking, snazzy clothes, good grooming, and a generally pleasant appearance. Fifteen per cent want to marry a blonde, and the other eighty-five want brunettes, and thirty-three per cent say they wouldn't take a blonde under any circumstances. Maybe to look at, but not for marrying purposes. And about seventeen per cent said that they wanted a gal who is anywhere from plump to frankly buxom. Maybe they figure the fatties are better cooks or something. I wouldn't know. But they prefer two hundred pounds of curves to one hundred pounds of nerves. Very few wanted a little lady, under five foot four; five foot six and up is preferred, but of course there's limits in that direction, too, although most of the men of average height said they'd be perfectly happy to have wives taller than themselves, and some preferred them that way. And they were just about unanimous in declaring that if the gal has a few features which appealed to them, they wouldn't even see others that aren't too good. She don't have to be perfect, just as long as she's got something. The idea is that a real fancy pair of ankles can make up for a button nose, and big blue eyes can take a guy's mind off buck teeth.

The boys agreed that the only really ugly gals are either ugly because they're crude, or they're sloppy and messy, or they look ugly because they have unpleasant expressions. And they're agreed on another thing, too. If a gal happens to have some disfiguring feature, a bad chin or an unfortunate nose or something like that, even a scar, they don't hold it agin her if she hies herself to a plastic surgeon and gets done over. They're all for that.

It's kind of interesting to note that John Powers, the famous model agents, puts perfect features last on his list of beauty requirements. His top ingredients are: a radiant personality, integrity of character, complete self-assurance, and intellectual curiosity. That's what he thinks the boys want, and he might be right.

Oh, and by the way, you know how the Bedelias talk about wanting their guys to be "tall, dark, and handsome"? Well, statistics show that only one man in every two hundred gets to be six feet. So that search ain't too promising. Maybe they dream of Gary Cooper, but they'd better settle for a Joe with a good disposition, even if he don't have his head way up in the stratosphere.

JUST FOR TODAY

Just for Today—I will be happy. This assumes that what Abraham Lincoln said is true, that most folks are just about as happy as they make up their minds to be. Happiness is from within, it is not a matter of externals.

Just for Today—I will adjust myself to what is and not try to adjust everything to my own desires. I will take my family, my business, and my luck as they come and fit myself to them.

Just for Today—I will take care of my body. I will exercise it, I will care for it, and nourish it, and not abuse it, nor neglect it, so that it will be a perfect machine for my soul.

Just for Today—I will strengthen my mind, or try to. I will study. I will learn something useful. I will not be a mental loafer all day. I will read something that requires effort, and thought, and concentration.

Just for Today—I will exercise my soul in three ways. I will do somebody a good turn, and not get found out. If anybody knows of it, it won't count. I will do at least two things I don't want to do, as William James suggests, just for exercise. I will not show anyone that my feelings are hurt today. They may be hurt, but just for today, I'm not going to show it.

Just for Today—I'm going to be agreeable. I'll look as well as I can. I will dress as becomingly as possible. I will talk low. I will act courteously. I'll be liberal with flattery. I'll criticize not one bit, nor find fault with anything, and not try to regulate, nor improve anyone.

Just for Today—I'll have a program. I'll write down just what I expect to do every hour. I may not follow it exactly, but I'll have it. It will save me from the two pests—hurry and indecision.

Just for Today—I'll have a quiet half hour all by myself and relax. In this half hour I'll think of God, so as to get a little more perspective to my life.

Just for Today—I will be unafraid, especially I will not be afraid to be happy, to enjoy what is beautiful, to love and to believe that those I love, love me.

All these things I will do just for today!

Anonymous

SARAH BERNHARDT'S CORSETS

It's a funny thing, how a little thing like one particular woman's whim about a dress style can change a whole industry, but that sort of deal goes on all the time. Empire styles came in with Josephine, Napoleon's ever-loving wife. The Empress Eugénie set a whole train of styles, and we had a revival of them a few years back when every gal went around with one of those little tippy hats on her head.

But there was one woman who knocked the dress business into a cocked hat, and then gave it a comeback that swamped the wildest dreams of the style authorities, and that woman was Sarah Bernhardt.

Up until the 1870s, fashion decreed that the gals wear tight-fitting, wasp-waisted corsets that warped the human form into such a strange shape that every dress had to be fitted individually to the woman who was going to wear it. Ready-made dresses were unheard of. You can't have ready-made dresses when no two women, strapped in wasp-waist corsets, bulged out in the same places, upper and lower, where the corsets left off.

Sarah Bernhardt, the greatest actress of her day, and, perhaps, of any day, decided she was having none of that wasp-waist stuff, and what Sarah said was law to every woman in the world, as far as styles went, anyhow. So her dressmakers had to design an entirely new type of corset for her, a much looser and freer garment with a straight front. So of course every other fashionable woman had a straight-front corset, too.

It didn't take the boys long to find out that women who wore straight-front corsets could be sorta catalogued according to definite size and shape, and one size sixteen was just like another, as far as the fit of dresses went. The sewing machine had been invented by Elias Howe some twenty years before, but its use had been confined to the home. Now that ready-made dresses had become practical, factories were set up, and the wholesale dress industry, as we know it today, got its first start. In the beginning, working conditions were bad, but today hundreds of thousands of people, many of them women, have jobs because Sarah Bernhardt changed the style of her corsets.

THE USE OF THE WORD "LOVE"

A while ago I read a discussion of the loose and unsatisfactory way we use the word "love." This was in a book called *Faith and Freedom*, by the Rev. Russell J. Clinchy, who has his pulpit up Hartford way.

Now this isn't about speaking of love the way the gals do when they say, "Oh, I just *love* that darling dress . . ." or "Don't you *love* Clark

4

Gable's mustache?" Using "love" that way is just an affected little trick of speech that don't mean much of anything.

What Dr. Clinchy points out, and I'll admit I've sorta puzzled over this myself, from time to time, is that we use the word "love" to cover a whole slew of situations and emotions that haven't got the slightest thing to do with each other. They don't even belong in the same league.

For one thing, there's romantic love. Romantic love covers everything from the deep and abiding affection and companionship of two people after a lifetime of happy marriage to the flush of infatuation a guy feels on his first date with a pretty girl that he wants to make a good impression on. And the psychologists use the phrase "love impulse" practically synonymous with "sex impulse." It can mean anything from a tender flutter of attraction between boy and girl to the mad and dangerous urges of the sex maniac. Seems to me we kinda need a couple of extra words in the language to cover these different meanings.

Then there's the love we bear for members of our family. Love for our fathers and mothers differs from love for our brothers and sisters, and love for our children is still another kettle of fish. It isn't that we love one more than the other; we love them differently, and it seems as if there ought to be some simple easy word to describe this difference.

We love our friends. That's still another kind of love. And we love our country, but we don't love our country quite the way we love a helpless little child or a mother or a father of our best girl. It's all a little mixed up.

And there's another kind of love which has nothing to do with any of these; it's a kind of combination of charity and mercy and forgiveness and loyalty put together. You know how in the Bible it says: "Love thy enemies" . . . well, anybody who ever gave this any thought knows that you aren't supposed to love your enemies the way you love your wife, or the way you love your country's flag. That don't make sense. What's closer to it is good will and not bearing grudges. "Love thy enemies" really means "Don't get burned up with hate for your enemies." It also means you should do a good turn for your fellow man, friend or enemy, without expecting a reward or being afraid of the consequences. It ties in with the Golden Rule—"Do as you would be done by"—but it definitely don't mean anything like your love for your family or friends or sweetheart.

Now, as it happens, the ancient Greeks managed this business better

5

than we do. They had one word for all possible love relations between man and woman, and that word was "*eros*." We have it today in the word "erotic." Then they had another word for love of family and friends, "*philias*." We have it in the name "Philadelphia," the city of brotherly love. Then they had a third word, "*agape*," which means exactly that mixture of good will and not bearing grudges mentioned in the Bible. And love of God is still another kind of love.

Now, I don't suppose, at this late date, we can unscramble the problem and put into popular use all the simple, understandable words that would be needed to designate these different kinds of love, but it would be just as well to take heed and not add to the confusion by using the word "love" to describe how you feel about the latest styles or a new hair-do or the picture you saw Tuesday night. The way some of you gals use that word, you'd think it was the only verb in the English language. Of course, that's better than if you "hated" everything and everybody. That'd lead to a fine state of affairs. But just sorta try not to overwork that "love" deal so it stretches over everything from your new parlor curtains to dear old Grandma, because if you do, it don't do either Grandma or the curtains credit.

MRS. WHITEHOUSE'S PUBLICITY STUNT

Every once in a while, you hear about some extraordinary and extremely effective publicity stunt. There was a publicity man named Harry Reichenbach who was famous for them. He was the guy who took a lion into the old Waldorf-Astoria Hotel to stir up a little comment on lions in general, and the current stage production of George Bernard Shaw's *Androcles and the Lion* in particular. The play hadn't been doing so well up to then, but when Harry bust loose with his bright idea, there weren't enough seats in the house to hold the clamoring customers.

Well, back in 1919 and 1920, when women's suffrage was the hottest issue in the land, Mrs. Norman de R. Whitehouse thought up a publicity stunt which was just about as effective, on a national scale, as Harry's was with the New York theatergoing folks. Mrs. Whitehouse was a prominent leader of the suffrage movement, and she came up with the bright idea of throwing a scare into the masculine world, who insisted that "women's place is in the home," by asking that all women stay home for just one day.

Well, she sent copies of her plan to the newspapers, and chaos broke out on the spot. Department stores, telephone companies, hospitals and schools, and every employer of women's labor rose up and howled, because if all the women stayed home, even for one day, the business of the country had to stop until the gals came back to work. And the bluff worked. All those employers saw, right off, that if women were getting so important that business couldn't go on without them, they might as well give the gals the vote and keep them happy. Maybe it proved that old saw about "You can't live with 'em and you can't live without 'em," but there it was. And not long after Mrs. Whitehouse's little idea, the ladies were voting, and that's all there is to that little tale.

HOUSEWORK AS IS HOUSEWORK

You know that old saying: "Man must work from sun to sun, but woman's work is never done"? Well, maybe it seems that way; when the old man comes home from his job he's through for the day, while the gals still have dishes to wash and the kitchen to sweep up and a big basket of mending waiting for them to spend the evening on. But no matter how hard you work at housework nowadays, you can be mighty sure you don't do anywhere near as much as women used to a few years back. I don't know what they made the Bedelias out of in the pioneer days; it must have been cast iron. I don't know how a farm wife, for instance, lasted long enough to raise a family, with all the work she had to do, and, as a matter of fact, they didn't last too long. About fifteen years of it was the average of what they could take, and then they retired to permanent peace and the farmer married himself another gal to take over where the first one left off.

Some of the boys have researched the old New England cemeteries out in the farm districts, and the findings are that the father of the family lasted out the full threescore and ten years allotted to him in the Old Testament, and, more than likely, he wore out three wives in the process. The first one, married at sixteen or seventeen, probably wore out around thirty, and there's her headstone to prove it. The next one, also married in her teens, would last for another fifteen years, and after Old Abner buried her he picked himself out a middle-aged widow who usually outlived him. At least, that's what the records say.

Of course, the reason why life on a farm was so hard on women in the early days is that each household had to be sufficient unto itself. In addition to cooking and cleaning and looking after the kids, some-times nine or ten of them, because they had huge families, a farmer's wife made all the clothes the family wore, and she made the cloth, too. She took raw wool from the farm's sheep and raw flax from the farm's fields, and prepared the fibers and spun them into thread. She wove the thread into cloth on a heavy, homemade loom. Sometimes she got to go for a walk in the forest, not to look at the pretty scenery, but to gather barks and herbs to dye the wool and flax with.

Everything pertaining to the henyard was her business, including the feather beds she made out of feathers from the chickens the family ate and the wild fowl the menfolks shot. Of course, she made the bedquilts, too, and they had to have plenty for those cold winter nights before anybody ever heard of steam heat. She made the hooked rugs; that was supposed to be recreation. She brewed the family medicines, from herbs brought over from England and planted in her herb garden, which she tended herself, and from wild herbs she learned about from the Indians. Of course, the farmer tended to the main crops of the fields, but she raised the family vegetables, just like her husband raised the cows and sheep, but she had the chickens and ducks and geese and turkeys on her hands. If Hubby was a good egg, he plowed the land up for her in the spring, and he might give her a hand with the heavy stuff, like pumpkins and such, at harvest time, but the rest of it, all the planting and weeding and cultivating, she did herself. And if he didn't happen to be a good egg, she did the plowing, too, and maybe helped him with his, out in the main fields.

Then the farmer's wife made all the candles they used around the house, out of tallow and beeswax, and if she was lucky enough to have beeswax to make 'em out of, that meant she had a few beehives to take care of, too. She made all the soap the family used, out of grease saved from cooking and lye which she made herself out of hardwood ashes which she, naturally, took out of the fireplace. Could be, she split that wood to make the fire in the first place. And she cooked the meals over the open fire in that same fireplace, too, which ain't exactly like nowa-days, when you cook on a modern gas or electric stove which will even turn on and off of itself.

She got a chance to get outdoors and see the flowers in the summer-

8

time, though; that is, she saw 'em while she was picking berries and lugging them home to make jam out of. She put up the winter's supply of food—mincemeat, salt meat, smoked hams, corned beef, salt fish, and so on—and she sun-dried bushels of apples so's she could spend her spare time making pies in the winter.

Of course, a couple of times a year, she got to a quilting bee, sewing quilts, or a harvest supper, which she had to pitch in and help cook. But about the only regular rest she ever did have was sitting absolutely still on a hard bench listening to those three- and four-hour-long sermons they used to have of a Sunday. That was the only time she ever got to sit down and fold her hands and do nuthin'. I bet sometimes she wished the sermon would last five hours instead of four.

Of course, the old man didn't have it too easy, either, back in the pioneer days. It was hard labor, from dawn to dark, but at least he got off fishing or hunting with the boys once in a while, and in the winter he didn't have so much to do, aside from taking care of the stock. Mostly he did some carpentry around the house and repaired his tools and harness and such, but that was easy compared with what the women did. Their work went right on, winter and summer and spring and fall. There never was any letup at all. So of course they wore out early. Nowadays the boys who mess around with statistics figure that a woman is likely to survive a man by anywhere from six to eight years, but not in those days.

THE HIGH COST OF MARRIAGE

I don't know if anybody has figured out exactly what the average bridegroom spends on his bride before the parson says those fatal words. Probably some of the boys have worked out those figures, because they're always making up statistics, about one thing and another. But if they have, I haven't seen it.

However, I do know just what it costs to get a gal into a marrying frame of mind down in East Africa. A list came out a while back telling how much a bride costs in those parts, and how the payment must be made. And it's pretty steep. In fact, it's enough to consign quite a few young men to lifelong bachelorhood—which may or may not be a good thing, depending on how you look at it. But if the boy wants his girl,

9

it's gonna set him back one hundred and eighty bucks and ten cents. There's a flat rate on brides in East Africa, a rate established by law in 1906 and still holding today. He pays out the hundred and eighty in the following order:

6000 spears	$100.00	5 hats	2.50
12 guns	30.00	13 pots of salt	6.00
2 barrels of powder	1.00	2 knives	.50
70 boar tusks	15.00	2 packages of beads	.50
2 sheep	12.00	2 packages of flints	.20
2 iron pots	2.00	1 hatful of buttons	.40
10 pieces of cloth	10.00		

HABITS THAT DESTROY LOVE

During courtship and honeymoon days, you've been up on Cloud 7 sailing through the azure skies without hitting a single air pocket. But three days ago Joe went back to work at the office, and just this morning you noticed he has kind of a funny habit of sipping his coffee audibly, and, though it never occurred to you until right now, that custom of his of hanging his pajamas on the floor in the morning and his clothes in the same spot at night is gonna get kinda monotonous as time goes on.

If you're just noticing these things now, maybe you're lucky. Many honeymoons hardly begin before these annoying little habits and a few dozen others make themselves evident. And don't think he's got a corner on the habit department. You've a collection of your own that he'll start noticing sooner or later, if he hasn't already.

However, these annoying habits are by no means glaring faults of character. Their insidious power to sour an otherwise happy marriage lies in their eternal repetition, like the drip, drip, drip from a leaky faucet that frazzles the nerves past endurance. In this way a minor annoyance becomes unexpectedly powerful in making or breaking marital happiness.

Of course, your Joe may have a set of habits that are kinda on the weird side, and nobody else on earth has anything like them. But probably both he and you annoy each other with the same annoyances that practically every other husband and wife rasp each other's nerves with, all the while being themselves quite unconscious that they're doing anything at all. For instance, most men complain that their wives talk too much, and the wimmenfolk counter with the argument that their husbands are unresponsive, and that it's impossible to find out what a man's thinking except when he's in the mood to criticize something. The psychologists say that these are just the normal differences in temperament between the two sexes, but it's as well to guard against these natural tendencies becoming irritating habits.

Some gals can practically drive their husbands to the happy house by reading aloud magazine and newspaper items in which the poor guys haven't a speck of interest. However, as far as bad newspaper habits go, few things are more annoying and unflattering than for a husband to hide himself in glorified isolation behind the double-spread sports section at breakfast. Believe it or not, that one particular little item has caused a lot of couples to split up the blankets.

Another very annoying habit to a fastidious wife is a husband's disregard for his personal neatness. Dropping his clothes where he takes them off, failure to shave daily and bathe regularly, messing up the bathroom with wet towels and stray toothpaste caps and leaky shaving brushes and used razor blades that lurk for unwary fingers, carelessly sprinkled ashes and crumpled papers, all these are slow death to any wife who takes particular pride in her home. Of course, overcleanliness can work both ways, too, because sometimes it's the wife who's personally careless, who clutters the bureau drawers and cupboards with miscellaneous junk. She's the gal who has no regard for the sanctity of her husband's desk and no interest in whether he has a supply of clean socks and handkerchiefs or whether he's down to the last rag he owns.

A woman who is habitually untidy about her dress or person runs a serious risk of losing her husband's esteem. There's little that's more disconcerting or discouraging to a man than to have his wife sit down to breakfast with her hair done up in barbed wire and herself in an old robe that looks like a discarded bird-cage cover.

A lot of women become slovenly in appearance at home because, they complain, their husbands never notice what they have on anyway, even though they may have taken particular pains to doll themselves up. It's a wise husband who will make a point of complimenting his wife on her new hair-do or her dress or her housecoat. If she's earned a spontaneous compliment, she ought to be sure of receiving one.

Then there's the jerk who brings a couple of the boys (and their wives) home for dinner without first investing a nickel in a phone call

11

to break the news. If he and his friends get that lowered brow and that steady look from the little woman, he has only himself to blame. Like as not, he'll have to end up taking the whole crowd to some snazzy restaurant that his wife has been hankering to go to for ages and hasn't had the nerve to suggest before. Seeing as how he brought it on himself, if he gets out of the predicament at something under ten dollars a plate, he's a very lucky guy. These guests-for-dinner-at-the-last-moment deals have carried many a domestic fracas far into the night. If the dinner is to be at home, a wife has a right to at least a full day's notice, and preferably two or three. In addition to the necessary extra shopping, she probably has to break out the extra spoons and Aunt Minnie's lace tablecloth, not to mention getting her hair done for the occasion.

Here are a few more habits that both men and women can get awfully tired of: unnecessary and repeated lateness, lack of faith, unreasonable jealousy, moodiness, bossiness, demands for rigid accounting for every penny, repetition of the same old jokes, public love-making, bragging, and juvenile horseplay before spectators. Except for lateness and unreasonable jealousy, both of which the gals give free rein as the whim comes over them, I'm afraid that these annoying habits are almost entirely masculine. However, neither sex has a patent on needling one another, public ridicule, petty lying and deceit, any one of which, grown into a flourishing habit, can turn your Garden of Eden into a vacant lot.

Every one of these habits can be faced and overcome. Every marriage is affected by a few of them at the beginning, and they can destroy love just as completely as can the more serious troubles such as brutality or drunkenness or depravity of any sort. Nevertheless, most of us weed them out as we adjust to our marriage partner; if we didn't, there would be no happy marriages at all in the world. All life is growth, and marriage is only a very important part of life. Good will, understanding, intelligence, and, above all, kindness are the unfailing antidotes to habits destructive to love. If we are truly kind, we cannot bear to wound our loved ones, even by whistling off key or leaving the soap in the bathtub.

TELL HER SO

Amid the cares of married life,
In spite of toil or business strife,
If you value your sweet wife,
Tell her so.

When days are dark and very blue,
She has her troubles, same as you.
Show her that your love is true,
Tell her so.

Your love for her is no mistake,
You feel it, dreaming or awake,
Don't conceal it. For her sake,
Tell her so.

Never let her heart grow cold,
Richer beauties will unfold,
And she is worth her weight in gold,
Tell her so.

Anonymous

I BEG YOUR PARDON

One time a friend of mine got into a little discussion with me about all
the wishes and salutations that we hand out without particularly thinking them over first. We were just kicking around the subject of how
many times in his life the average guy says Hello, and How are you, and
Merry Christmas and Happy New Year when he ain't even noticing he's
saying the expression, and he don't particularly care if the person he
says it to has a Happy New Year or goes and jumps in the lake.

Some of these common social expression become a habit after a while.

13

I don't suppose that when people say How do you do to one another, they care in the least how the other fellow does. They don't want to know how he does at all. It's just something to start a conversation with, like Hello, or How's tricks. They have no desire to inquire into the guy's health, or the state of his business, and the last thing they want is to get a long earful about it. Did you ever say How do you do to somebody and have him take half an hour to tell you about how he does, just as if you were really interested? You wish you'd never bumped into the bore in the first place.

Then there are the folks who say some simple phrase in such an insulting manner that you'd like to hit 'em over the head with a flower-pot. Suppose you get into a crowded elevator and bump into somebody accidentally, and before you get your mouth open to say Excuse me, he raps out with an *I beg your pardon?* in such an insulting tone of voice that about all you can do is give the guy a steady look and hope he'll slip on a banana peeling. Actually, the bump was accidental, and as much your fault as his, or his as yours, whichever way you want to think of it, and it don't make a speck of difference which one of you said the necessary Excuse me or I beg your pardon or whatever phrase first came to mind to prove that you were both civilized people who don't crash into strangers on purpose.

I can't help wishing we could put a little fresh meaning into these common everyday phrases. I wish that we'd either say How do you do and really mean it, or we'd use some other expression that wouldn't tempt people to tell us how they do. And I wish we would never use that *I beg your pardon?* deal in an insulting tone. And I wish that when we say Merry Christmas and Happy New Year we'd really take a little interest in whether the other guy is having one, or whether he's so miserable he don't even know what day it is.

Not long ago, I heard about a movement afoot to cut all the stilted salutations and form phrases out of business letters. I think I'd go along with that. Take some little item in your morning's mail that starts out "Dear Mr. So-and-so: Yours of the nineteenth instant to hand, contents duly noted and beg leave to state." And then the real part of the letter starts, about two paragraphs down.

Of course, you aren't his "Dear Mr. So-and-so." He never laid eyes on you. So why not just write your name, or even start the letter with plain Hello? Then you start reading all that "nineteenth instant to hand" monkey business, clear down to the "Very truly yours" and the flourishing signature. After you've figured out the fancy stuff, all the letter boils down to is that you owe some money, and if you don't pay up they'll be over to take away the piano.

Maybe I'm wrong. Maybe the "Dear Mr. So-and-so" softens the blow, and the "Very truly yours" makes you feel as if it ain't such a harsh world after all. If we did pitch all this stuff out of the window, we'd have to go to all the trouble of thinking up some other salutations and closing expressions, I suppose. But I think we could get along very well by using fewer of them, and letting the ones we use really mean something. "I'm glad to see you" should mean just that, with no under-lying connotations of "Gosh, how can I get rid of this bore?" And "Good morning" should mean that your morning is okay, and you hope the other guy's is, too. Sometimes I think just cultivating a reasonably pleas-ant expression would take care of all those shopworn phrases without ever uttering them.

LEARN HOW TO WORK

Have you noticed that most of us feel constantly under pressure about not getting our work done, about having it pile up until it's unsurmount-able? You aren't the only one whose work gets so far behind that life ain't worth living. It happens to most people, and the reason it happens is that they actually don't know *how* to work.

Dr. Edward Spencer Cowles, the author of *Don't Be Afraid* (and by the way, that's a book you ought to read sometime; there's a lot of swell stuff in it)—Dr. Cowles says that he constantly has to teach patients who have been working hard all their lives *how* to work.

Some people work with their hands, and some are supposed to work with their heads. The trouble is that most of the head-work people don't work with their heads at all—they work with their emotions.

For instance, take the businessmen who rush all the time. They have to be taught the value of making haste slowly. Instead, they seem to feel that they are not doing anything unless they're running themselves ragged and their tongues are hanging out. They have no time for lunch; they bolt a sandwich at a counter or have something sent in to their desks. The telephone rings; they can't pick it up; they leap at it. When they interview a client, they sit on the edge of the chair and fume inwardly. Sometimes the fuming is not so inward. Even the client notices it. If someone comes to sell them something, even something as valuable as a new idea, they're too busy to listen.

Guys like that believe that they are accomplishing a great deal. They talk about how hard they work to build up the business. Well, they ain't building up the business, or anything else, as far as that goes. They're breaking themselves down. They are losing valuable energy all day long, not because they do so much but because they do not know *how* to do what they do.

They are not making use of their heads on the job. They are working with their emotions.

Dr. Cowles says that these businessmen could save themselves all that wasted nervous energy, and could accomplish a lot more, and have time out for relaxation, if they would only arrange their time the way a librarian arranges books on a shelf. You know how it is in most homes— the books are in the bookcase any old way, and if you want to read any particular book you have to hunt through the whole kit and ka-boodle to find it, and it's never in the same place twice. But a trained librarian keeps all the history books on one shelf, all the science books on another, all the novels on a third; the books that are used a lot are kept right out handy, and the ones there isn't much call for are put out of the way of the others.

So the idea is for a businessman to arrange his day the way a librarian arranges his books. If the day is planned in advance, either by himself or by his secretary, if before each appointment he has before him a note about each man he sees, and the nature of the business at hand, he'll lose no time or energy in coming to the point. He can sit back and make his visitor feel at ease, which is not only common courtesy: it helps to get the interview moving quickly, because there are no obstacles that take time for the visitor to surmount.

Dr. Cowles says also that it's very important not to set up prejudices and challenge everybody to overcome them. A business interview that turns into a wrestling match leaves the businessman in no shape to take on all the other guys who are waiting to see him. If he knocks himself out with just one interview, and has maybe thirty more scheduled for the day, it's easy to see where that leaves him.

And another thing: in business, pay strict attention to what the other guy says. You can't do it if you're listening with half your mind and making mental notes with the other half to call up So-and-so and send for the factory superintendent and remind Miss Frizzlewhiff to get those figures on the government contract. Three minutes of undivided attention will get the gist of what the other guy has to say. Then you can say to him: "Am I right in thinking that you offer me *this?* Is what you propose to do for us that?" In this way you can cut short any rambling he may be disposed to do, and you can dispose of the whole deal in about five minutes. Then spend the other five or ten in which you would ordinarily be wrestling with his proposition in friendly talk, a good laugh with the guy, cordial inquiries about himself or his family, and so forth. In this way, you can work with ease and humor. Instead of beating your brains out for fifteen minutes, you've actually been working for only five, and resting and rebuilding your nervous energy for ten minutes. What's more, you will send the guy away feeling that you've paid him every courtesy in giving him your undivided attention and in taking a personal and cordial interest in him and his proposition. You will have made a friend of him. And no business can be really successful without friends.

OUT OF THE MOUTHS OF BABES

I always did like those yarns about kids saying their prayers. Here's one that tickles my funnybone.

Little Suzybelle was listening very quietly while her father and a neighbor discussed politics at some length.

That night she knelt at her little bed and said her prayers as usual, but she wound up with a brand-new conclusion. "Bless Daddy, and bless Mommy, and please take good care of Yourself, because if anything happened to You, we'd only have the President, and he hasn't come up to Daddy's expectations."

MAKING THE HOME ATTRACTIVE TO WOMEN

In all the loose talk that goes on about the home being the foundation of a nation, nowadays we've kinda forgotten to make home life attractive to the one person who has most to do with it, the woman. We read a lot of books and magazine articles, and hear a lot of lectures on what wonderful careers there are for the gals in the modern world, but we kinda forget the one career that's essential to keep a country going, the career that our ancestors sure didn't forget, because if they had, we wouldn't be here. That's the career of being a wife and mother and running a home.

Now, since it looks as if women were here to stay, but if they don't stay home once in a while, humanity ain't going to stay long on earth, we'd better figure out ways to make home more attractive to the gals. Between a twenty-four-hour job of cooking, washing, baby-tending, and husband-soothing, and a nice desk job on a forty-hour-a-week basis, with your pay check all your own, you dames would be a little stupid to hold out for love, marriage, and kids, unless there are added inducements. And I'm not kidding—this is just common sense. The fact that a lot of women marry and then find out they've lost their freedom, and taken on a thankless job that barely gives them board and room, and they're overworked and bored stiff—well, that fact is responsible for an awful lot of divorces in our time. Back in the days when the gals stayed home because they didn't have any other place to go, folks didn't have to think about this problem, but nowadays it's pretty important.

So, what can we do to make home more attractive to the ladies?

For one thing, we can kinda remove the stigma of the word "housewife." You ask a gal what she does, and she says, "Oh, I'm just a housewife," and she says it kinda apologetically, as if she was ashamed of it—and she is. Why wouldn't she be, with Suzybelle, whom she went to school with, in the movies, and Daisy an executive in a big department store, and Lily a magazine editor, and here she's just a little old housewife, and she feels inferior. "Housewife" is kind of a bad word—it implies doing all kinds of menial tasks. It fairly reeks of dishpan hands and scrubbing down the cellar steps with yellow soap and sewing patches on Junior's overalls. A wife and mother probably has to do all these things, and a lot more, at one time or another, and maybe all the time, but she don't like to be reminded of it. She ain't exactly wild about that "housewife" tag being hung on her. We oughta hunt around and drag out some more attractive title to call her by.

Then there's the gal who has to take care of her home and her family, but there ain't quite enough money to go around, so she gets a job to help out in the financial department. If she's a very strong physical specimen, an active type who plans her time well and can take it, that's all right, if she feels that way and it's necessary, but it's really quite a strain on her, especially if the kids are small, and she's likely to skimp

18

her duties at home. If she skimps at the office, the boss will fire her. So if she neglects anything, it's the old man and the small fry. She'd really love to keep a nice home, but she ain't quite got the strength to do both, and they need the money. Something ought to be done to release her from this outside work so she can raise her family without strain and worry. Some sociologists have suggested government subsidies to relieve the economic pressure. In Germany the Nazis gave bonuses for babies; maybe that helped get the women back into the home, but it sure didn't keep them there, and it's doubtful if anything was accomplished except an increased birth rate, often without benefit of clergy.

Then, home would be more attractive to women if they took a more active part in the education of their children. But when a kid is around six, he's sent to school, and from there on his education is all in the hands of his teachers. Nowadays schools even like to have all the homework done in study periods during school hours, so Mom don't even have a chance to help with the arithmetic and spelling. Going over the schoolwork with the kids may not sound like a very exciting pastime, but actually it's very companionable and it brings the family close together. Women can supplement this by reading books with the kids, by sharing scrapbooks of poems and stories with them, and, later on, by taking courses with them in subjects of special interest. There's no reason why Mom and Sis can't take an art course together, or why young Oswald and his ma, and pa too, for that matter, can't all learn figure skating or carpentry or anything they have a mutual interest in. It gives them things to do together at home, interesting things that Mom can look forward to after a daylong session with the vacuum cleaner.

Then, most women like their homes a lot better if they have outside interests that give them a little rest from the housework, which, in spite of all the modern gadgets, is kind of monotonous. It wouldn't hurt Pop to pitch into the house cleaning every week so that Mom can have a few hours off for constructive work outside the home. She may enjoy social service, or Red Cross work, or she may teach a class in music or languages; she may be a consultant in some special field like catering or dressmaking or interior decorating, or she may want to devote a little time to whatever kind of work she did before she got married. She'll come back with renewed interest in her home if she has something else to do, a few hours a week, that's interesting and constructive and worth doing.

19

Then, the world could take a little interest in what a housewife—there's that word again—what a housewife does, and praise her accordingly. All too often her work is just taken for granted. When you drop in on a friend, it don't hurt a mite to mention how nice the new curtains look, and how clean and neat everything is, and what a pretty dress she made for Sister, and how good the cookies she's baking smell. It sorta gives the gal a boost and lights up the whole day. And of course it's part of a husband's job to praise his wife's housekeeping; anybody knows you can get more and better work done if you scatter a few kind words occasionally. So, even if her biscuits aren't exactly as good as Mom's used to be, maybe they'll get better if a guy at least gives her credit for trying. If she was working in an office, she'd get both praise and pay for special efforts and overtime work, so around the house time and effort ought to count, too.

It takes a lot more general capability to run a house than it does to run a typewriter or to follow a filing system or to operate a machine. Let's try to put homemaking on a par with other skilled labor, and somehow make the rewards at least as attractive as that weekly pay check the single girl gets from her job. If we don't, I, for one, can't exactly blame women for cold-shouldering the cares of a house and a family in favor of a forty-hour week and the rest of her time to herself. Home ought to be love and security and a paradise on earth, instead of a trap to be avoided at all costs.

HORSES HAVE FUN

If you've been around horses much, you've noticed that a well-treated dobbin, especially one that don't have to work too hard, usually has quite a sense of humor. Horses really have fun, no foolin'. And they're particularly fond of adopting other animals as companions and playmates.

For instance, fine race horses often have another animal in the stall with them to play with and to keep them from feeling lonesome. Animals get lonesome just like people, as you know if you've ever had a new puppy in the house, one that's just been taken away from its mother. That's one good way to be kept awake at night.

The famous race horse Seabiscuit never had a playmate, or mascot, as these animals are called when they're just kept around to keep the horses happy. Seabiscuit never seemed to need or want anything except to be alone, until one time a cat moved her family of kittens into his stall. He promptly adopted them and they were welcome to anything he had in the joint. They shared his dinner, and you wouldn't think kittens would be interested in the sort of stuff a hayburner gobbles up, but they were. They climbed all over him and played tag up and down his back, and he liked it. And they bedded down with him at night. After they grew up and drifted away from home, as cats do, Seabiscuit moped until his trainer hunted up another family of kittens, and that went on as long as Seabiscuit was in the racing game.

One of the most famous horse-and-mascot teams was that of the Kentucky Derby winner, Exterminator, and a fat little Shetland pony named Peanuts. For seventeen years these two romped and ate together, and slept side by side in the same stall. When they were out in the pasture they played the same game over and over: Peanuts would suddenly dart away, Exterminator would give him a head start and then take out after him, dash past, and turn around and give the little fellow a horse laugh. And sometimes Exterminator would tease Peanuts by suddenly leaning sidewise against him. When the pony thought things had gone far enough he'd try to kick, but the big horse would pin him right to the ground. Of course, he could have squashed him flat as a pancake if he wanted to, but he knew just how to keep Peanuts held down and helpless without hurting him a mite. Then they'd both stand up and Peanuts would lean against the big fellow and shove with all his might, while Exterminator stood there with his lip curled back, laughing his head off.

When visitors came to see the famous race horse, Peanuts always got shy, and hid in the corner of the stall. After Exterminator came out and met the folks and took his bows, he'd go in and get hold of Peanuts by taking the pony's mane in his teeth, and haul him out to meet his public, same as a mother has to drag Junior into the parlor by main force when company comes.

There's another example of a playful horse that comes to mind. This is a race horse, too, maybe not as famous as either Seabiscuit or Exterminator but still quite a critter. His name was Flood Town. Flood Town's constant companion was a little gray donkey named Christmas Night. The two were together constantly. They'd rather play tag in a pasture than eat. But once in a while Christmas Night got too fresh, and then he annoyed Flood Town so much that the big horse would make the little donkey stand in the corner as a punishment. He'd just take so much, and then he'd butt the little fellow into the corner and tell him in horse talk to stay there until he was told to come out. And Christmas Night would do it. After the two had been together for about a year, Christmas Night got so he could tell by the look in Flood Town's eye when he was due for a session of standing in the corner, and he'd trot over by himself and stay there quiet as a mouse until Flood Town whinnied at him that all was forgiven.

Maybe in the cold light of scientific study, it's right and proper to say that animals don't have a sense of humor, but I've always thought that any scientist who says that is just proving he don't have much of a one himself. I think they have just as much fun as people, and maybe even more, because they don't have so many things to worry about. Could be, what this world needs is a few more horse laughs.

WHAT DO YOU TALK ABOUT?

Ever notice how you can pick out the married couples in a restaurant or hotel dining room by the way they chomp away on their groceries and don't have much to say to each other? If Buster gives out with more than "Pass the salt," or "It looks like rain," it's a seven days' wonder. Momma may want to talk, and heaven knows she does enough of it when she's out with the girls, but there just don't seem to be much left to say to Father. Some couples are completely silent, and some talk only of money and bills, or the state of their health. Consciously or unconsciously, they take the attitude that they've been married for so many years that they're all talked out, and while they can get up a brisk wrangle over the price of having Junior's teeth straightened, they have nothing to say to one another about subjects of general interest. On the other hand, in some families the husband and wife discuss everything: their work, the books they've read, politics, world affairs, the kitchen plumbing, and the new family who's moving in next door.

There's no doubt that the folks who like to talk things over get more fun out of life. Of course, if two people are happy together, they're also happy in their silences, and it doesn't particularly matter if they do a lot of gabbing or not, or if one does more talking than the other. For instance, many women live rich and happy lives by seeing the world through their husband's eyes. They don't contribute much themselves, but they're perfectly content to listen to the man of the house telling about what a great little guy he is.

On the other hand, very few men can listen to a running stream of talk about the house and the kids without developing what is known as "husband deafness." Husband deafness is a protective technique which sets in early and soon becomes chronic, and once a wife has hardened her guy's ears to the point where he pays very little attention to her, it's pretty difficult to get any important news through to him. She could yell "Fire!" and he wouldn't hear her. Of course, there's the equivalent in "wife deafness." A woman who's married to a Great Authority stops listening to a word he says, and he could be telling her that he's mortally wounded and she'd just smile and figure Joe was sounding off about his corns again.

Your conversation with your marriage partner is likely to be a good clue to the state of your marriage itself. If everything you talk about is dull and shopworn, with occasional rows about money and in-laws and other problems, perhaps a conscious effort to liven up the conversation by introducing new and interesting subjects would also liven up the marriage. You both had interesting ideas before you got hitched. There seemed to be a world of things to talk about. Why not talk about them now? A pleasant, lively discussion about important topics is just as good for a marriage as it is for a courtship. There are no set rules as to what to talk about, but if you enjoyed pleasant conversations before marriage, you can keep right on enjoying them afterward.

But don't be afraid of silence, if there's understanding and sympathy between you. There are silences that soothe and comfort. The perfect proof of a deep and abiding love between husband and wife, and the greatest tribute which they can pay that love, is to enjoy a rich, companionable silence together—like the rests in music. On the other hand, the dead silence of utter boredom, or the silence that bristles with unspoken grievances, can kill love more thoroughly than open quarrels.

Some time ago I ran across a list of suggestions for keeping husband-and-wife conversation on a pleasant and lively plane. I wish I knew who drew this list up, because I'd like to give credit where credit is due, but this has been buried in my notebooks so long that I've lost the source. Nevertheless, here it is, and in my opinion it's one of the most helpful lists of do's and don'ts that I know of:

1. Beware of unburdening. We all need outlets, and we need to share the trials and triumphs of the day, but they shouldn't form our

entire conversation. Frankly, they may be kinda fascinating to us, but they're dull as ditch water to the other fellow. He's aching to go into a long discussion of his burdens, you know.

2. Don't whine and complain. It's tiresome to the listener, and you'll feel worse, because through repetition anguish is likely to be increased rather than relieved.

3. Don't discuss your health—or his—unless some important medical decision must be reached. Don't use your marriage partner as an audience for a daily going over of your minor aches and pains, and never use ailments to get attention.

4. All couples have to discuss money, but don't make it the sole basis of conversation. Out-loud worrying about money solves nothing and puts a serious strain on marriage.

5. Try to make your conversation the expression of a rich personality. Make new friends, read important books, listen to good music, go to lectures or art exhibits.

6. Don't be a "groove" thinker or talker. There are guys who can't hear the word "steak" without going on for the next half hour about how it should always be et rare, or well done, according to their particular lights. There are wimmenfolks who, if glasses are mentioned, have to go into details about their struggle to wear bifocals. During rationing, some folks couldn't talk anything else. There are people who sound off continuously on taxes, or military training, or any other pet subject they're fond of working over, and, while such conversations are merely tedious to the casual listener, they're positively bad for the husband, or wife, who has to endure them over and over.

7. Delve into the newspapers for real news and for interesting human-touch items, not merely for the household hints and the editorials which echo your opinions.

8. Last, but not least, listen to each other. Don't get that glassy stare when your marriage partner starts a topic that you're already bored with. See if you can't contribute something of your own to pep things up. Some poor unfortunate folks go through life counting the laundry and mentally mixing the baby's formula or running over the budget every time the other person opens his mouth.

Good talk and attentive listening are, after all, forms of sharing experience. Constant, scintillating brilliance is not the aim. But constant interest is. Try to be as amusing for your mate as you would for an attractive stranger. Use some of that wit and charm that you save for the office or your friends. It might surprise you to find out how far good talk and a friendly interchange of ideas can go toward making a better marriage.

TOLERANCE

"When the other fellow acts that way, he is ugly; when you do, it is nerves.

"When the other fellow is set in his ways, he's obstinate; when you are, it's just firmness.

"When the other fellow doesn't like your friends, he's prejudiced; when you don't like his, you are simply showing you are a good judge of human nature.

"When the other fellow tries to treat someone specially well, he's toadying; when you try the same game, you are using tact.

"When the other fellow takes time to do things, he is dead slow; when you do it, you are deliberate.

"When the other fellow runs great risks in business, he's foolhardy; when you do it, you are a great financier.

"When the other fellow says what he thinks, he's spiteful; when you do, you are frank.

"When the other fellow won't get caught in a new scheme, he's backwoodsy; when you don't, you're conservative."

Anonymous

WHO IS GOING TO HANDLE THE MONEY?

I suppose that more trouble is caused between married people by money than by any other single bone of contention. Even in-law trouble can't hold a candle to money trouble when it comes to causing squabbles. And money that monopolizes the conversation, with accusations of stinginess on one hand and extravagance on the other, invariably leads to violent and unpleasant quarrels about other subjects that come up along the way. Seems that if a pair get to squabbling about money, they latch onto every other disagreeable thing they can think of and drag it into the quarrel until there's such a donnybrook going on that everybody's feelings are hurt. So many sore spots get opened up that it's practically impossible to get back to normal.

It's only common sense for young people to decide, before marriage, who is going to handle the family finances. Every boy and girl ought to know the value of money early in life, from the time he or she is old enough to realize that even though a nickel is bigger than a dime in size, it's only worth half as much. But plenty of kids never know the value of money until they're grown up and married. That's a fine time to start finding out. That fixes everything up good.

But, for the sake of argument, let's assume that with a certain young couple starting out in life together, each has a good understanding of the value of a dollar, even in these precarious times when that value don't stay the same two days running, at least as far as what it'll buy is concerned. Well, the smart thing for this young couple to do is to decide who is going to handle the family cash box, and the smart way for them to decide it is that they both will. Together. Like teamwork. But that happy arrangement isn't always possible. All too often, one party or the other is incapable of handling money either because he or she is too stingy or too extravagant. In that case, some kind of budget that will allow for the failings of the erring partner has to be devised.

Generally speaking, husbands complain that their wives spend too much money, and wives complain that the old man is tighter than the bark on a tree. Sometimes it's the other way around; you'll occasionally find a very saving type of Bedelia nagging the liver out of some guy whose coin dribbles through his fingers like water through a leaky sieve. But that ain't so usual.

The reason men are often stingy and women extravagant is fairly simple. A guy before he marries has, like as not, been living on his own hard-earned cash for some little time, and he's found it perfectly adequate to cover his needs. If it isn't, he cuts down expenses and works for a raise. But most bachelors make out all right. Then what happens? They get married, and they earn that same adequate amount, or maybe even a little more, but somehow there never seems to be enough in the pay check to go around any more. He has to whittle down on his own little luxuries, and there don't seem to be anything so wonderful around the house to show for it. Naturally, he blames his wife. She's the only new thing that's been added to the establishment so far, and she don't have a word to say. She's let bills go unpaid because the guy just didn't give her enough dough to keep groceries on the table and nylons on her legs and pay the gas bill, too. So he says she's extravagant. She probably ain't, or if she is, she can't help herself—not in these times, anyhow. She's probably doing the best she can, the guy just don't realize all the little things that nibble away at the household cash. But, extravagant or not, she isn't going to take kindly to criticism of her household management. It's easy to see how that kind of a squabble over petty cash can lead to a real quarrel.

Actually, there's nothing more annoying to a wife than a husband who doles out the simoleons as if he was making a donation to a charity he didn't take much interest in. The gal has got to have enough to run the house on, and a little bit over for herself, and she gets to thinking, very quick, how much better off she was when she was single and had a job and spent to suit herself, if he gives her that minor charity treatment. On the other hand, there's the type who handles all the cash himself, buys everything that comes into the house, and never lets his wife handle a penny. She's got rings on her fingers and a mink-trimmed bedspread, but if she has fifty cents in her purse from one year's end to the next it's unusual. He gets her everything she asks for, or he thinks she wants or should have, but she never has a chance to get anything for herself. This can lead to trouble, too, bad trouble, because that kind of a guy is usually convinced that whatever he likes is right, and if he likes turnips they eat them every night of the week even if the very smell of them makes Suzybelle ill. I once knew a woman who always wore red—red suits, red dresses, even red shoes. Her husband bought every stitch of clothes she wore. So after forty years, he up and kicked the bucket, and she got rid of every bit of clothing she owned, because all those years she'd hated the color red and never dared peep about it, on account of dear Henry liked red so much and it was so sweet and kind of him to buy so many clothes for her. Sweet and kind in a pig's eye. All he was doing was asserting his authority over her. Maybe she did have six times as many dresses as any other woman in her circle, but she hated every one of them.

Another money trouble that can crop up in a family is when the wife works, especially when she earns more than her husband does. And that's not too uncommon nowadays, with a lot of gals who got into high-salaried positions during the war far outstripping their ex-G.I. husbands in the matter of the weekly pay check. It creates a pretty ticklish situation, requiring a great deal of tact. Once she gets in the habit of mentioning her superior earning capacity she's practically issuing an invitation to come to see her in Reno. There's a whole new set of problems

27

concerning money in the case of the working wife, but nothing that can't be solved with common sense.

I don't know if anybody has ever made a list of the troubles money can cause, but if they did, broken marriages would be right there on top. It's an individual problem for every couple to settle for themselves. The mistake that most make is that they never settle it at all. They just let it grow on them until they're swamped. And that ain't good. It's got to be decided on ahead of time, and that's one decision that both parties better stick to if they want peace and quiet.

PRAYER IS NATURAL

There is nothing more natural in the world than prayer, even though some of us act unnatural about it. Some of us feel mighty self-conscious and childish and ashamed when we pray, or admit we pray. And yet praying is as natural as breathing, or being afraid, or hoping or wanting or believing. Here's what Bishop William T. Manning said once about prayer:

"Prayer is the highest and most natural action of the human soul.

"Prayer is not a matter of theory. It is one of the universal facts of human experience. We are brought to prayer not by argument but by normal impulse.

"Prayer is the action of a normal human life. It is the life without prayer which is abnormal and needs to be explained.

"Prayer includes all that the soul feels and desires to express concerning its relationship with God. It is not always necessary that our prayers be expressed in words. Some of our truest moments of prayer are those in which we simply feel that we are in harmony with the universe. Prayer is a far deeper thing than words.

"Prayer gives to our lives serenity, self-control, courage, unselfishness and cheerfulness. It gives us strength, spiritual, mental and physical.

"But we must not expect to know the power of prayer without effort. The power of prayer, like our other powers and faculties, must be developed by practice and use. In public and in private our prayer and worship must be a reality. We must take trouble about it. We must give to our prayers the same thought and care and effort that we give to any other serious business of our lives."

28

KNOWING YOUR PARTNER—AND YOURSELF

One of the most significant questions of modern-day living is "How can marriage be made to last?" And that's no joke either. Not long ago the statistics read to the effect that nowadays one marriage out of four is headed for the ash heap. The boys have now come out with a new set, in which the ratio is more like one out of three. One third of all our marriages are a publicly declared mistake, and heaven only knows how many more of them are secret tragedies that never get aired in the open. And it's a pitiful thing that most of these unhappy marriages and broken homes could have been avoided if people would just use their heads instead of losing their heads, before the fatal knot is tied.

For instance, it's the little things that make the difference between a really happy marriage and one that just manages to be endurable. If your interests match those of your partner in life, and your ideas of what makes a happy life are the same, you've got a lot better chance for a good marriage than if you picked the guy out because he reminded you of Gregory Peck.

There's a book, *Marriage Is on Trial*, by Judge John A. Sbarbaro, which every married couple and every single person who is thinking about marriage ought to read. It might save a lot of trouble. Judge Sbarbaro has had long years of experience on the divorce bench of the largest court in the world—Cook County, Illinois—and he's one guy who ought to know what he's talking about. Judge Sbarbaro takes up many aspects of marriage, from sex adjustment to troublesome in-laws, and from budgeting to infidelity, in an attempt to find some remedy other than divorce for a bad marriage. He says divorce is no remedy at all, because it leaves both parties emotionally and financially insecure, and its effect upon children is so disastrous that it should be avoided at all costs. And the best way to avoid divorce is to make marriage a real serious consideration, and to use more than a little sense beforehand— if only to save more than a few tears afterward. I particularly like his first chapter, on knowing yourself—and your partner.

There are any number of reasons why people marry, but the most valid reason is because they have fallen in love with the right person. The most effective insurance for a happy marriage is to know as much as possible about the man or woman you are marrying. Courtship has a great many pitfalls which only time can eradicate. In courtship, both are on their best behavior, and both completely overlook any flaws in the other party. The old phrase, "Love is blind," may be trite, but it's still true.

The only way, then, to become thoroughly acquainted with the real person who is your intended mate is to know him for a reasonable length of time, a year, for example, and even two or three years isn't too long. You should have time to find out how you get along together when the going is rough, when you don't see eye to eye, when the fresh glow of a brand-new romance has worn off a little and you can get a peek at the clay feet of your idol. Remember, it's those clay feet that are going to walk all over your heart for the next twenty or thirty or forty or fifty years, and it's your business to find out if they step light or heavy. The important thing is not only how well you agree, but how well you disagree.

The quality of your courtship is important, too. Sipping cocktails to the accompaniment of a night-club orchestra ain't a smart way to prepare for marriage. Neither is strolling hand in hand under a summer moon for that matter. The fact that you enjoy it is no sign that you have found the one person in the world with whom you want to spend the rest of your life. If you're young and impressionable, a moonlight walk with practically any guy short of Dracula would seem pretty romantic. And moonlight can soften a gal's eyes and put golden lights in her hair and an unsuspecting boy never notices that she's really got a kinda mean set to her mouth and the way she laughs would rasp the souls of the dead. Well, there'll be plenty of nights when the moon ain't out, but he's gonna see that mouth and hear that irritating laugh and wonder what the heck ever got into him to make him pop the question. If, during courtship, folks could go through some hard times together, and find out how each acts in times of trouble, there'd be a lot fewer mistakes in marriages.

Also, in courtship, you should have plenty of opportunity to talk to each other, often and at length. Your conversations don't have to be studied and deadly serious, but, after all, the only way you can really know one another is by an exchange of ideas, so your talk shouldn't be just jabbering away for the sake of filling a social vacuum. If you have thoughts, express them, and listen intently to what your intended has to say. In this way you will learn to know him, and to know yourself, too. Don't be afraid to talk about important things, such as religion and politics, and any prejudices which either of you happen to have. These subjects are going to come up sooner or later, and if they crop up unexpectedly, they can make an awful lot of trouble.

It matters very much that you and the love of your life agree on your ideas of how to have fun, and the way a home should be run, and who should manage the money, and how to bring up children. You don't have to see alike down to every last detail of your way of life, but the more you agree about, the better. Because if your views are divided, eventually you will find yourselves traveling different paths entirely. But the small pleasures which people can enjoy together—a shared hobby, some game or sport, an interest in collecting books, or records of classical music, even a fondness for some particular pet—can not only save a marriage that is otherwise unstable, but can even make it full and happy. If you're the impractical, dreamy type whose money slips through her fingers, you may have trouble getting along with a hardheaded businessman who knows so much about budgets that you suspect he's the guy who invented them, but if you both enjoy the same kind of music, and like to play golf, and think that cooking a steak over an open fire is the best sort of good fun, then you have a pretty fair chance to make your marriage work. It's the little things that count, as well as the big ones, and a whole slew of little things that you agree on can compensate for just one big disagreement that might wedge you apart. That old saw about opposites attracting one another may be true, but the attraction quickly wears off. The more alike you are, the more your interests coincide and your personalities click, the more likely it is that your marriage will be a success and you'll never see the inside of a divorce court.

This business of preventing divorce, and the necessity for divorce, is one of the most important questions we have before us today, and we ought to learn everything we can about it. Let's try to get that "one divorce in every three marriages" back to "one in every four," anyhow. That's bad enough.

HINTS FOR THOSE THAT WOULD BE RICH

Every once in a while I turn to the writings of old Ben Franklin, and I never dip into them without coming up with something worth while. Here are some of Franklin's remarks on the use of money, which you

31

can find in *Poor Richard's Almanack* for 1737, in case you're interested. Now Old Ben wasn't exactly a miser, but you wouldn't be stretching the truth if you called him—well, careful with that government lettuce. I think you'll like his "Hints for Those That Would Be Rich." This is just the way he wrote it, only I've taken the liberty of translating the monetary terms he uses into the ones we use today. Back then we were still English colonies, of course, and Ben talks about groats and pounds and shillings, but of course if he were around today he'd be saying dollars and cents like the rest of us. Here goes:

"The use of money is all the advantage there is in having money.

"For six dollars a year, you may have the use of a hundred dollars, if you are a man of known prudence and honesty.

"He that spends two pennies a day idly, spends idly above six dollars a year, which is the price of using one hundred dollars.

"He that idly loses a dollar's worth of time, loses a dollar, and might as prudently throw a dollar into the river.

"He that loses a dollar not only loses that sum, but all the advantages that might be made by turning it in dealing, which, by the time that a young man becomes old, amounts to a considerable bag of money.

"Again, he that sells upon credit asks a price for what he sells equivalent to the principal and interest of his money for the time he is like to be kept out of it; therefore, he that buys upon credit pays interest for what he buys. And he that pays ready money might let that money out to use; so that he that possesses anything he has bought, pays interest for the use of it." (Maybe you think that's a mouthful, but think it over. Ben ain't kidding. No matter what, you're still done in the eye.)

"Consider, then, when you are tempted to buy any unnecessary household stuff, or any superfluous thing, whether you will be willing to pay interest, and interest upon interest, for it as long as you live; and more, if it grows worse by using.

"Yet, in buying goods, it is best to pay ready money, because he that sells upon credit expects to lose five per cent by bad debts; therefore he charges, on all he sells upon credit, an advance that shall make up that deficiency.

"Those who pay for what they buy upon credit pay their share of this advance.

"He that pays ready money escapes, or may escape, that charge.

"A penny saved is twopence clear,

"A pin a day is a penny a year."

So . . . how're you feeling now? Kinda poor? You know, the old boy knew what he was talking about. Figure it out for yourself. It may make you feel like crawling in a hole and pulling the hole in after you, but you'll get over that after a while and maybe be just a little careful with that green stuff that's burning a hole in your pocket. Try it out.

OUR SEPARATE PATHS

Did it ever occur to you how much we go along our separate ways, cut off from one another, just as if we weren't all members of the human race, living in the same world, or the same continent? If you don't belong to my church, and you don't pray as I do, you're an outsider. If you don't belong to the same club, you're an outsider. If I vote one way and you vote another, you're an outsider. We make laws against this and that, with a tongue-in-the-cheek attitude that the strong among us will break them and the weak will live up to them. The powerful guy with a lot of dough figures he has rights and privileges not accorded to his lowlier brethren.

Then along comes a war, and overnight everybody says that we're all brothers and all equal. Suddenly I'm as good as you are, and you're as good as your neighbor. The Presbyterian fights alongside the Catholic, and the Jew alongside the Methodist, and the atheist stands shoulder to shoulder with the Baptist. The white and the black and the sinner and the saint are all brothers.

We can get along with each other when we kill, but not when we're just plain living. Funny, isn't it?

I think it was Charles Brandon who wrote some lines along this subject, and here's what he said:

Life is like a journey taken on a train,
With a pair of travellers at each windowpane.
I may sit beside you all the journey through,
Or I may sit elsewhere, never knowing you.
But, if fate should mark me to sit by your side,
Let's be pleasant travellers; it's so short a ride.

I wish we could all paste that in our hats and think about it once in a while, as we go along so busily minding our own business and pretending that everybody who doesn't happen to belong to our own little circle is an outsider.

33

WHAT'S IN A NAME?

Out in San Francisco, in 1897, a judge and jury were faced with a pretty little problem, if ever I saw one. You know how a criminal must be tried and sentenced under his true name, no matter how many fancy aliases he may happen to have?

The particular guy I have in mind was tried and convicted on circumstantial evidence and, because of an error in the judge's instruction to the jury, was granted a retrial and convicted a second time . . . all under an alias. And the reason was that if they'd taken the time and trouble during the court proceedings to use his real name, the trial would probably be going on yet.

This man, who brutally murdered a harmless old woman who employed him to do odd jobs, was named "Hoff" in the trial. That's what they called him, all through the proceedings. Now, anybody who tries to pronounce his real name is risking lockjaw. I'll spell it for you. The first part was Albert Frederick George—that's easy enough. But his last name was V-e-r-e-n-e-s-e-n-e-c-k-o-c-k-o-c-k-h-o-f-f. I'm not kidding. Twenty-two letters, arranged so they're practically unpronounceable. You can warp your jaw, just trying.

BOREDOM IN MARRIAGE

I don't suppose there are any figures available on marriages which reach the breaking point because one party or the other is bored. Figures on marriages which go on the rocks for this reason don't appear, because they are invariably hidden behind a screen of fancied complaints. But Judge John A. Sbarbaro says that in his opinion boredom is one of the commonest of all causes for broken homes. He says that if the true reason were known for divorce—and the true reason seldom is aired at the court proceedings—many a plaintiff could sum up his entire case in the phrase, "I'm simply fed up with the whole thing."

Judge Sbarbaro has some pretty interesting things to say about this unfortunate state of boredom that settles down over so many marriages.

He says the primary cause of people becoming bored with marriage is that they enter wedlock under the deluding influence of rosy-hued romantic dreams. The shock of finding that the little vine-covered cottage has a furnace that has to be tended and a kitchen full of dirty dishes to wash is just too much for them. They start to daydream, wondering if they might not find the idealistic existence they originally sought if they only had a chance to start over again with a new mate. Of course, the fallacy in that line of thinking is that, eventually, the same old difficulties and realities would crop up, and it's a lead-pipe cinch they wouldn't be faced with any better grace the second time than they were the first.

Now there's no doubt in Judge Sbarbaro's mind that magazine stories, romantic novels, and movies must take a share of the blame for the honey-and-kisses concept of marriage. In most stories and most pictures, the marriage happens on the final page or the last close-up, and the implication is that this pair will live happily ever after, with absolutely no trials and tribulations, and Joe will never have a nasty disposition before breakfast and Suzybelle will never burn her thumb learning to cook, and the kids will be little angels, and never a moth will eat his way through the clothes closet.

But then it ain't exactly the fault of the writers and movie producers, because the whole Anglo-Saxon culture of chivalry, on which our modern social customs are based to a great extent, has a highly romantic tradition concerning relationships between men and women. And if our whole psychology of courtship and marriage dates from the days when knighthood was in flower, and every Bedelia was a beautiful damsel in distress—well, that ain't exactly a likely sort of preparation for figuring out a budget and coping with a cookstove. When you're draped over a washtub scrubbing out Junior's dirty overalls, and you think of all those lovely promises and how wonderful marriage was going to be and how your Joe was going to give you the moon on a silver platter, and look at you now—well, it just ain't right, that's all. Maybe this is what marriage really is, but if so, it ain't what it's cracked up to be. And it's the same with Joe. Maybe you used to look like a movie queen when you went out on dates with him, now you look—and act—like a harassed wife and mother, and marriage ain't a realm of sweetness and light, not by a durn sight. Especially with unpaid bills.

Here's another angle. In this country today female beauty—that is to say, sex attractiveness—is strongly emphasized. "Cheesecake" is a high art, and every billboard and advertisement, practically, displays the

35

physical charms of a pretty baby with just as little on as the law allows. Handsome (and not-so-handsome) screen celebrities are mobbed for autographs. Young girls band together in "fan clubs" and shriek and swoon. Here in America we are actually in a state of hysteria over sex attractiveness—artificial hysteria, it is true, but it's sufficiently widespread to affect the average American marriage.

Thus we have a whole set of traditions and customs and psychological attitudes toward romantic love and realistic marriage which are probably the most demanding in history, and yet our young people go into marriage blindly, apparently under the impression that if the other party is physically handsome enough, unutterable bliss is automatically insured. So it's no wonder that disillusion and boredom set in.

Judge Sbarbaro says that we fail to recognize that it takes a very mature mind to realize that marriage is not a dream existence, but simply another kind of life; it's a good kind, but it has problems. You have to work to make a marriage go. And, believe it or not, that work is extremely interesting, perhaps the most interesting job in the world, only it'll be extremely boring if you shirk it. Work neglected, or badly done, is always a bore. Just walking down that flower-strewn aisle and hearing the bells ring out don't do the trick. And look at your job, if you have a job—aside from the job of marriage, I mean. It has its dull moments, even though it may be truly your lifework. But because of a few dull spots you don't give it up in a moment of disgust. And how about your hobbies, and your friends? They're pretty boring sometimes, too, but you'd be awful lost and lonely without them. Nothing on earth is uninterruptedly fascinating, every single minute, and there's no reason why marriage should be either. But if you're bored, you can do something about it. If you feel you aren't getting enough out of marriage, you probably aren't putting anything into it. You can exert yourself a little to provide the missing elements: excitement, love, adventure, companionship. You will be pleasantly surprised, and so will your marriage partner, because neither of you will be bored any more.

ON STANDING STILL

There's a legend, among some of the primitive tribes of the Belgian Congo, about how the native guinea fowl got their spots. These guinea fowl are beautifully marked birds, with their glossy dark feathers evenly spotted with clear, pure white.

But, the story goes, the guinea fowl weren't always beautiful. They used to be drab, dull gray, but they appealed to the gods of the forest to make them beautiful, and the gods of the forest told the guinea fowl to stand very still and be patient, and the gods painted the birds with neat, shining white spots.

Well, the guinea fowl went back to their homes, and did considerable swelling around the joint, on account of they were all pretty now, and the other animals were still just plain colors. So the other animals went and told the gods of the forest that they wanted to be prettied up, too, and the gods of the forest told them to hold still and be patient and they'd paint them with white spots, just like the guinea fowl.

But this deal didn't work out so good. The hyena was surly and cringing, and afraid of the paintbrush, so he got just a few spots. The leopard was bold and restless; he shoved the others aside, and demanded to be painted at once, and then he wriggled around so much that the paint ran and some of his spots became stripes, and some were large and some were small. And the antelope was so timid that he jumped right out of the hands of the forest gods, and only got one spot, on the tip of his tail.

You might work that little yarn off on junior, sometime you're combing his hair or washing behind his ears or something, and he starts to wiggle. It may not help the wiggling much, but it'll pass the time faster.

YOU HAVE KNOWN ABOUT HIM ALL THESE YEARS: BUT HAVE YOU REALLY KNOWN HIM?

Back some years ago, when Bruce Barton was putting out so many of his wonderful little essays and editorials, I clipped out every bit of his stuff I could find and put it in my scrapbooks. Since then I've collected every book that Bruce Barton ever wrote, and in my considered opinion he's one of the really great writers and teachers of our time. My only quarrel with him is that he's quit writing, and I wish he'd start up again and give us some more of his fine, sound ideas.

Probably you're well acquainted with that thumbnail word sketch of Jesus which Barton wrote maybe thirty years ago, and which is reprinted over and over, every Easter. Just because I'm sure you've seen that piece many times, I'm not going to include it here. Instead, I am going to include a less well known and slightly longer portrait of Christ which Bruce Barton wrote as a Christmas editorial.

"Since we stand upon the threshold of His birthday, let me introduce you to the most attractive, most delightful young man in the world.

"You have never known Him as He really is: all the pictures ever drawn misrepresent Him. They have made Him out a weakling, a woman's features with a beard . . . He who for years swung an adz and drove a saw through heavy timbers, who for long days tramped the borders of His loved lake, and would not sleep indoors if He could slip away into His garden.

"An outdoor man He was, a man's man who could stand watch when all His friends deserted Him in sleep, and could face the tempest in a little boat calm-eyed and unafraid.

"They have called Him a pacifist. How could they forget that day, I wonder, when in the midst of the hard-faced crowd He stood, and, braiding a little whip, drove them out before Him?

"Think you it was only the glance of righteous anger in His eye that sent them scurrying? I tell you that behind that little whip were muscles of iron, made strong by many years of labor, and a spirit that never once knew fear, not even in the presence of the cross.

"I have met men long-faced and sorrowful, wagging their heads bitterly over the evil of the world, and by their very joylessness adding to that evil. And in their hearts they supposed that they were representing Him.

"Think of it—representing Him, to whom little children flocked with joyous laughter, and men, beseeching Him to have dinner with them in their homes.

"You remember the first of His miracles—or perhaps you do not. Too often those who claim His name have preferred to forget that miracle. It does not fit in with the picture of Him that they have wrought.

"He was at a wedding party with His mother and some friends where the merriment ran high. In the midst of it they came to Him in consternation. The wine had given out.

"So he preformed His first miracle. Just to save a hostess from embarrassment—and He thought it worth a miracle. Just to save a group of simple folk from having their hour of joy cut short—it was for such a cause, He thought, that His divine power had been intrusted to Him.

38

"No one ever felt His goodness a cloud upon the company. No one ever laughed less heartily because He had joined the group. His was the gospel of joyfulness; His the message that the God of men would have them travel happily with Him, as children by a Father's side, not as servants shuffling behind.

"They killed Him, of course, in the end, and sometimes I am almost glad—glad that He died at thirty-three, with youth still athrob in His veins, and never an illusion lost or an ideal dimmed by age.

"Claim Him, you who are young and love life; let no man dispute your claim.

"For He too was young and is; He too loved laughter and life.

"Old age and creeds have had Him too long: I offer Him now to you —not in creed but in truth—Jesus of Nazareth, the joyous companion, the young man whom young men can love."

AVOIDING FATIGUE IN HOUSEWORK

Housework can be a series of dull, burdensome tasks that leave you whupped down to a nubbin, or it can be a rewarding job that you get through in a reasonable amount of time so that you have the best part of the day left over to do other things. The second way saves wear and tear on your health, and that of your family.

There's a book by Marion Hurst, *The 1-2-3 of Homemaking*, which is a streamlined basic guide to a smooth-running household. There's a lot of valuable information in this book for everybody, but especially for the woman who's always behind in the housework, who never can seem to get caught up, and who's tired all the time. It's the tired house-wife who neglects the safety rules and has accidents.

Miss Hurst says the worst enemy of the homemaker is fatigue. She says that housework undoubtedly is tiring, and takes a lot of time, but even if you have six kids and a Monday wash that, laid end to end, would stretch from here to Timbuktu, you can axoid excessive fatigue. She's got some kinda tricky little suggestions for making the work seem easier and for cutting down on long hours. If you're doing housework fourteen hours a day, you have a right to be dead on your feet. You would be if you worked in a factory fourteen hours, too. But you've got no business doing housework fourteen hours a day, and you won't, if you're smart about it. Here are a few of Miss Hurst's suggestions for cutting down on time and getting a little more rest:

1. No matter what, make time for a short nap in the afternoon, with your shoes off and the shades pulled down. Just drop what you're doing and lie down for half an hour. Whether you sleep or not don't make much difference, but you probably will.

2. Take a breather every hour or so. Sit down, read the paper, listen to the radio, or twiddle your thumbs, but lay off for five minutes once every hour, especially if you're doing some heavy work like washing or house cleaning.

3. Have a chair or stool of the proper height so that you can sit down while ironing, peeling vegetables, and such tasks.

4. Practice good posture while working. Wear comfortable, well-fitted shoes. This is no time to wear out your old evening sandals or to slop around in bedroom slippers. You can break down your arches and hurt your spine doing that.

5. Have the windows open when you're cleaning and provide plenty of fresh air for all strenuous work.

6. Double up on tasks whenever possible. Gather up the laundry as you make the beds; that saves an extra trip. Or sterilize the baby's bottles, or start the pot roast going, while you do the luncheon dishes.

7. Spend five minutes straightening up the living room before you go to bed at night. Then you've got some chance of getting some co-operation from the family in folding up newspapers, brushing away crumbs, and so forth. If you wait till morning, you'll be doing it yourself.

8. Set aside a time for quantity cooking once a week. You can make a week's desserts, bake pies and cakes and cookies, fix sauces and salad dressings. If you make a business of it for one afternoon, it's out of the way for the whole week.

9. Make Sunday a real holiday. You need a day of rest, too. Limit what you do to real necessities, and encourage the rest of the family to wait on you a little bit.

10. Cut down on excess trips up and down stairs, to the basement or the back yard. If you get everything you need together before you start a job, you won't be chasing to one closet for a broom and to another for the vacuum, and upstairs for a whisk broom and out to the kitchen for soap.

11. Limit interruptions as much as possible, so you'll have more time later. A five-minute chat with your favorite neighbor is fine, but if Mrs. McGillicuddy parks in the parlor and tells you her troubles for upwards

of three hours, you're as tired out as though you'd been plowing the north forty. You may have to brush her off, as gently as possible, but be firm. Tell her that you'll be through with your housework later on, and she can come over and tell you then. Or, better still, you go to see her, and then you can walk out when you want to.

12. Use both hands for your work. It goes faster and isn't so tiring.

13. Follow a heavy day by a light one. If you washed and baked and cleaned house all day Monday, and got a company dinner because your old man brought the boss home on short notice, then on Tuesday you ought to do something kinda mild, like catching up on the mending, or sorting the linen. And don't forget that you need a little recreation. You're supposed to run the house, not let it run you.

ODD ADVERTISEMENTS

I thought I'd heard about every possible crazy collection that people could make, and people who collect things go in for some crazy ones. That is, they seem crazy to the rest of us. Probably they don't, to the collectors. Books, stamps, postcards, photographs, buttons, match covers —they're all within the normal bounds of collecting. Chess sets, playing cards, old valentines—they're a little more unusual. Some folks collect big things that you can't keep in a glass case. James Melton, the singer, goes in for old motorcars, and Ed Stettinius, the white-haired boy of U. S. Steel and formerly a big shot in the New Deal setup, collects old locomotives, old covered wagons, everything and anything that tells the story of transportation in America. You've got to have space to spread around a thing like that. You can't keep a flock of old locomotives in a two-room apartment.

Then there was the child prodigy, William James Sidis, who died so tragically a year or so ago. Sidis collected streetcar transfers. A woman named Katherine Powers, a screwball miser who died in Brooklyn in 1940, left a collection of uncashed dividend checks, although, from the way she lived, you'd think she was in dire poverty. She also left a vast collection of milk-bottle tops; she lived entirely on milk, being possessed of the nutty notion that somebody was trying to poison her food. And she saved the caps. When she conked out, there was a whole roomful of the things.

41

George IV of England saved every coat he'd ever worn, and, being a king, he must have had a closetful. Tommy Manville collects wives, and they, in turn, collect plenty. And there was that horrible creature hovering around the German concentration camps, who collected the tattooed skins of human beings, and made them into gloves and lampshades.

But there's a guy up in Pelham, New York, who collects something pretty odd, and he must get a lot of laughs out of it. His hobby is original with me. I can't say I've ever heard of anybody going in for this one before.

His name is Mr. Lockwood Barr, one-time public relations chief of General Motors. How he got into this collecting bee of his I don't know, but what he saves is odd advertisements. Any time he sees an advertisement that's a little out of the way he copies it off or cuts out the clipping, and he's got thousands of 'em now. A lot of people know about his hobby and send him stuff, too. His mail is full of clippings from acquaintances in all parts of the country, people he's gotten to know through this unusual hobby of his. He even gets copies of odd ads from China and India.

So here's a few of the prize gems of his collection:

"Young man who gets paid on Monday and is broke on Wednesday would like to exchange small loans with a young man who gets paid on Wednesday and is broke on Monday."

"Positively no more baptizing in my pasture. Twice in the last two months my gate has been left open, and before I chase my heifers all over the county again all the sinners can go to purgatory."

"If J.M., who twenty-two years ago basely deserted his helpless penniless wife and infant son Michael, will return home, Mike will take pleasure in knocking the (censored, censored, censored) out of him."

"Brown, the furrier, begs to announce that he will make up coats, capes, etc., for ladies out of their own skins."

"Found: Lady's purse left in my car while parked. Owner can have same by describing property and paying for this ad. If owner can explain satisfactorily to my wife how purse got into car, will pay for ad myself."

"Anyone found near my chicken house at night will be found there next morning."

"For sale: De Soto sedan. Looks like De Soto himself might have used this one, but she runs fine."

"Brave man wanted to curry lions. Funeral expenses guaranteed."

"Monday morning breakfast: Pitcher of ice water, glass of tomato juice, two aspirins, cup of black coffee and our sympathy, all for thirty cents."

And here's the top-off: "Wanted: An attractive salesgirl. Must be respectable, till after Christmas."

DOES PLAY REST US?

Ever know a tired businessman who goes out on Saturday afternoon and whales the stuffing out of a poor little innocent golf ball and comes back so tired out that all day Sunday he lies on a couch groaning about his aching back and the crick in his neck and his arm that's so sore he can hardly lift a spoon to feed himself?

So, you sort of wonder why he plays golf on his day off, if it's going to do all that to him. Seems like play and rest and recreation ought to refresh a person, instead of leaving him all tired out like that.

Well, the proof of the pudding is that the aching back and the crick in his neck aren't a bit important; Monday morning he snaps into it at the office with renewed vim and energy, and if he'd taken things easy all week end he'd probably feel just as dragged out as he did Friday night, after a week's work.

A fellow by the name of S. R. Slavson—just one of those guys who's curious about behaviorism—has gone into this question in a book called *Recreation and the Total Personality*. Dr. Slavson says play is very, very necessary to the human race, mostly because few of us find any outlet for the urge to create and to express ourselves, either in our work or around the house. For instance, most of us have fighting or aggressive impulses which we have to keep bottled up. It don't do to take a poke at the boss in the office; all you'll get out of that is fired. And it doesn't work so well around the house either, if the little woman or your father-in-law or somebody annoys you. The best thing to do if you feel like giving somebody a good walloping is to go to a baseball game or a fight or something like that and let off steam by watching somebody else do the fancy fist and foot work. Or take it out on a golf ball, like our tired businessman.

And about that urge to create, the fulfillment of which is so necessary to our mental health: maybe you think it's sort of childish if a big husky truck driver comes home and hunches for hours over a stamp collection, or some insignificant little piece of whittling. Well, it isn't childish; it's just normal. He's been swinging his muscles around all day with big coarse heavy objects, and now's he's relaxing with something that's just the opposite, something small and colorful and comparatively useless. It's his safety valve. And if you have somebody in your house who is the studious, bookworm type, don't get excited if he suddenly takes up mountain climbing or jitterbugging as a hobby. It's as natural as it is for a cow to crave salt. He may come back tired, bruised, and banged up, but he's really been resting.

REWARD

With shining eyes and lifted nose,
   A million dogs lined up in rows
And stood before the throne of God,
   While He, with just a smiling nod,
Bade all the household pets sit down
   Upon their haunches on the ground,
Or I should say, upon the sky,
   For they were spirits. As for why
God wanted dogs, that seemed to be
   Much more than anyone could see.
Each ear upon each spirit head
   Was up, to hear each word He said.
"You've all led lives untouched by greed,
   And love and honor seemed your creed.
So now, because of that, you've come
   To dwell with Me in this your home.
You'll not have any crowns to wear,
   But you'll have bones and meat to spare,
And friendly fires 'round which to sleep,
   And too, some spirit fleas to keep
You busy when you've naught to do
   But haunt the homes of masters who
You loved in other happy days
   When once you walked in earthly ways."
They all lay down just where they sat,
   While God gave each a loving pat.

44

And as he walked between the rows
   They each rubbed a cold friendly nose
Against His robe as He passed by,
   And strolled on down the windy sky.

Galen Drake

STRAWS FOR THE CAMEL'S BACK

You know how you feel when a lot of minor calamities pile up one after another, and then, just when you're cheering yourself up by muttering, "Anyhow, things can't get any worse . . ." they suddenly do. And you want to scream once, very loud, and then go off and get lost somewhere where nobody you ever saw before can ever find you.

Dr. Rhoda Bacmeister, the expert on family relations, has a real interesting section in her book, *Growing Together,* on the subject of what to do when the straw that broke the camel's back suddenly gets loaded on yours. She says the only solution is a large dose of sense of humor, followed immediately by a period, which needn't be very long, of complete rest and relaxation.

One little thing can loom mountainously large, if it follows a whole train of bad luck. For instance, Dr. Bacmeister tells about one young mother whose big clean washing, just hung out, fell in the mud because the clothesline broke. The gal went right in the house without saying a word and prepared to commit suicide. And every one of us knows just how she felt, even if we don't let things drive us so far.

What happens is that we allow tensions to build up and up, fighting our battles doggedly, but without relief. It creates a vicious circle of trouble, effort, extra strain, fatigue, irritability—more trouble, more effort, more strain, and so on. Finally, there's a snapping point; yet it can arise very gradually and very naturally.

We all know some gal whose reaction to feeling below par is an orgy of house cleaning. When you feel miserable and irritated and sore about something, all the little untidy corners that lurk in any house, the corners that you've been meaning to get at for some time, bother you more than usual. So you start furiously to clean them up. Pretty soon you feel worse, and the whole room looks drab and dull. You hate the sight of the same old stuff, and you start pulling everything apart, beating the carpet, hauling the furniture around, wasting more strength and energy than if you were cleaning up Buckingham Palace.

Well, you're just lucky if you don't land flat on your back and really sick. It's a wise woman who reaches for a sofa instead of a scrub brush when she feels that sense of pressure and irritation sweep over her. Some Bedelias act like they were real proud of laying themselves out, as if "not ever knowing when to stop" was a badge of honor and a tribute to their housekeeping. But it ain't.

Ever hear about the housewife who said, "There's just so much work to do, I don't know where to start . . . so I think I'll go to bed"? Well, maybe she had something. Don't take on that extra straw that'll break your back. Leave it for the camel; he's used to it. He's been doing it for a long time.

KAMALA, THE WOLF GIRL

In October 1920 the Rev. J. A. L. Singh, a serious and responsible clergyman in charge of the orphanage of Midnapore, near Calcutta in India, had occasion to visit a little isolated village—its name was Godamuri—which lay within his jurisdiction as visiting missionary, a work he carried on in connection with the orphanage. While in Godamuri he heard wild tales of a Ghost Man who was supposedly haunting the surrounding jungle. Naturally, Dr. Singh didn't take stock in ghost stories, but he figured he'd knock this superstition on the head once and for all by sitting up in a tree all night overlooking the path the supposed ghost had been seen on. So up the tree he went, and he saw three grown wolves and two wolf cubs emerge from a hole, followed by something else he didn't at all like the looks of. In his own words: "Close after the cubs came the ghost—a hideous-looking being, hand, foot and body like a human being; but the head was a big ball of something covering the shoulders and the upper portion of the body, leaving only a sharp contour of the face visible, and it was human. Close at its heels came another awful creature exactly like the first, but smaller in size. I at once came to the conclusion that these were human beings."

Several days later, with the help of the terrified but obedient natives, Dr. Singh succeeded in capturing these two wolf children and bringing them to his orphanage at Midnapore. Now Dr. Singh had had all kinds and conditions of kids under his care ever since he started in his chosen career, but he'd never come up against anything like the two wolf children he'd caught in the forest of Godamuri. When he got them cleaned up a little, he found that what he had on his hands were two little girls, one about eight years old and one about a year and a half. They had completely lost all human behavior. They'd lived with wolves and they acted like wolves, and the older one, which Dr. Singh named Kamala, even had taken on some of the physical characteristics of a wolf; she had great calluses, like the pads of animals, on her hands and the soles of her feet; her arms and legs were very long and her shoulders abnormally broad, but her hips were unusually slender and flexible. Since she ate by tearing her food like a wolf, her jaws opened wider than is normal in human beings, and her canine teeth were huge and very sharp. She sniffed the air through abnormally wide nostrils; her ears trembled and in the dark her eyes shone like a wild beast's. The littler child, named Amala, didn't show any of these physical changes; evidently she had not lived with the wolves long enough. Neither child could walk upright, but they ran very fast on all fours and when they weren't in a hurry they crept on hands and knees. Like their foster parents, the wolves, they slept all day and were awake at night; in fact, they couldn't even open their eyes fully in broad daylight. At night they prowled around restlessly, occasionally emitting weird wolf calls that were answered from the surrounding jungle. They snapped up raw meat from the floor, making no attempt to use their hands, and they lapped milk in the way of all young animals. They slept piled up like wolf cubs, and according to the records, they did not perspire, even on the hottest day, but panted with their tongues out.

Now, not only was it amazing to find one child reared by wolves, but here were two—apparently adopted by the same wolf! It's a fact that hundreds of children are carried off every year by wolves in the jungles of India, but these children are killed and eaten. What must have happened is that the wolf who seized Kamala was nursing her own cubs at the time, and, not being particularly hungry, she accepted the human baby right along with her own brood. Having raised one human and kept it with her seven years or so, she seized another and started raising it, too.

The Rev. Mr. Singh wasn't interested in the scientific aspects of the case; his anxiety was to keep the truth about the wolf children concealed, at least until he could get them kinda tamed and fit to associate with normal human beings. Mrs. Singh assumed the care of the wild little creatures, and after they got over being afraid of her they were loving and gentle. She massaged them daily to loosen their muscles so that they could learn to walk upright and little Amala was already beginning to walk and talk eleven months later, when she died during an epidemic. If she had lived, it seems quite likely that she would have grown up completely normal and unmarked by her experience.

Kamala was now a sad and lonely little creature. With love and care and patience she became reconciled to the loss of her little companion. She learned to wear clothes, to do simple tasks such as working the overhead fan that hangs in every house in India, and she was so gentle and obedient that she was allowed to mind the babies in the orphanage, and she seemed to enjoy this very much. She had a happy disposition; she liked small children and her greatest joy was tending them or, during the summer, herding a flock of goats kept for the babies' milk. Everybody loved her and she loved everybody. But two things she never learned to do well: walking and speaking. She was over thirteen before she could walk upright, in spite of Mrs. Singh's daily care and training, and even then she was awkward and unsure, and when she had to hurry she ran on all fours. As to speaking, in all she learned only forty-five words, some of which she could combine in phrases of two or three words.

In the fall of 1929, when she was seventeen, Kamala fell ill of an organic disease which, it seems likely, was brought on by a two-legged creature learning to run on all fours and then straighten up and walk the way she was born to. All this while no word of the wolf girl had reached the world; Dr. and Mrs. Singh had thought it best to let the pathetic and simple and happy little creature live without the eyes of the curious upon her. But because of her serious illness a doctor had to be called in from the outside, and when this doctor examined her he found the physical evidence of her life among the wolves: her queer big teeth, her unnaturally broad shoulders and distorted hips, and the calluses which never wore off her hands. So the cat was out of the bag and the news spread around and even as poor little Kamala lay dying the world started taking an interest in her.

Of course, it was pretty hard to believe. But such cases have been reported before. As a matter of fact, there are on record thirty-five well-authenticated cases of children being brought up by wild animals: wolves, leopards, wild pigs, sheep, and bears. And Dr. Singh, during the nine years Kamala lived in his household, kept a very careful diary in which he set down her progress every day. So Kamala and her little

48

foster sister Amala took their place as genuine wild children in the scientific records. It's just one of those things that you have to stretch your believing department a little to take in, but it's guaranteed to be true.

WHAT ABOUT HAVING CHILDREN?

There are about as many reasons for getting married as there are marriages, and only a few of them, such as companionship, the desire for a home, security, and affection, are valid and legitimate. Some are just as silly as they sound, and the people who marry on account of them can't expect much good to come of it, even though their intentions are the best in the world. Like marrying a guy to reform him, for instance; that ain't even as sensible as it would be to marry him just because he's got long black eyelashes. However, let's turn to one of the few sensible reasons for getting hitched, the desire for children.

It's as true today as it was back in the days of the very beginnings of mankind on this earth that children are the basic reason for marriage. And all the laws and customs and ceremonies surrounding marriage are put there to safeguard the children that are to be, and these laws and customs are designed to create a family unit that is sturdy and can withstand the shocks of life, the trials and disappointments and troubles that everybody has to go through. Of course there are plenty of childless marriages that are perfectly happy, but the vast majority of marriages are strengthened as the family unit grows. And yet there are marriages that actually go on the rocks because one partner or the other didn't want kids around the house.

Now this is a question that young people ought to ask themselves frankly, and ask each other, before marriage. If it crops up afterward, and they disagree, it can cause an awful lot of trouble. It's something to find out about before it's too late.

Of course, if you both want a family, there's no problem. It's a good idea, before marriage, to have a physical checkup, and let a competent doctor go over you and find out if you're fit for and capable of parenthood. If he gives you the green light, then you're all set.

But suppose one of you wants to have a family and the other doesn't. If you are thinking about marrying somebody who is decidedly opposed to having a child, you'd better have a thorough discussion of the matter and try to find out why. Because in finding out why your guy or gal, as the case may be, don't want kids, you may find out some other very interesting and important things about his or her character, things you never suspected were there, and that you ought to know about before you take any drastic steps such as ordering the orange blossoms and soft music.

For instance, if you find out that the boy friend is opposed to having a family because he is basically a very selfish person and can't take the idea of sharing you and your love with anybody, even his own children, you can decide right off that he just ain't got it in him to be the makings of a good husband. Same with a gal; she may be just too self-centered to take care of anybody except herself. She may have all sorts of preconceived notions that having children will spoil her figure or her looks. If she has, you've got hold of the wrong Bedelia, and you better lose her quick and find yourself another—that is, unless you want to play nursemaid to a spoiled, bratty wife for the rest of your days.

Then there are the young folks who say they don't want children because they don't want to be "tied down." If your intended is that kind of a guy, who don't want to be hampered with a family, he just might find out, after the first flush of married bliss has worn off, that he don't want to be hampered with a wife, either. When they start giving you that "don't want to be tied down" routine, they're good lads to stay away from.

Of course, it ain't fair to bring kids into the world if you can't possibly support them, at least as far as the necessities of life go, but most excuses about not having children because of economic problems are just a cover-up for selfishness. A young couple who can afford all the comforts and some luxuries for themselves can certainly manage to raise a family, if they really want to. Even a young couple operating on a shoestring can swing it, and plenty have. But the whole problem should be talked over before marriage, and if there's any basic disagreement between you and the person you're thinking of spending the rest of your life with, you'd better think twice.

It's not a question to be decided for today, or for tomorrow. It has to be decided on a lifelong basis. Once you have the kids, there you are, whether you're a born parent or you positively dislike everything about it. And once you decide on a childless marriage, you'll drift along in it until suddenly, one day, when you're too old to do anything about it, you'll find that you wish you'd had a family after all. It's an even bigger problem than just you and your partner in marriage. It affects your parents, if they're still living, and your brothers and sisters if you have any. It affects your relationship with your church, particularly if you belong to a faith that frowns upon birth control. It affects your whole place in a community, your old age, even your disposal of your worldly goods when your time comes to pass them on.

So think it over while you still have time, and talk it over before you marry. You might save yourself, and others, a lot of heartache. And you'll learn a good deal about yourself, and about the person you intend to marry, by doing so.

TEN WAYS TO KILL AN ORGANIZATION

1. Don't go to the meetings.
2. If you do, go late.
3. If the weather doesn't suit you, don't think of going.
4. If you do attend a meeting, find fault with the work of the officers and members.
5. Never accept office, as it is far easier to criticize than to do things.
6. Get sore if you are not appointed on a committee, but if you are, do not attend committee meetings.
7. If asked by the president to give your opinion on some matter, tell him you have nothing to say.
8. After the meeting tell everyone how things should have been done.
9. Do nothing more than absolutely necessary, but when other members use their ability to help matters along, howl out that the organization is run by a clique.
10. Hold back your dues or don't pay at all.

Anonymous

ACCENTUATE THE POSITIVE

Accentuating the positives in marriage is one of the best ways to earn real happiness. If you've never thought about real happiness as a thing to be earned, rather than as a gift dropped in your lap, then you'd make some headway toward emotional maturity by beginning right now to think of happiness that way, particularly in reference to marriage. A child may be extremely happy because Santa Claus brought him a longed-for toy, or because he's going on a picnic. No grownup can be truly happy in quite that way, just as no food, however elaborate, ever tastes as good as that slice of bread and butter, piled high with sugar, that your mother told you to take outdoors and eat so's you wouldn't get it all over the living-room rug.

So, right off, accept the fact that a good marriage has to be earned. And a large part of earning it lies in concentrating on its positive, rather than its negative, aspects. No matter how grand your marriage partner (or your mother or your brother or your sister, for that matter) may be in many ways, if you keep them constantly aware of their faults and failings and the negatives in their conduct, you'll stack them up against overwhelming odds.

You take the guy who says to his best friend that he and the missus are having a pretty tough time of it. He launches into an elaborate explanation of how he can't get along with her any more. He describes her faults, what she didn't do, and what she did, why she almost drives him crazy, how she's failed him and what he wishes she would do. The relationship seems to be pretty hopeless.

Now suppose this best friend says to him: "Well, if the gal hasn't any qualities that you like at all, why did you marry her? Seems like you used to tell me how charming and attractive she was, and how intelligent, and what a swell sense of humor she had."

So the guy kinda squirms, because he don't like these questions much, and he says: "Well, when we were first married, I thought she was pretty and intelligent and her sense of humor was working all right, but lately she's kinda lost her good looks and she never laughs any more."

And the friend says: "Well, do you ever mention how pretty she is? Do you ever try to make her laugh, or tell her how much you always liked her fine sense of humor, or how good it is to talk things over with her?"

The guy has to admit that he doesn't do any of these things. And, of course, his negative attitude toward his wife is the reason why she's lost that old verve and sparkle that made her so attractive, and why she looks on the grim side of everything, and why she don't bother any more to fix up her face and tidy her hair and put on a fresh dress, like she used to when they were courting and she felt he appreciated her and cared how she looked. No one on earth can take an emotional diet of steady criticism without showing signs of it—and all she's heard out of Henry for the past three years is why don't she make pies like Mother used to, and how pretty and neat that Mrs. Humperdink down the street always looks, and why don't she make the kids stop yelling.

If this guy with the negative attitude would take a couple of weeks, just as an experiment, and devote them to telling his wife how cute she looks, and how he likes to hear that little giggle, and what a swell cook she is, and what a grand job she's doing with Junior, and how the boys at the office compliment him on having the smartest, prettiest wife in the crowd, he'd get a real shock. He might not feel like saying those things, but he can't help noticing how she perks up right away. She'll be a little bit suspicious at first, but after a while she'll fall right in line, and she'll get just as pretty and trim as she ever was, or maybe even prettier, and he'll begin to enjoy himself and find out what an idiot he was with that critical, nagging, negative attitude that was making her drab and dull, and the pair of them will be on the way to a happy marriage again.

It takes a pretty good Joe to do a thing like that, because he has to admit that he wasn't always right and his wife always wrong. He has to have the courage to give up his own ego and put the accent on hers. And he deserves a lot of credit. It's a difficult thing to start, but very easy to keep up, once he learns how to accentuate the positive at every opportunity.

What happens with this former negative attitude of his is that he used to talk about her faults all the time and never mention her good points, and pretty soon the mental image of being a slovenly, homely, dull woman came into her mind. She felt rejected, and as she grew more and more hopeless of being understood or even wanted by her husband, she lost all her positive and charming qualities. She grew to look and think like that drab, uninteresting creature he was always sniping at. If you focus on the negative in a person, you bring out the negative in that person in ever-increasing proportions.

And it works both ways. When a husband finds himself the object of continual fault finding, he becomes a different person, too. He comes to believe that whatever his wife says is criticism, even when she doesn't intend any. His negative picture of married life grows and grows. His spontaneity in the matter of love-making ceases to exist. Finally, he becomes emotionally incapable of inspiring love or responding to it at home. Unless he seeks some extramarital sexual satisfaction (which certainly is not to be recommended) he may find that he is undergoing serious damage to his health.

At the same time, the wife suffers, too, although her suffering is unconscious, because she's too angry to realize it. She can't escape the effects of her constant criticism; they bounce back on her like an echo. She has to live with a husband who's becoming less and less interested in her by the hour, and pretty soon he's not her husband any more at all; he's just the guy she fights with and cooks for. She probably feels justified in her criticism, but that won't help her any. Life is as dreary for her as it is for him. Her negative attitude has not only ruined her husband's chances for happiness, but her own as well.

The main secret in the art of getting along happily in marriage, or in any other human relationship, for that matter, is to turn the favorable attention of the other person toward you. And you can only do that by turning your favorable attention toward him. That's what love is—a mutual understanding and appreciation of the positives in each other, and understanding and appreciation so real that the negatives become of no account whatsoever. It can never be accomplished by carping criticism. Accentuating the positive is the only thing that will do it.

HOW TO STEAL A WHALE

You know, great scientific minds are not above crossing one another up, if they get a chance. Mental giants are just like anybody else in getting there fustest with the mostest, if they can add to their own glory by doing so.

There's one case of thievery among the great that I wish I'd seen. That was when Professor E. D. Cope of the Academy of Natural Sciences of Philadelphia calmly walked off with a whale right under the nose of Dr. Alexander Agassiz of Harvard. Dr. Agassiz always claimed afterwards that Professor Cope was the greatest thief in the world, because he stole the largest object ever stolen. Here's what happened.

A Captain Atwood of Provincetown, Massachusetts, once notified Dr. Agassiz that a strange whale had drifted ashore up on the Cape, and Dr. Agassiz at once sent a crew of naturalists down to look over the specimen. Well, the whale was very dead, and it happened to be an

54

entirely new species, so with considerable excitement the boys prepared the skeleton for shipment and loaded it on a flatcar for transportation to Cambridge.

But Professor Cope, down in Philadelphia, had his spies out, too, and when he heard of the whale the Harvard boys had found, he went up to Provincetown and took a room in a farmhouse where he could watch proceedings and still keep out of sight. Finally the bones of the whale were all loaded, and the Harvard boys went home, and that night Professor Cope went down and had a little conversation with the station agent, and somehow or other the waybill on that flatcar got changed from a Cambridge waybill to a Philadelphia one, and the whale ended up as a new species described in detail by Professor Cope and its skeleton is still preserved in the Academy of Natural Sciences in Philadelphia. This happened around eighty or ninety years ago . . . and the boys are still mad about it. If you want to raise the hackles on any guy in the Science Department at Harvard, just mention that whale.

ARE YOU FIT TO BE A PARENT?

It's a funny thing how a lot of us, who wouldn't think of practicing law or medicine without passing examinations and getting a license, or trying to bake a perfect cake without reading the cookbook, or planting a garden without examining the type of earth the seeds are to grow in, will rush into parenthood without knowing anything about the business of raising babies. Oh, sure, they probably know enough to fix the kid's formula, and to hold his head up out of water when they're giving him a bath, but that ain't all there is to parenthood. Not by a long sight. It's only about one per cent of the deal. And the other ninety-nine per cent is the part they don't know, and the part they oughta find out a little about, before they begin operating on the younger generation.

Did you ever stop to think that parenthood is a social relationship, and social relationships require a whale of a lot of responsibility, and parenthood is probably the one and only social relationship that you can't possibly get out of, once you've gotten into it?

For instance, if you have a job, you have a very definite social relationship with your boss, and by social, I don't mean friendship outside the office. But you gotta say good morning to the guy, and make reports and take orders; you have a thousand and one occasions for social relationships with him. And if you don't like these social contacts with the guy you're hired out to work for, if they're sufficiently irritating to make your work thoroughly objectionable, you can quit. You can get out of the relationship. What's more—I got news for you. If that boss of yours don't like you, he can get out of it, too.

Same thing with friends. You meet somebody and like him real well, then maybe after a while you find you don't care to pal around with him, so you drop him. Or you meet somebody you don't like right off; you give him a fast brush-off. You can get out of such social relationships with comparative ease. You can even avoid contacts with members of your own family, if you have to, and sometimes even that is necessary for your peace of mind and theirs. But the relationship of parent and child—uh-uh. You can't get out of it if you're the parent. Maybe the kid will grow up and start avoiding social relationship with you, but from the time he's born till he can stand on his own two feet and give the world back as good as he gets, you're stuck with him.

Of course, the feeling of being stuck with the kid is no natural notion for any parent to have, but let's face it, and then forget it and figure out whether you, yourself, are fit to entertain this great responsibility of parenthood. Of course, we can't solve that problem in the next five or six minutes, but there are two or three little tips some of the psychological boys have figured out that may set you thinking.

In the first place, it ain't exactly enough to love your kids, and take care of them and feed them right and keep them clean. That's only half the job. The other half is that you've got the full responsibility for teaching Junior how to live in the world. If he succeeds, you succeed, and if he fails, you fail. And if you have to apologize for his shortcomings, remember, you're apologizing for your own, right along with his. So you've got to teach him to become a mature and independent member of society, and give him all the opportunities he's got coming to him; in short, make him into the kind of an individual you truly wish that you yourself could be. That's kind of a large order.

By the way, don't get the idea that maybe you and the Mister aren't entirely perfect now, but the minute a little stranger comes into your life everything will be different. Junior will make his own weather, all of it sunny, and you and your old man will stop throwing the plates at one another and turn into angels. The boys who mess around with psychology have found out that there's nothing much to that popular notion that the great and inspiring experience of becoming a parent is gonna uplift you right into having the disposition of a saint. If anything, the worry and responsibility of having a child acts just the other way. So you gotta be a pretty decent sort to start with, if you're going to make a go of it.

The main thing to remember is that the personal qualifications for being a fit parent are pretty much like the personal qualifications for being a fit wife, or a fit husband, or a fit friend, or being a success in your business or your profession. Nobody likes a sourpuss or a complainer, not even a baby. Nobody likes a shrill or strident voice; it grates on day-old ears, too. Nobody likes a poor sport, or a person with a streak of cruelty, or a nagger, or a conceited show-off, and kids notice those things awful fast. A nice, sunny, tolerant disposition can do more for a kid's well-being than anything else, and nice, sunny, tolerant people are the ones that fit in best in every walk of life. You don't have to be a pollyanna and bubble over every minute. That kind of person can be as irritating as the folks who go around acting as if they'd been weaned on a pickle. But have fun. Have fun with the kids. I guess about the nicest compliment a grown-up boy or girl could pay to his parents would be to say that maybe the going was a little rugged now and then, but they always had fun together.

And remember that no matter how surprised you may be by Junior's actions, he learned those actions from somebody, probably you. In school a smart teacher can usually tell, the minute a new kid walks into a schoolroom, just about what kind of parents he has. She can tell by the way he hangs up his coat in the locker and bangs his books down on the desk. So, no matter how nice you act out in company, you ain't fooling nobody if little Alcibiades shows you up by acting the way he usually sees you act around the house when nobody's looking.

To be a good parent, you don't have to live by the second hand on your watch, nor by the last drop of the special formula that you're feeding Little Sister and the last spoonful of spinach that Junior just can't down. Neither do you have to be one hundred per cent enthusiastic one hundred per cent of the time. The pleasures of bringing up kids so far outbalance the tiresome difficulties so heavily that there's no need to pump up fictitious cheerfulness. You've got to have good emotional balance to be a good parent, and maybe, after all, there's just one real good test. If you and the old man can pull in double harness, sharing life with happiness and deep enduring satisfaction, then you're fully qualified to be a good parent. You won't even have to work at the job. It'll all come natural.

SHORT SERMONS FOR YOUNG MEN

The famous clergyman and author, Dr. William Barret Millard, at one time wrote some terse rules for young ministers, rules which could be just as well applied by any smart young man who's starting out in life.

"Pray every night and shave every morning.

"Keep your conscience clean, also your linen.

"Let your light shine, and shine your shoes.

"Press your advantages, your opportunities, and your trousers.

"Brush the cobwebs from your brain and the dandruff from your collar.

"Beware of a reputation for bad breath or rancid jokes. Both alike offend.

"Covet a golden tongue more than a greenback.

"Don't mix your metaphors, but, at the same time, be a good mixer.

"You can't put fire in your work unless there is fire in your heart.

"Two things cannot be imitated: God's sunset and man's insincerity.

"It is better to establish a good precedent than to follow a bad one.

"It is better to lose a good fight than to win a bad one.

"Always be content with what you have, but never with what you are."

SUGGESTIONS FOR A BUSY FATHER

Here's a list of suggestions for a busy father. It was drawn up by Dr. Anna W. M. Wolf, the specialist in child care, with an eye to cementing friendly relations between a busy and harassed father and his eager small fry. I think you'll get an idea or two out of this.

1. Father and child should breakfast together as soon as the child can sit in a high chair. If baby has already finished his breakfast, let him have a small portion of bread and milk at the family table.

2. Father and child should have some time together in the evening, if schedules can possibly be arranged. This time should be spent in quiet activity—not too much rough play and shouting.

3. Father shouldn't get impatient with the kids if they run in and out of the room when he's shaving. It's a good time for conversation, believe it or not, and for some reason kids are absolutely fascinated by the spectacle of a guy taking his whiskers off. It's pretty near impossible to keep them out, so let them come on in.

4. For part of Sundays and other holidays Father should find time to play with the kids, either in his own room or any place in the house where he can be free and easy and not worry too much about scarring the furniture. This does not mean merely watching the child at play, but actually taking part, building with blocks, playing house, drawing pictures, looking at picture books and reading. Keeping a scrapbook together is a good idea, and if Pop has a hobby such as carpentry or photography or such, he can carry the kid right along with him. And collections of all kinds can usually be made interesting to children. Father mustn't set his standards too high; kids will be kids, and carelessness will crop out and interest will fluctuate and doubtless some rather precious equipment will get broken sooner or later. But if he's willing to compromise with the incessant questions and the clumsy fingers of his four-year-old, he'll find something very rich and rewarding. Naturally, he'll have sense enough to keep delicate and expensive apparatus out of the way at this point, and he won't let anything real sharp or any poisonous chemicals come into their hands.

5. Don't neglect the obvious outdoor activities—running, jumping, ball-playing, handicap races, and any sport the old man used to be pretty good at when he was a kid. If he's still any good, he'll get a kick out of it and the kids will be right proud. And he shouldn't neglect trips with the kids down to the waterfront, over to the airport, to the fire station, to the local factories. Such ordinary sights of your home town can be as much fun as a circus if Junior has Dad along to take an interest in everything with him. You're doing strictly nothing for the kid if you take him on a solemn walk or a formal call upon adult relatives or friends. But if he gets to go down to the firehouse or along with Dad to the barbershop, swell time will be had by all.

6. Occasional visits—very occasional—to his father's office or place of work are almost essential for a child. Let him see what Dad does all day; let Dad explain *what* he does, as clearly as possible. Be simple. Don't make it an all-inclusive sight-seeing tour, but watch to see what

captures his interest. It's better for the young'un to learn a lot about one small side issue than to come home all mixed up about everything. Father will get a real thrill out of introducing his offspring to other workers in the office. Keep the visit brief, and afterwards tell him about the other guys down in that place: what they do and what their families are like, so that the office seems human, and not some dim mysterious place that swallows Pop every morning and spits him out just in time to get home at night.

7. After the child is about five or six, his father ought to take him once in a while to a restaurant, and this is a strictly stag affair. No wimmenfolks allowed along. It's best if he takes the kid to a place where he goes often with his business friends and where he knows the waiters and where things are quite different from home—a man's world. And let the kid have what he wants to eat. For once, forget that balanced diet. Of course, don't deliberately poison him, either; if you know from experience that he gets sick each and every time he eats a certain food, don't tempt fate by letting him have that food in large quantities. But let him go the limit, within reason.

8. For the six- or seven-year-old, one of life's greatest treats can be the big ball game he attends with his father, when Dad acts really young again and whoops and hollers and stamps and cheers and yells for the annihilation of the umpire. If the kid don't already know the game, Pop may have to explain as he goes along, but it's a sure thing he won't have to the next time he takes the kid out. By that time Junior will be telling *him*. And Father shouldn't forget to be generous with the peanuts and the pink sodas, either. The chances for a stomach-ache are very slim; not worth balancing against the good-fellowship.

9. Another important and private bond between father and child is often the funnies. As a rule, women don't care for comic sheets. They just ain't interested; they think the funnies are stupid and vulgar and unsuitable for the young and tender mind. But the psychologists say the gals are all wrong about this. Father knows better, for the very good reason that men go right on enjoying the funnies after they grow up, which may be just one more proof that a man is always a little boy in some ways and the gals are kind of superior in cultural attainments. And then again it may not prove any such thing. It may prove that all children and most men have a natural robust sense of humor, which gal babies kinda lose as they graduate into girlhood. At least that's what the psychologists say. Don't quote me on it.

Well, you may go along with Dr. Wolf on that list of suggestions as to how a busy father can keep friends with his kids—then again you may not. I just gave it to you the way the book says. And personally, I think there's something in it. Might be worth trying, anyhow.

COUNTING THE PRIBILOF SEALS

Most of us have real ordinary routine jobs. Some of us have jobs that are a little unusual, and every once in a while you run across a guy who holds down a job the like of which you never heard before. And it's always interesting to find out how the guy got this unique job, and how he likes it, and how much it pays off, and stuff like that.

One of the most unusual jobs I ever heard of was the one held down in 1914 by Dr. George Howard Parker, the famous zoologist. He was the guy sent to the Pribilof Islands to count the seals.

You know the Pribilof Islands, those two little rocky specks in the ocean that we acquired with the purchase of Alaska in 1867. They're the breeding grounds for the seals that yield those silky golden-brown fur coats that are supposed to make any Bedelia glamorous, even one with a puss like she'd been weaned on a pickle. Nobody had paid much attention to the seal herds on the Pribilof Islands. The fur trade used to send a flock of ships up there every year and the boys would get out and whap as many seals over the head as they could pack hides in the holds of the ships, and consequently the seal herds were in serious danger of being extinct. The hunters would take seals in the open water, which meant that each cow seal killed while she was out swimming left a baby seal to starve to death back on the rocks, because the Pribilof Islands were where all baby seals, or pups, as they're called, were born. So about 1910 the United States Government took note that if things went on as they had been, in a few years there wouldn't be any seals at all. The boys clamped down on hunting the seals, and there was an agreement between America, Russia, and Japan, the three nations chiefly interested in sealing, that no seals could be hunted in the open sea. And then, in 1914, Dr. Parker and two other men, one from the Smithsonian Institution and one from the Department of Agriculture, were sent up there to count the seals and see if the herds were increasing. This was a very important and ticklish assignment, because the Russian and Japanese fur hunters claimed that we'd put something over on them by demanding that no more seals be hunted down in the open sea.

Counting those seals wasn't as easy as it sounds. You have to know a little about the habits of the fur seals to know how the boys did it. Seems the male seals, which are called bulls, swim to the Pribilof Islands around the end of May. Each bull is a big husky critter weighing in the neighborhood of four hundred pounds. The female seals, or cows, don't arrive on the Pribilofs until around the first of June. Each big bull has picked out his own rookery on some rocky corner he takes a fancy to, and as the cows swim in he snags himself off a harem of maybe thirty or forty wives and they set up housekeeping, right there and then. The cow seals have come to the islands to have their baby seals, who are, you might say, souvenirs from the last season they spent there. So one big old bull is surrounded by his harem of thirty or forty cows, each one with a pup. Incidentally, the cows are relatively small, weighing only about eighty pounds, and the big four-hundred-pound bull has no trouble bossing them around. It's the cows' skins that are valuable in the fur trade. The hide of the bulls, especially the old ones, is too stiff and tough.

In addition to these large family groups, there are a lot of young bulls who weren't strong enough to snag off a rookery or grab themselves a batch of wives. They stay on the islands until early autumn, and then bulls, cows, and pups swim off into the open seas, where they live a free life until they return to the Pribilofs the following year. When they're there, they're in residence by the tens of thousands, all bellowing and grunting and squealing at once. People who've seen them say the place is bedlam. And when they're out in the ocean, not a seal can be found in the Pribilofs.

Well, Dr. Parker figured out a way to count these seals—a very ingenious way, because it never in the world could be done by counting one after another. The critters are in and out of the water all the time.

So first they counted the bulls, who are so big that they stuck up like telegraph poles among the restless squirming cows and pups that covered every inch of rock on the islands. Then, when they figured all the pups had been born that were going to be, the boys chased the cows into the sea to get them out of the way, and herded the pups together, and counted them. Since each cow gives birth to one pup a year, the number of pups born in a year must be the measure of the number of cows on the islands. Then, by calculation, for it was impossible to count them, the boys figured out the number of young nonbreeding animals and bachelor bulls and such to be expected in such a herd.

So a problem which was apparently insoluble was worked out, and they came to the conclusion that there was in the neighborhood of a quarter of a million fur seals still left in the world. Now, with proper protection and laws governing the taking of fur seals, there are close to three million seals in the Pribilof Islands, enough to provide plenty of furs and still keep the herds flourishing.

I think that's kinda interesting, about three dignified gentlemen of science standing up there on the rocky cliffs of the Pribilof Islands, with the bulls bellowing and the cows shrieking and the pups pulling at their coattails like real puppies the world over, confronted with the problem of counting a quarter of a million animals that don't stay put for more than a second at a time. I don't think I'd want the job, but you gotta admit it's mighty unusual. There wouldn't be very many dull moments.

MAKE UP YOUR OWN MIND!

Do you know that there's a real thrill in making up your own mind? It's kinda like taking a plunge into real cold water. After that first shuddery shock is over, you feel real exhilaration in plowing through the briny deep, and you wonder why you never did this before. Maybe you had to get up a lot of nerve for the plunge, but now it's worth it.

Ever read a book called *Make Up Your Mind*, by Margery Wilson? It's not a real new book. It's been out for eight or nine years now, but there's a lot of good stuff in it. Here are a few things Margery Wilson has to say about making up your own mind.

For one thing, it's surprising how few people ever know the superb thrill of making up their own minds. Probably most of us think that we do make up our minds, when, if the truth were known, we're only parrots. Most of our opinions are canned, packaged, precooked, and predigested. What do you suppose would happen if, next time you hear some guy come out with a very positive statement, you snap back with, "Is that your own opinion, or is it merely an acceptance of what you have read, heard, and been told, with no weighing of the facts on your part?" Well, the guy will be insulted—that's what'll happen—but it's the truth. It's a rare person who's able and willing to admit that he

63

does very little independent thinking, and that he's just a bundle of carbon copies of all the opinions he's heard lately. Take it from me, if you do not make up your own mind, someone else will!

Ever see a hypnotized person who will do whatever he is told? Ever see a sheep get caught in brambles or a barbed-wire fence? It'll stand there and starve to death rather than pull away with one quick wrench. That actually happens, in sheep country, a dozen times a day. Guys have to go around doing nothing but unhooking sheep from things that any other animal would have backed out of slicker'n scat. Well, if you can't make up your own mind, you're kinda like those sheep, standing there caught up on the barbs of other men's opinions. Of course, you probably won't physically die of it, but mentally and emotionally you'll grow awful old and dull.

Another thing: if you don't learn to make up your own mind, you get in the habit of mental drifting. Mental drifting is about the worst menace that can creep up on you insidiously. If you do not exercise your "decider," it gets creaky and rusty. And one day you may need it something fierce, and it goes back on you completely, and it takes a long time to build a lax-muscled mind back to firmness again. Maybe you remember that one method the dictators always use in a conquered country is to reduce the inhabitants to confused, undirected thinking. Nothing, not even torture, breaks a man quicker than to lose hope and direction and live in a state of listless waiting. It's not a state you'd get into willingly, and yet it creeps up on you unless you learn to make up your own mind.

Even if at times it is really necessary for you to let other people make up your mind for you, then, in self-defense, you should be the one to make the decision to let them do it. Don't let it just happen to you. Even deciding *not* to decide for yourself is better than being a mental drifter.

Well, let's say you can make up your own mind. You know how to, and none of the boys and girls are putting anything over on you, and you've been doing it all your life. There's a danger there, too. Of course, make up your own mind, but put some kind of a little gadget on it so you can turn it off, or change it, before you get like that guy who made up his mind to fish in a certain pool, and the pool went dry, but there he sat with his hook stuck in the mud. He'd made up his mind too much.

Miss Wilson says that "it is the careful examination of an idea, considering it from all angles, and then acting upon your own interpretation of it that makes you a strong and valuable person. Vacillating, easily persuaded, childishly bored minds are no permanent asset to either side of a discussion, or to any group. They are easy prey for the next persuader, the next propagandist."

And that's the most important thing, I think, about making up one's own mind. If we ever needed to think for ourselves, it's today, when there's a self-appointed opinion pusher in every gathering; when you can't pick up the morning paper, or walk down to the corner store and do your shopping, without being barraged by other men's opinions, not to mention the insidious opinions the propaganda artists sneak in on us in sugar-coated doses. There was never a time when we needed more to starch up our own deciders, to use our own powers of discrimination, and not to let ourselves be led by the nose, however gently. Remember those Indians who were so enraptured by a few strings of bright-colored beads that they sold Manhattan Island for twenty-four dollars' worth of trinkets! Probably old Peter Minuit gave the Red Men a line something like this: he says, "And in exchange for these valuable beads, all we ask is just that little old island over there, which ain't much good and you oughta be glad to get rid of it even if we only offered to haul it away free of charge." That's a swell example of getting led downstream and not even knowing it.

Don't let's forget how important it is to make up our own minds, if we want to have any hand in planning the world we are to live in. And even beyond world affairs, or affairs in our own town or our own block, there's one little core of individuality inside every one of us into which no idea can enter without our consent. Each of us knows that deep down inside there's a point where we're individuals, separate from every other person. We don't have to drift helplessly. All we have to do is learn to use that individuality, learn to make up our own minds, consciously and with due consideration. Think about it a little. It's worth—making up your own mind about!

LEATHER GOODS

Yes, people collect the darnedest things, and sometimes these things end up in museums.

A while ago I read a book about Hermon Carey Bumpus, who was the first director of the American Museum of Natural History, where they have more collections than you can shake a stick at. This book is a biography of Dr. Bumpus by his son, who is also Dr. Bumpus, and I think I got interested in it mostly because I sorta like that name, Bumpus, as a collector of things.

Dr. Bumpus, in his long life as a collector and museum director, ran into some weird little collections, but there was one that really takes the prize. Here's what happened.

In 1904 Dr. Bumpus was traveling in England looking for odd objects, and he ran into an English officer who early in life had been stationed in New Zealand, where he had collected some forty tattooed human heads. Now, as it happens, in the early days this native tattooing of the New Zealand aborigines was so beautiful and so highly prized that, when a member of the family died, especially one with fine tattooed patterns all over his face, his head, properly tanned, was preserved. In this way the natives were able to keep in personal contact with their ancestors, so to speak.

With the advent of the white man, these ancestral heads came to have commercial value, and the natives were tempted by high prices and so sold them off, until they became pretty scarce. So the natives kinda started manufacturing these heads for the trade, as it were. There's a yarn to the effect that a sea captain, upon inquiring if there were any to be had, was told: "Not right now, but if you'll look over the live ones and tell us which one you would like, we'll have it tanned and ready for you on your next voyage!"

Of course, the English kinda frowned upon this incentive to homicide among the local boys, so they forbade the exportation of tanned heads under penalty of a heavy fine and imprisonment, and as a result the natives confined themselves to preserving only the heads of those friends and relatives who died naturally, and they didn't help them ease off this planet, because after the English clamped down on this head-selling deal there wasn't any profit in it. Consequently there were very few specimens in even the largest museums, and the retired officer's collection represented more than were to be found in all the museums put together. Of course Dr. Bumpus was delighted to get it for the American Museum of Natural History.

He packed the heads in his personal luggage, because he didn't want to trust them to the tender mercies of the hold of the ship, on the voyage back to America. Everything was fine on the way across, because Dr. Bumpus was used to things like tanned human heads, but when the customs officer opened the trunks in New York and saw forty dried and tattooed human faces staring him in the puss, he was kinda at a loss for words. He proclaimed that during his many years as a customs inspector this was the most unusual consignment he'd ever been called on to check through. And he didn't know how to classify them for customs duties, either, but he hit upon the notion of listing them as "leather goods" and that took care of the matter.

I don't suppose that inspector ever felt the same about opening trunks, though. I think if a thing like that happened to me I'd change my job.

NON-BIBLICAL PROPHETS

Prophets never have been very popular, in their own country or any-where else. That's because the medicine they hand out usually has a bitter taste.

I'm not going to talk about any of the biblical prophets; if you've read your Bible you know all about them, and if you haven't, go read it. It's a mighty interesting book.

But there have been a lot of other fellows besides those in the Bible who not only prophesied terrible things but also sort of rubbed it in about what was going to happen if folks didn't behave themselves. Sometimes they were right and sometimes they were wrong. Take Mother Shipton, for instance. Around the end of the fifteenth century she prophesied the discovery of America in 1492, the Great Fire of London, the French Revolution, the discovery of potatoes and tobacco in the New World, the Napoleonic Wars, and Hitler; that is, some folks read all that into the jingles she made up. But she was dead wrong about one thing: she said the world would come to an end in 1881, which it didn't, and, moreover, Hitler wasn't even born by that time.

As a matter of fact, Hitler was no mean prophet himself. In 1920 Bad Boy Adolf declared that Germany could never win a war with England fighting on the opposing side—and how right he was!

Some of the poets have seemed to have a prophetic sort of vision: Tennyson wrote about something that sounds suspiciously like aerial warfare, long before airplanes were invented:

There rain'd a ghastly dew
From the nations' airy navies grappling in the central blue . . .

Tennyson talked about something else that's in the news today: "The parliament of Man, the Federation of the world." According to his version, the United Nations worked out all right. Let's hope.

And the German poet Heine got in a few good licks about the Nazis a hundred years ahead of time, when he said, "There will come crashing and roaring forth . . . the insane Berserker rage. The old stone gods will rise from the long-forgotten ruin and rub the dust of a thousand years from their eyes, and Thor, leaping to life with his giant hammer, will crush the Gothic cathedrals!"

But the champion prophet of all time was an obscure country doctor named Michel de Nostredame, who lived in France about the middle of the sixteenth century. Nostradamus, as he's generally called, enjoyed an enormous vogue as a soothsayer from the time he set up in the fortunetelling racket until today. Right this minute there are a whole lot of people who believe in the prophecies of Nostradamus, and when something happens in the world they give out with: "See? I told you so. It's right there in the book!"

Nostradamus made literally hundreds and hundreds of detailed prophecies concerning his own time and far into the future. In fact, they're going on yet, and they will be for some little time. His prophecies are couched in rhyme, and some of them are so obscure that the meaning can be interpreted several ways, which certainly leaves a loophole for Nostradamus. If the thing doesn't pan out, somebody can always say, "Aha, you didn't read the right meaning into it." But he was astonishingly detailed, and astonishingly accurate. He prophesied his own death, to the day, hour, and minute. He got in Queen Elizabeth, and the death of Oliver Cromwell; he said the Great Fire of London was set by firebugs, a theory which has never been disproved; he went into some very detailed stuff concerning the French Revolution, Napoleon, the formation and growth of the United States, the two World Wars. Just about anything and everything of world significance that's happened since the sixteenth century can be found in Nostradamus, if you interpret his words to cover the situation.

One thing he states for sure: the world is going to be at peace for the first time in history in 1953. A whole lot of prophets agree on that particular date as the beginning of the Golden Age. I just hope they don't mean we're gonna have peace because we're permanently out of commission on account of being blown sky high by our own inventions. I can see how an atomic bomb or so could spread around a whole lot of permanent peace for a whole lot of people . . . maybe an entire worldful.

USING YOUR WIFE'S BRAINS

I suppose it's just human nature to take credit where credit is due, and then run over where it ain't due a bit and take some credit there, too. We're all inclined to blow our own horn, no matter how weak a toot comes out. That's the reason why so few men are big enough to credit their success, at least partly, to their wives.

Just the same, a lot of the boys achieved their place in life because of the little woman. We've mentioned how a wife can harm a man in his work; now let's turn to what she can do for him. And do it she does, because the lads who mess around with statistics have figured out that in six cases out of ten, where a man succeeds in business, it's because he used his wife's brains as well as his own.

If men would only realize the wealth of potential help—sound, practical, effective help—the average woman is capable of giving, there'd be fewer male mediocrities, and more successful, happy marriages. But unfortunately not so many men are able and willing to talk things over at home and pick up some much-needed advice. Man seems to have a special variety of ego that dazzles and dazes him. He can't look around or beyond it. He becomes mentally myopic, especially toward his own shortcomings. And his ego expands until he becomes the traditional stuffed shirt.

Let's face it: women are the practical sex. And, contrary to the general opinion, it ain't half as easy to wound a gal's feelings or snub her or step on her pride as it is to do the same thing to a man. A man will throw up a perfectly good job for a real or fancied slight that a gal would shrug off with a couple of well-placed wisecracks. A man will open his yawp and let a lot of unconsidered stuff run out when a gal, in the same position, will keep mum and bide her time. Men discourage easier than women; they get fed up quicker than women, and, believe it or not, they're a dozen times more impulsive. If a guy has sense enough to realize this, he'll ask advice at home, and talk over his problems, and go down to the office in the morning with a better perspective on things than he took home with him the night before. Of course, some bird-brained gals can't be talked with, because they have nothing to offer in return, but the average woman is a doggoned good manager at home, and home management and office management are closer than you'd think, offhand.

Men may sound off a lot about their excellent snap judgment, but oftener than not they're merely jumping to conclusions which, on the one hand, may be as wise as the decisions of Solomon, and, on the other, may be pitfalls that even a half-witted rabbit would have sense enough to keep out of. And they've also got a habit of keeping their own counsel when things go wrong at the office or when there's some big deal afoot. They hang their heads at home; they're grouchy; they criticize the dinner and yell at the kids.

If the wife senses that something is amiss, she's eager to share the burden and ease the pain, and if the husband gives her a brush-off, she's likely to aggravate him all the more by insisting that he can't fool her and pretend he isn't worried. Right off she tells him that she hasn't lived with him all these years for nothing, and he gripes back that he can't talk to her, because she don't take an interest and wouldn't understand anyhow, and right there is a beautiful opening for a domestic ruckus. Of course the ruckus only makes things worse, because he can't think things through when he's in the middle of a quarrel, any more than he could if he had a splitting headache. If he'd been willing to give his wife a chance, and explain things to her, and lay it right on the line, she'd not only be able to cope with it, same as she does with the price of meat or the braces on Junior's teeth, but she'd probably have some real sensible suggestions to offer. Even if she didn't, the pair of them would be in full understanding of the problem together, and he'd have the assurance and confidence of her faith in him to back him up. A man needs a woman's psychological and spiritual help as balancing factors, just as a woman needs his.

No matter how highly gifted a man may be, no mattter how well developed his logic and his reasoning, if the premises from which he starts thinking are faulty, he stubbornly keeps on and on in the same old wheel track. It's one of the things about men, even the smartest of them, that makes wives turn gray. It's pride that keeps a man from turning back, a funny kind of mistaken pride that may wreck him.

As much as we'd love to believe it, the average of us males just ain't no genius. Most of us are pretty good Joes, but we need help. And that's where the real boss of the household comes in. Man, being a supreme egotist, sometimes discusses his business affairs with his wife because he wants to be "yessed" or to show what a big shot he is, same as Junior comes in to tell Momma that he just killed ten Indians with his bow and arrow. If the light of his life turns on her intuition, he becomes sarcastic and sometimes downright insulting. He's missing a great opportunity to get the same smart advice he may shell out a few hundred bucks to a lawyer for, later on.

Aside from this matter of talking things over, most women help their husbands in any number of ways which, alas, are all too often totally unappreciated. They'll go all out socially to foster a husband's career. They'll make important contacts in a friendly way by attending an important luncheon or giving one. They'll budget and save in order to dress well to make a good impression on a man's business associates. And they'll make every effort to stimulate the male ego to do and dare and achieve. They'll give him trust and confidence, if he wants it or not.

Unless there's a specific and sound reason for not doing so, every wife should be consulted regularly about business affairs, not only that she may have a full grasp of the family finances and prospects, but that the husband may have the advantage of her advice, impressions, and decisions. In fact a man's a dope if he don't give his life partner an opportunity to demonstrate what she can do, and, moreover, is eager and willing to do, to help him.

HERE LIES AN OLD WOMAN

Here lies an old woman who always was tired;
She lived in a house where help was not hired.
Her last words on earth were: "Dear Friends, I am goin'
Where washin' ain't done, nor sweepin' nor sewin';
But everything there is exact to my wishes:
For where they don't eat there's no washin' of dishes.
I'll be where loud anthems will always be ringin',
But havin' no voice I'll be clear of the singin';
Don't mourn for me now; don't mourn for me never—
I'm goin' to do nothin'—forever and ever."

Anonymous

HOW TO TAKE OUT STAINS

Taking out spots and stains is something every wife and mother has to do all the time. Everybody else has to do it once in a while, if they haven't got wives and mothers to do it for them. You can be the Sheik of Araby and still get spots on your vest—and feel just as foolish as the next guy until somebody gets it out for you. Here's a list of a few things to do when you start seeing spots where spots shouldn't be, and the spot expert of the family isn't within earshot.

Bloodstains will set in hot water, but soaking in cold water will take them out of washable material, and a good commercial bleach is all right for white material, except rayon and silk. If the stuff isn't washable, call for the nearest professional cleaner.

Candle wax may be scraped from the fabric with a dull knife. Then you put the spot between two layers of blotting paper and press it with a warm iron. If it's washable, wash it in plenty of soap, and if it isn't, sponge it with grease solvent. If the wax was from a colored candle there may be a dye stain which probably will come out with wood alcohol.

Chewing gum, which is always a menace, has become a triple threat now we have bubble gum. Scrape off what you can with a dull knife, and soften up the spot with egg white, or soak in turpentine or gasoline for stubborn cases. Then wash the material as usual, or if it doesn't take to washing, any solvent with carbon tetrachloride will get out the rest.

If a stain is fresh and the fabric washable, chocolate and cocoa stains will come out with lukewarm water. Old stains on washable stuff should be soaked in wood alcohol to which a few drops of ammonia have been added, and non-washable fabrics may be treated with carbon tetrachloride followed by hydrogen peroxide; but test the peroxide first—it may take the color out.

Cod-liver oil stains, which are the bane of young mothers' lives, will come out of washable stuff with banana oil and soapsuds, or unwashable material with carbon tetrachloride.

Pour boiling water through coffee stains, wash, and bleach if the material will stand it. For non-washable stuff, sponge with warm water and peroxide, being careful not to take the color out. If the coffee had cream in it, you'll have to use a grease solvent, too.

Egg stains are set with heat. Soak them in cold water, and, for stuff that can't be washed, sponge with lukewarm water. They're hard to get out. Maybe you'd better send it to the cleaner's.

Fruit stains on delicate or non-washable goods are nothing for the amateur to tackle. If the fabric is white or fast color, and washable, fasten the material over a bowl with a rubber band or string, and pour boiling water through the spot at a height of two or three feet. It may work and it may not.

Grass stains come out with washing and bleaching. If the goods won't take a good scrubbing, it's a job for the professionals.

Grease and oil stains come out with soap and water or a good solvent.

Inkstains are kind of discouraging, but sweet milk will take them out. Try soaking the stain, and change the milk when it becomes discolored.

Iodine stains respond to a good soaking in a cold starch solution.

Iron rust is tough to get out. You can try steaming the spot over a boiling kettle while you drip lemon juice on it. You may have to rinse it out and repeat several times, and if there's any stain left, moisten salt with lemon juice, and spread the paste on the stain and put it in the sun.

Mildew can sometimes be gotten out by soaking the goods overnight in sour milk and spreading them in the sun, or you can give the stains that lemon-and-salt treatment.

Paint stains look bad, but they're easy. Turpentine is all you need.

A scorch mark will come out, if it's not too dark, with plain water and sunlight. Of course, if you let your iron burn all the way through, that's different.

Tar can be removed with carbon tetrachloride.

Tea stains, which set with heat, will come out if soaked in a borax solution, or, if the fabric is white, lemon juice and sunlight are all you need.

The main thing to remember about stains—any kind—is to get them out as quickly as possible. Remember that a little judicious dabbing with cold water when you first get the catsup on your necktie is better than a bottle of cleaning fluid two weeks later. And, if you send your clothes to the laundry, don't forget to take the stains out first. They don't mean a thing to your laundryman unless you particularly call his attention to them.

If you use a solvent around the house, don't use an inflammable one. Never use gasoline or kerosene or anything like that. Buy a good brand of solvent and read the label before you use it. And no matter what it says, don't use it around open fires. There's no sense in taking chances.

Anybody can take stains out intelligently, but being intelligent also means to know enough to stop if the thing is beyond you, and hunt up a good cleaner who makes his living specializing in such things. More material is wasted because of what people do to spots and stains than because of the spots themselves.

TALES OF THE YELLOWSTONE

Folks are always talking about the seven wonders of the ancient world. Well, there are plenty of spots right here in the good old U.S.A. that are pretty wonderful, and in addition to their natural wonders, some of the boys have fitted them out with a set of tall tales that kinda knock the spots off everything from the Pyramids of Egypt on down.

Take Yellowstone National Park, for instance. Everybody knows how full of wonders Yellowstone is, with its fantastic geysers and hot springs and weird rock formations, but to listen to some of the old boys tell the story, it isn't just half out of the world; it's plumb out altogether. You know how the storytellers can't leave the truth alone; even if it's too amazing to believe anyhow, that's just a temptation to pile up startling embellishments.

But in Yellowstone the embellishments don't even add up to the reality, because the reality defies exaggeration. After the geologists got to work and analyzed and catalogued the natural wonders, the spectacular truth about them was so startling that the old legends seem pale beside it.

There are the geysers, probably the most awe-inspiring phenomena, and they sure inspired awe in the Indians. Those columns of gushing water, accompanied by thunderous rumblings, scared the red men half to death. They thought a terrible continuous battle between infernal spirits was going on, and they kept well away from the valley. The earliest explorers brought back tales of geysers shooting a thousand feet into the air; actually there are more geysers in Yellowstone than anywhere else in the world, and the clockwork regularity of some of them, like Old Faithful, is more amazing and interesting than the tall tale of a thousand-foot spouter. Seventy feet is high enough for average geysers, especially as there are hundreds of them and some of them are boiling hot.

74

Then there was the notion that Satan conducted his business right under Yellowstone. There are plenty of bottomless pits, belching smoke and sulphurous fumes, where unwary trespassers could take their chances on meeting Old Nick face to face, if they were careless.

The legend about the Firehole says that the water comes out cold as ice, but rushes over the stones so fast that it heats up, and comes out boiling hot in a pool at the foot of the waterfall. It does come from a spring as cold as ice, but there's a steam vent leading into that pool, so you get the effect of one of those hot-and-cold mixers on your bathtub faucet.

There was the tale of Alum Creek: if a horse forded it, his hoofs would shrink to pinpoints, and the alum was so strong that it could pucker distance itself. Actually the water will give you a wry face for a week, if you dare taste it, but the very fact that alum is there at all in concentrated doses is miracle enough. There don't seem to be any sensible explanation for a river whose water is full of alum, just one river in the whole world. How did the alum get in there in the first place?

According to some stories, there was a petrified forest in the Yellowstone country, with petrified trees, and petrified birds on them singing petrified songs, and the sun and moon gave petrified light! There is a petrified forest, although those petrified birds and petrified songs are stretched a little far. Some of the geysers which spout hot water actually do go up to two hundred feet of scalding spray, and this spray is supersaturated with lime. So when the wind blows it over nearby trees they are covered with glittering particles, which gradually make a sparkling crystal coating on the geyser side of the trees, while the other side bears living branches.

Then we have any number of accounts of Crystal Mountain, supposedly a real mountain of solid transparent crystal, like a great lump of clear glass. You'd walk right up and bump into it, because you wouldn't see it. You'd take aim at a deer and fire, only to find the deer didn't even hear the shot, because he was on the other side of the mountain. The geologist boys found that was only an inexpert attempt to describe the Great Obsidian Cliff, flint-hard, smoky in color, and, instead of being transparent, it's a perfect mirror on a vast scale, reflecting the whole landscape, so that the deer those early hunters were sniping at were really behind them, reflected in the obsidian, instead of around on the other side, as they thought.

One place the boys improved on nature, though, was in their account

75

of the echoes in Yellowstone. The yarn ran that opposite a certain camping ground rose a sheer mountain, without a tree or a wisp of grass growing on it, and the echo that bounced off this mountain made an excellent alarm clock. When you crawled under your blanket at night you just hollered "Time to get up!" at the mountain, and back came the echo, at exactly six o'clock the next morning. That I gotta see. It's about the only tall tale around the Yellowstone that isn't backed up by wonders more miraculous than the storytellers could dream up.

FEAR! MAN'S COMMONEST DISEASE

The most ordinary thing for any human being to have the matter with him, next to the common cold, is some kind of a morbid fear. Just about everybody has one or two of these whingdings, and he knows he has it, he knows it's utterly foolish and makes him ridiculous, and he feels completely baffled as to how to cope with the thing.

I'm not going to discuss the ordinary fears that most of us experience at one time or another, usually in childhood. Fear of the dark, of strange animals, of heights, of loud noises—those aren't morbid fears, because most of us get rid of them in the process of growing up. Of course, if we keep them and nurse them along and suffer with them when we're adult, they can become morbid fears, but that's another story.

No, I'm talking about the funny little eccentric fears that just about everybody has, like a woman I heard of once who could walk into a lion's cage and never turn a hair, but an ordinary little piece of fuzzy cotton wool would send her right off into a fit of the shakes. A psychologist found out what was the matter with her: years before, she'd reached out in the dark when she was half asleep and put her hand on something soft and fluffy and it turned out to be a mouse. Then of course the psychologist had to go back still further and find out why she was afraid of mice, but he finally got her all straightened out.

Now probably you aren't afraid of cotton wool, but it's a lead-pipe cinch you're afraid of something. These neurotic fears are legion; one small dictionary lists seventy-six of them, all with fancy Greek and Latin names. Claustrophobia is one of the commonest—that's fear of being in enclosed places. A fine way to insure your kids having that one when they grow up is to shut them in a dark closet as a punishment. Then there's agoraphobia, or fear of wide-open spaces. You've heard about these people who never venture more than a block or so from home? That's what they've got. A famous American poet, William Ellery Leonard, had agoraphobia so bad that during his entire life he was hardly able to cross a street, and he was scared of locomotives, too, for some odd reason, so even when he was able to get more than a block away from home he still couldn't go very far, or he'd see a train or a set of railroad tracks and that would take all the starch out of him. Of course, he was an extreme case; the average guy who has agoraphobia just feels mildly uncomfortable and don't know why, if he's out in a wide flat space.

Related to these two common fears are fear of being aloft in the air, fear of tunnels and basements, fear of mountains, fear of the ocean. And you probably know somebody who just can't stay alone two minutes. He has to be with somebody all the time; either he's rushing from one engagement to another or friends come in to see him, and the minute they leave he's on the telephone trying to scare up somebody else to spend an hour or so with. Well, he's got monophobia, or fear of being alone. It ain't that he's just sociable—he can't stand being by himself.

There's pantophobia, or fear of being in a crowd, and xenophobia, which is fear of meeting strangers. There are morbid fears of being in the company of men, or of women. There are fears of being contaminated by dirt or germs, of catching some particular disease; fear of certain colors, such as the color red, which is associated with blood, and a guy who has that particular fear is often terrified by the sight of blood. Some folks are afraid of dogs or cats or horses, or snakes or spiders. Some are afraid of blushing or showing embarrassment. There are actually people afraid of sunlight, or of a cold wind, or of a drop of rain, and of course the fear of thunderstorms is almost too common to mention. There's fear of death, and fear of water, and fear of fire, and fear of being poisoned. The list is endless.

Now, as I mentioned earlier, there's hardly a human being on earth who hasn't got a touch of these fears. With most of us, the fears don't count. Of course, we'd be better off without them, and we could get rid of them if we wanted to, but we just don't bother because they're only a very mild inconvenience. But if they're so bad that they're really making a nuisance of themselves, then we oughta do something about them. They can waste a lot of time, and the extreme reactions of sweating, palpitation of the heart, pallor, and tremors put an awful drain on the whole body.

Most people can't get rid of their fears without help from a trained psychologist who recognizes that the fear of some specific thing, such as a spider, for example, is only a symptom of what's wrong. The spider is a symbol, not the thing that's really scaring you. And as soon as you realize that, half the battle's won. The other half is when the brain mechanic helps you to find out what it's a symbol of, and once you know that, you're over it. Some folks can figure the thing out for themselves, and if you can, you're lucky. But if you have some little mild fears and they aren't enough to bother you, don't worry about them. Everybody else is in the same boat.

NEVER TROUBLE TROUBLE

Better never trouble Trouble
Till Trouble troubles you,
For you only make that Trouble
Double-Trouble when you do.
And that Trouble, like a bubble,
That you're worrying about,
May be nothing but a zero
With the rim . . . soon . . . out.

David Keppel

GETTING RID OF BAD HABITS

There's a routine that some of these self-righteous individuals like to pull, which goes something like this: "I don't believe in forming habits. It's all a matter of will power. Just as soon as I find I'm forming a habit I break it at once."

Anybody who sounds off like that is talking a lot of nonsense. In the first place all behavior is made up of habits, one way or another. We have learned the habit of walking to get from place to place, talking in order to make our wants known, and putting food in our mouth when we're hungry. A person with no habits at all would be just as helpless as a day-old baby, and in fact he'd act pretty much like one. He probably couldn't even focus his eyes to look at something. So when anybody gives you that "I have no habits" stuff, try pointing out what he'd be like if he really didn't have any.

So you can take it for granted that any guy with a mouthful of conversation like that is really trying to prove that he's superior to you, in that you have some habits he doesn't approve of. He's just boosting up his own ego.

And when he says it's all a matter of will power, don't take that too seriously either. The psychological boys say that "will power" when used to break habits can make a person nervous and irritable, and it can start up a whole chain of new bad habits, and it probably won't work anyhow. You just try for five minutes to *stop* thinking about something you want to stop doing—eating candy, for example—and what do you wind up thinking about? Candy, of course. Remember the Popeye comic strip a while back, when Wimpy was trying to break himself of the habit of eating hamburgers?

But there are things people can do to get rid of habits, and when a habit is either bad for your health or annoying to other folks it's just as well to know how to ditch it.

For instance, take fingernail biting, an unpleasant little habit that spoils your nails and is decidedly aggravating for other folks to watch. It can start up in childhood. A lot of mothers have gotten gray hairs and a lot of kids have gotten spankings on that one. Or it may start up in grownups after some disappointment or emotional crisis.

If fingernail biting is a recent thing with you, it's possible that if you kind of ignore it and keep your mind off it, it'll go away and get lost of its own accord. When you find you're biting your nails, stop, and give your fingers something to do to keep them busy. You can't bite your nails if you sew, or knit, or whittle, but if you force yourself to keep your hands perfectly quiet in your lap you just ain't going to get rid of fingernail biting. First time something distracts your attention, you'll be chewing away for dear life again.

Or you can take somebody into your confidence and say: "Look here. I want to get rid of this fingernail gnawing. Every time you notice my doing it, I want you to make me put ten cents in this piggy bank here. And don't let up on me once. Nag me into doing it." Then you put the piggy bank in some place that's hard to get to, like a high shelf that you have to climb up to reach, and if your friend keeps at you, the inconvenience of taking a dime and getting at the piggy bank with it will annoy you and your habit—so much that your habit will worry itself plumb out of existence. Your conscious mind is so bothered by all this piggy-bank nonsense that your unconscious will kill off the fingernail chewing in no time. Nobody likes to be nagged.

Or you can analyze the habit in your own mind. Why do you bite your nails? When did you first do it? You can think about how silly you look while doing it, how unsanitary it is, and how ugly your hands look. Maybe you can rationalize yourself out of it. As to the looks of the thing, lots of young girls who chew their nails stop doing it when they learn to manicure their hands and apply nail polish. Sometimes boys quit when they begin having dates with girls and start trying to make an impression and put their best foot forward.

The whole thing forms into a pattern: to get rid of a habit you have to make the consequences unpleasant, like hunting up a piggy bank and putting a dime in it—that could be an awful nuisance if you have to do it several times an hour. And while you're breaking the habit you want to get loose from, try doing something else as a substitute. If you have the habit of losing your temper, for instance (and that's a habit, too), inflict some little punishment on yourself, and at the same time think about something pleasant that you really enjoy. It sounds complicated, but it really is easy as pie. Scowling people can learn to smile; touchy people can stop getting their feelings hurt; naggers can quit nagging and liars can quit lying.

But don't break a habit just to show off your so-called will power. If you do, you'll make a habit of that, too, and you'll end up with a whole set of jittery whingdings, not to mention that your friends will consider you a self-righteous bore, and they'll stop making a habit of you.

ABRAHAM LINCOLN SPEAKS

What is this talk on every hand I hear?
This alien babble of distrust and fear?
Is this the language of my native land?
Is this the spirit of the pioneer?

Hark, from the din of voices one sure voice
That cries: Take heed, my people, and rejoice!
I am your free, unconquerable soul:
Choose in my name; you have no clearer choice!

Pluck up your hearts, and be you undismayed!
Your fathers flinched not; shall you be afraid?
A brave new world is rising from the ruins:
Build it and say, "Here is the world we made!"

Joseph Auslander

THE LOST CONTINENT

There has always been a great deal of interest and speculation about early cultures, those dim records of our past that promise so much and are really so fragmentary. When you come right down to it, man's history, as we know history, began with the earliest records, roughly something over five thousand years ago. The honor of being the birthplace of mankind has been claimed by a good many places and in a good many continents. Some of the historians say it was the Gobi Desert, and some the valley of the Euphrates River, and some insist that the ancient Mayan culture in southern Mexico and Central America, and the pre-Incan Indians of Peru, antedate them all.

Some of the boys say that the earliest civilizations of all weren't in any of these places. In fact, they were in places that don't even exist any more, because they're sunk beneath the waters of the Pacific and Atlantic oceans. And the boys make out a pretty good case for their theories. They claim that there was either a vast continent in the Atlantic Ocean, which they arbitrarily call Atlantis, or there was an equally vast continent in the Pacific, which they call Mu. And they get into very hot controversies over these supposed continents, which, even if they did exist—and that's none too sure—certainly aren't around now and probably never will be again.

There's a certain Colonel James Churchward who happens to be on the Mu side of the argument and who makes out an excellent case for the existence of a big continent in the Pacific. Colonel Churchward has done untold research on this, and he's written several books on the subject. Some of the conclusions sound awful farfetched, to me, and he drags in everything but the kitchen stove, and at least three lids off that, to prove his points. But when he gets through you have to admit he builds up a logical case.

First, he says that certain ancient writings, particularly various ones found in Burma and India, prove that the people who wrote them were descendants of the original folks from Mu, who escaped whatever catastrophe engulfed the continent and made their way to those parts. Second, he says that hundreds of other ancient records, scattered from Mexico and Peru to Egypt and Greece, tell the story of a vanished continent. Third, there are certain ruins, like the giant stone heads on Easter Island, that have actually survived on points of land, possibly mountain peaks of Mu, which still stuck out of the ocean after the continent sank into the water. And there are prehistoric ruined temples in Mexico and Yucatán, bearing symbols which the experts translate as referring to "the Lands of the West, from which we came." Fourth, there are certain curious symbols and customs which are absolutely identical, and yet are found in such widely scattered parts of the world as Egypt, Burma, India, Japan, the South Sea Islands, Central and South America, among the North American Indians, in Scandinavia and Ireland and every other seat of ancient civilization. And, considering that they didn't exactly have airplane transport service in those days—in fact, travel of more than a few miles was almost unknown—these symbols and customs must have come from one central birthplace of mankind.

So Colonel Churchward put all these early records together and came up with a detailed description of the continent he calls Mu. He says it was roughly five thousand miles from east to west, and three thousand from north to south, extending more or less between Hawaii and the Fiji Islands, taking in a whole vast body of water. The islands we call the South Sea Islands are supposed to be mountain peaks that didn't quite get covered over when the land sank.

He pictures Mu as a beautiful tropical land, full of lush vegetation. He says it was the haunt of elephants and other tropical animals, and that it was the homeland for possibly sixty-four million people, according to these ancient records, who lived in a high state of civilization. There were seven principal cities, and many smaller towns and villages, with a well-organized road system connecting them. These people were far enough along to start colonizing, and they sent their ships to China and Burma to the west, and Mexico to the east. They were peaceful folks, who didn't have anything to fight about, and they were sun worshipers, with enough knowledge of engineering to erect huge ornate stone temples. They had records and conducted trade and commerce and built palaces and enjoyed considerable art and science.

Now Colonel Churchward figures that this civilization began maybe two hundred thousand years ago, and it reached heights of culture that we're still striving for. And then something happened. About thirteen thousand years ago a series of volcanic eruptions simply blasted Mu out of existence, and a few miserable survivors were left on mountain peaks to which they clung, and these survivors were forced to descend to the lowest depths of savagery in their fight for existence. The few colonies of Mu in Burma and Central America struggled along for a while and then died out, leaving tantalizing traces in their ruins of a great vanished race and a civilization, the first on all this earth.

TECHNICOLOR SQUIRRELS

You know that out in Africa they've got squirrels that are bright lustrous green on their backs and vivid golden orange on their faces and underneath? I ain't kidding. These squirrels are written up in any number of nature books; I read about them in Ivan T. Sanderson's *Animal Treasure*.

Not only are they bright green on top and orange underneath, but they change color at night. That green-and-orange deal only goes in the daytime. At night the green turns to brindled gray and the orange to a dull brick-red.

I know you don't believe this. Well, neither did Mr. Sanderson. He thought it was some kind of optical illusion, and then he figured that the squirrels he caught during the day had mysteriously gotten loose and a couple of other squirrels had gotten in, and then he decided that the other men on the expedition, the purpose of which was to get specimens of rare animals for the British Museum—well, he figured these other guys were playing games with him.

And then his native hunters brought in one of these green-and-orange squirrels dead, and he started preparing the skin for a museum specimen. It was getting dusk, and there, right in his hands, the colors changed, and I wouldn't be surprised if the color of his hair changed,

83

too, right there with the squirrel skin, into a kind of dingy brindled gray. But it didn't change back to green and golden orange in the morning. It stayed gray, and when Mr. Sanderson got back to the British Museum and told his story he had an awful time persuading the authorities that he wasn't a little teched in the head. They didn't believe it either. And it didn't help much when he said these squirrels were flying squirrels; they thought he was half squirrel himself, to go around saying things like that. However, since Mr. Sanderson was out in the jungle, other naturalists have looked into this green-and-orange deal and found out that it's the real McCoy, and they really do change into gray at night, and a dead squirrel turns gray and never turns back. It's a neat trick, but nobody has ever figured out how they do it.

BROKEN FAMILIES

One of the most serious questions we have before us today is the problem of the broken home, particularly the effect of the broken home on the children. And there are more one-parent homes than ever, nowadays, what with one out of every three marriages ending in divorce, and with the tragedy of war which overshadowed us so recently and hung mourning wreaths on the doors of so many young people just starting out in life.

In the broken family one parent has to carry on for two: be the breadwinner, homemaker, court of last appeal, playmate, and refuge in time of trouble. That's the job of two people, and one person, however capable, simply cannot be two, and in particular two of different sexes! Even very young children need the balanced perspective that comes of knowing one man and one woman, working together to make a home. But, difficult as it is, one-parent homes are pulling through and making a go of it. We all know shining examples of a widow or widower with children who's doing a swell job of keeping the home together and bringing the kids up. When death steps in, life has an amazing, almost unbelievable power of rebuilding, right from the foundations upward. The house may not be as firm or luxurious as before, but all the necessities and most of the comforts are there. And it's possible that the broken home may be mended by remarriage; a good thing, too, if the new partner has genuine love for the ready-made family. But it's still not quite the same as it was at first. A home broken by death can be mended and rebuilt into a good solid structure, but it cannot possibly be exactly the home it would have been if nothing had happened. And hard as it is on the parent who is left, it's a hundred times harder on the kids. After all, the young widow had the companionship of her husband for a comparatively short span of her life. Before they met and fell in love and were married, she had her family and her friends. She has somebody to fall back on. But little Suzybelle had her poppa all her life, every moment, waking and sleeping. She's the one to whom half the world is lost.

Now, speaking frankly, in the face of cold fact, one wonders if people realize what they're doing when they apply for a divorce, especially when there are children to be considered. Granted that a broken home is probably better than a home reeking of mutual hate and distrust, it's a fearsome responsibility to break up a marriage. It's nothing to be done under the influence of anger, jealousy, or any other emotional hurricane. It's only permissible as a last resort, and even when it seems as though the last resort has been reached, maybe something still can be done. Are the discord and mutual distrust necessary? Probably not, if both partners direct a great deal of effort toward saving the family as a whole.

Suppose you've come to the end of your rope. Suppose this is the last time Joe gets away with the stuff he's been pulling lately. You'll never forgive him . . . he's incurable . . . no woman would live with a man with faults like his. But wait a minute. Not long ago you couldn't bear to have the guy out of your sight. You were promising to adore him until the end of time. Now, he's the same guy, ain't he? Maybe there have been minor changes, but nothing so radical as all that. And what's more, if your love for him was dead, it wouldn't hurt so. You don't get a broken heart over somebody you don't care two hoots and a holler about.

Now if you and Joe could get back just a hint of that vision of a happy life that you used to have before the trouble started, you can probably nurse it along until, one day, you find out that it's come true after all. It's a matter of getting enough common ground so that you can both stand on it together without crowding one another. And it's surprising what a small piece you can start with, and how that ground will grow, if you work for it. It's worth trying. If it fails, you're no worse off than before, and both of you may have a better view of what's to be done.

Of course, there are some marriages that never should have taken place, some people who are utterly unsuited to one another by temperament and inclination, and a few cases in which some shock or tragedy has so changed the personality of one parent that the family would be better off broken than whole and suffering. I'm not going to go into the religious aspects of the matter; if your faith forbids divorce, you can be sure that divorce ain't gonna solve any problems for you. But a separation, either on trial or permanent, may. Whatever way you split up the blankets, it's going to be hard on the kids. They have a right to two parents whom they can love and respect. No matter what happens, don't make them take sides. No matter how bitter one feels toward a former husband or wife, it's just making a bad matter worse to wave it in front of the kids. If they can keep respect for both parents, they won't go through life feeling that they are the children of an unworthy father or mother, and so are somehow tainted with unworthiness themselves.

Statistics prove without the shadow of a doubt that kids from broken homes rate high on the lists of delinquency, nervous troubles, mental disease, and unhappiness in their own marriages later on. So stop and think. Just because the old man tracked in some mud on the clean floor—and I'm using "clean floor" in the symbolic sense, meaning the even, calm beauty of mutual love and trust, as well as the kitchen linoleum you just broke your back over—just because he did that is no reason to decide This Is the End. Mop it up . . . or rub his nose in it and make him clean up the mess. Maybe that'll learn him.

Don't knock the house down, just to swat one fly. He ain't worth it. But the kids are, and they need a home to live in. They need the old man, too. Maybe he don't exactly look good to you at the moment, but he may improve by tomorrow.

ESKIMO JUSTICE

They've got a method of settling arguments, up Greenland way, that might be worth adopting for the rest of this crazy world. It makes more sense than some of the jurisdictional tangles we get ourselves into.

It seems that, whenever a Greenland Eskimo is wronged in some way, he challenges the offender to a song contest instead of dragging him into court and hiring a lawyer and going to a lot of expense. These song contests are used to settle all sorts of disputes—legal matters and criminal actions, in fact just about everything short of murder. It works this way: one Eskimo steals another Eskimo's wife, or his dog, or his cache of reindeer meat. Now if the wife or the dog is bad-tempered, or the meat is spoiled the man is well satisfied to be rid them, but if he considers his wife or his dog or his meat as valuable property, he demands that the other guy stand up with him before the assembled community and the two parties explain their cases through the medium of songs and dances worked out especially for the occasion.

While the plaintiff and defendant are out there yodeling their heads off, the rest of the villagers applaud or boo, depending upon who is especially friendly or a blood relative of which side, and also depending upon how good the songs and dances are. Sometimes a singer whose guilt is so obvious that there can't be a shadow of a doubt is able to put on such a good performance that he gets the crowd with him and the decision goes his way. But usually the guy with a guilty conscience can't seem to put out with the proper oomph to put the thing over, and justice triumphs.

Feeling runs high during such melodic duels, but it's considered very poor taste to show any anger or bitterness, and after it's all over the two contestants are expected to be the best of friends. As a matter of fact, it's not uncommon for the rivals to get so interested in their artistic performance that they forget what they were sore about in the first place. And the Eskimos don't miss movies and night clubs, because there's a free show going on in the village most of the time.

PSYCHIATRISTS, PSYCHOANALYSTS, AND PSYCHOLOGISTS

We've been mentioning psychiatrists, psychoanalysts, and psychologists at a great rate, without stopping to scare up a definition of the particular functions of each one. And unless you've looked into the field of mental hygiene pretty carefully, you're probably at sea about the special work each type of brain mechanic does. You've also probably wondered how you could tell the real article from the quack, in case you or any of the friends and neighbors have notions about consulting one. Psychologists, psychoanalysts, psychiatrists—what the heck are they, and why?

So here goes for a brief definition:

A psychiatrist is a guy who's earned his M.D. degree and then taken additional, specialized work at an approved institution that concentrates on the diagnosis and treatment of people who are mentally ill. He's a full-fledged doctor of medicine, and he brings a complete medical background to the field of mental health. He's the best, and also the most expensive, resource for people with mental and emotional upsets. In addition to being a genuine, certified M.D., he probably belongs to the American Psychiatric Association, although of course there are a few fine psychiatrists who don't. Nevertheless, if you find his name listed there, you can be sure he passes all the tests.

A psychoanalyst is a special variety of psychiatrist. He belongs to a small but respected group who use psychoanalytical procedures founded in the work of Sigmund Freud and the Vienna school. The term "psychoanalyst" is not legally protected as is the term "psychiatrist," and the legitimate analysts have unfortunately attracted a lunatic fringe of quacks and fakirs who are out to peel your pockets with highfalutin pseudo-scientific gibberish. A fine psychoanalyst is a true pioneer in science; a quack is right next door to a fake cultist.

A psychologist need not be a medical doctor at all, although the best ones usually are. He does not specialize in mental diseases; his field is the development of normal personalities and the understanding of normal behavior. He's often in the business of measuring children's abilities and interests, and he may specialize in child guidance and vocational guidance, in addition to helping adults adjust to life. He's earned his A.B. degree, gone on to a Ph.D., and he's put in a number of years in a good clinic. He's just as well trained in dealing with normal minds and normal adjustments as the psychiatrist is in dealing with sick minds and abnormalities.

Unhappily, there is no legal protection for the psychologist. Anybody at all can hang out a shingle and call himself one. And if you go to a fakir you have no comeback and no complaints. However, an out-and-out quack is found out sooner or later.

If you have need of consulting any one of these three very helpful specialists, your best safeguard to get a good one is through recommendation by a reliable and liberal-minded doctor. There still are hard-shelled medicos in the world who look upon the whole kit and kaboodle of workers in mental health and ill-health as screwballs. But such reactionaries are few and far between. If your good old family doctor recommends a man in any of these fields, you can be pretty sure he's all that is to be desired.

MADAME BLUEBEARD

I ran across a story the other day about a woman who, humanly speaking, was a monster—a female Bluebeard—but, psychologically speaking, she's just another case filed away in the fascinating archives of behaviorism. She was crazy in the sense that she had absolutely no regard for human life, except, of course, her own. But she was horribly sane in that she could turn this amoral, insane attitude of hers to good account. She made a business out of it, a good, profitable business. She was a one-woman Murder Incorporated. But there was a psychological reason behind her bloodthirsty actions.

This woman—her name was Belle Gunness—operated out of a pig farm near La Porte, Indiana, about forty years ago. Belle Gunness was a whopping big woman, very masculine in her appearance, and strong as an ox. She personally attended to all slaughtering chores on the pig farm, and as long as she kept her slaughtering to pigs it was all right.

But one day, only a few months after her marriage to Peter Gunness, Belle went into town and bought the cheapest coffin in the undertaking parlor, and she showed no signs of grief when she explained the coffin was for her husband, whose life had been unavoidably abbreviated the night before by a sausage machine which fell on his head.

Simultaneously with ordering the coffin, she put an ad in one of those lonely-hearts publications, and, sure enough, in a few weeks a fellow named Olaf Lindboe stepped off the train at La Porte with his straw suitcase and asked directions to the Gunness farm. I ought to say, right here, that the advertisement he'd answered was misleading in the extreme, because Belle had sent in a photograph of a pretty twenty-year-old girl and she described herself as being sweet-tempered and well educated. She had also stipulated that any prospective husbands who were intrigued by the ad were to come calling on her with as much cash as they could raise clutched in their hot little hands.

So Olaf Lindboe set out for the Gunness farm, his face shining happily, like an autumn crocus. Nobody ever heard from him again.

About that time, a dull-witted, dopey sort of guy named Roy Lamphere showed up on the Gunness farm. Roy was ten years younger than Belle, and he was just stupid enough so that he represented no threat at all to Belle and her nefarious operations, and he was crazy in love with her. So Belle let him hang around to do the chores, but she didn't return his affection. Sometimes he was heard gloomily repeating over and over to himself, "Why don't she love me?"

Belle put another ad in the lonely-hearts magazine, and a Mr. Anderson stepped off the train, just the way Mr. Lindboe had done. A few days later Roy Lamphere was muttering, "Now he's out of the way. Maybe she'll love me."

During the next three years three more strangers, all glowing with happy anticipation, disappeared into the never-never land of the Gunness farm. Roy Lamphere was still around, and still hopelessly in love.

And then a man named John Moo arrived in La Porte. John Moo was pretty well heeled, and he brought five thousand dollars in answer to Belle's beguiling advertisement. A few days after he signed up for a course of Belle's special treatment Lamphere was going around saying, "Oh, my goodness, the things that happened to Mr. Moo!" This caused the sheriff to go out to the farm and ask some embarrassing questions, but he couldn't find nothin' nohow. Everything seemed to be in order. There was some blood around, but Belle was bulldogging the pigs and cutting their throats that week, so a little gore could be expected.

Then a second Mr. Anderson turned up with a matrimonial gleam in his eye, but, coming from Missouri as he did, he was a cautious sort of critter and he spent a few days considering Belle's proposition before turning his five grand over to her. He'd just about decided that she was a good bet as a life partner, and he was going to join the firm in the morning, but that night he woke up to find her standing over him with a funny kind of glitter in her eye. Mr. Anderson left the farm in two minutes flat, and as far as is known, he's the only one of Belle's suitors who lived to tell the tale.

Right after Anderson's departure Belle put a stout log fence around the farm and heavy shutters over the windows and, while she had never been a friendly sort, now she stopped talking to anybody except her pigs. But she kept on putting ads in the matrimonial publications.

The next was Ole Budsberg, who counted out two thousand dollars the night he arrived. In the morning Belle spoke, for the first time in weeks. "You won't be seeing him around," she said to Lamphere.

And then an Andrew K. Helgelein turned up with three thousand smackeroos, and something snapped in Roy Lamphere. This long succession of boy friends who topped off the cream of Belle's affections, even though they themselves were topped off in the process, finally got on Roy's nerves. Coincident with the disappearance of Andrew Helgelein, Roy exploded with accusations that, for the past seven years, Belle had been slaughtering human beings as well as pigs.

The sheriff and his deputies loped out to investigate, only to find the Gunness farm in ashes. In the smoking ruins was the headless body of a woman, who may or may not have been Belle Gunness. Lamphere was tried for her murder, but acquitted when it was proved that the corpse was that of a considerably smaller and younger woman. If Belle escaped—and it seems likely that she did—she must have given up her murderous activities, because she's never turned up on a police blotter since.

In the cellar of the burned farmhouse the sheriff found nineteen corpses, some of them decapitated, and a whole set of butcher's tools, along with vats of quicklime which had obviously been used to destroy the missing heads.

Now that's a pretty strong story, and it sort of makes you wonder what kind of a person Belle Gunness was, before, at the age of thirty-three, she took up murder as a kind of hobby and profession combined. And that's where the psychological angle comes in.

Belle, whose maiden name was Sorenson, was the daughter of a wandering couple who worked the local carnivals and fairgrounds. Their big act was a decapitation scene, done with mirrors, of course, but little Belle, four or five years old, didn't know that. It was real as anything to her when she watched her father, dressed up to look like a red devil, chop her mother's head off. Little Belle was fascinated by the process of decapitation—so much so that she began chopping the heads off her dolls. When she was about eight, and had begun experimenting on cats and dogs, her mother insisted that they drop the decapitation scene, for fear it would produce a lasting effect on little Belle.

Evidently the Sorensons didn't drop their big act in time.

EIGHT LITTLE WORDS

I was reading a book a while back about Julia Ward Howe, who wrote "The Battle Hymn of the Republic." She wrote a lot of other things, too, but that's the thing we know her by, right off.

Mine Eyes have seen the glory of the coming of the Lord:
He is trampling out the vintage where the grapes of wrath are stored;
He hath loosed the fateful lightning of His terrible, swift sword;
His truth is marching on.

There's a song to put fire in your heart and wings on your feet, a song written by the light of the smoldering campfires of the embattled troops during the Civil War.

But that isn't what I'm talking about right now. Toward the end of this book there was a chapter which particularly interested me, concerning Julia Ward Howe's personal recipe for a long, happy, and useful life.

Seems that when Mrs. Howe was in her ninety-first year her daughter asked her what she considered the ideal aim in life.

The old lady paused a moment, and then replied, dwelling thoughtfully on each word: "To learn, to teach, to serve, to enjoy!"

And there was a whole philosophy, in eight little words: to learn, to teach, to serve, to enjoy. It takes care of just about everything.

Her daughter was so impressed by the wisdom and simplicity of these maxims that she asked her mother to draw up a list of rules of conduct, like a set of guideposts, by which one could live. So the grand old gal set to it, and in practically no time wrote out eleven rules for living, and even though the language she wrote them in seems a little old-fashioned today I don't know where you could find a better set of traffic signals to keep things running smooth along the highway of life. So here they are: all eleven of them.

1. Begin every day with a few minutes of retired meditation and prayer, in order to feel within yourself the spiritual power which will enable you to answer the demands of practical life.

2. Cultivate systematic employment and learn to estimate correctly the time required to accomplish whatever you may undertake.

3. Try to occupy both your mind and your muscles, since each of these will help the other, and both deteriorate without sufficient exercise.

4. Remember that there is a great inherent selfishness in human nature, and train yourself to consider adequately the advantage and pleasure of others.

5. Be thankful to be useful.

6. Try to ascertain what are real uses, and to follow such maxims and methods as will stand the test of time, and not fail with the passing away of a transient enthusiasm.

7. Be neither overdistant nor overfamiliar, be friendly rather than confidential; not courting responsibility, but not declining it when it of right belongs to you.

8. Be careful not to falsify true principles by a thoughtless and insufficient application of them.

9. High morality is not a matter of policy, but a real obligation.

10. Whatever your talents may be, consider yourself as belonging to the average of humanity, since, even if superior to many in some respects, you will be likely to fall below them in others.

11. Remember the three prime virtues: have faith in principles, hope in God, and charity with and for all mankind.

SUDS IN YOUR EYE

Remember the old medicine-show days, when the boys would come to town and put on an act, probably just in a little old tent or at the tailboard of the wagon, and then one of them would pass among the crowd with a bottle of Dr. Zilch's Cactus Compound, and bounce everybody in the audience for a buck?

I think the hecklers were the best part of the show. A few of the young bucks in the back of the crowd would start yelling out taunts and wisecracks, and sometimes they'd even break up the show.

Well, I got to thinking about those old medicine deals when I heard the tail end of a political speech some guy was making. I don't know exactly what the bird was running for, or even if he was talking for somebody else, but anyhow he was in there with a political pitch of some kind.

He was waxing pretty warm on the subject, and at one point he said: "Fellow citizens, the time has come when we must purge the party of socialism, and anarchism, and communism . . ."

And just then one old gaffer in the back of the room yelled out: "Let's get rid of rheumatism, too."

I think maybe the old boy had something there. Who wants any of them?

THE MIDDLE-AGED MALE FLIRT

A good many husbands, as they grow older, seem to go to one extreme or the other in the social life department. Either they mutter that they're too tired to take the little woman out more than one evening about every two years, or they wear out their wives by running down and accepting every invitation within miles, and if the wives are maybe a little tired themselves, the gay dogs don't mind going out alone.

I don't know which type is more trying—the guy who's wedded to his pipe, fireside, and slippers or the live wires of fifty-odd. But there's one thing to be said for a stay-at-home: you may get a little tired of looking at the four walls all day and him there snoring in his chair all evening, but at least you know where he is. The middle-aged male butterfly who has to keep flitting from flower to flower and who disappears at a party and turns up half an hour later with a strange shade of lipstick on his collar is no bargain.

Plenty of perfectly well-trained husbands seem to go a little wild at middle age. It may hit them in their forties or fifties; sometimes as late as their sixties. They don't seem to be satisfied with the interest of one woman; they have to have two or three on the string. They seek out the company of other women, and whether they do it on their own or at parties where their wives are present, it's pretty embarrassing and uncomfortable for all concerned, except, of course, for Poppa, who thinks he's cutting quite a swath. Of course, his bitter dose comes later on.

These middle-aged flirts aren't always exhibiting the call of the wolf. They're scared to death of the quiet years ahead. Men over forty fear old age far more than their wives do. They shudder when they discover that they need more sleep than they used to. They get frantic because their wind is short. And they're the people who keep the hair-tonic manufacturers in business.

Their makeshifts against the encroachments of old age are both pathetic and ridiculous. As a final gesture of defiance, they adopt a flirtatious attitude toward other men's wives, and, worst of all, toward gals young enough to be their own daughters. It's this search for vanishing youth, this consuming fever of rebellion which causes so much embarrassment and shame to their wives and families. And of course the poor jerks have the impression that by such antics they're renewing their youth, or at least concealing their true age, and they never realize that, in contrast to their fresh young companions, they appear even older than they actually are. And they're the last ones to see how unsound their reasoning is.

When a guy who's getting along in years starts up the monkey business with another man's wife, he usually picks one who's much younger than himself. He feels protected by the fact that she's married already, so she can't eventually get on his hands. He ain't wife hunting, you know, he's just out to prove to his own diminishing ego that he's still attractive to women. He's unconscious of gossip; in fact he may get quite a kick out of the fact that folks are referring to him as a Lothario. No thought of embarrassing the lady in question crosses his mind. He takes it for granted that she's flattered by his attention, and if she gives him the old heave ho, he writes her off as a fool and turns to someone more susceptible. Every once in a while he'll find a bored young wife who's ready for one of his rather pathetic little amorous adventures, and then of course his missus can either snatch out what hair he has left or sweat it out, according to whether she wants the leavings or not.

When the old boy turns to a cute young debutante for companionship, he's really to be pitied. In a way it's too bad that he can't hear how the lovely young things snicker and giggle behind his back. Youth is cruel, and they bait the poor old goat in a spirit of mischief. It never dawns on him that he's being kidded.

Like as not, he'll go on like that year after year, while his poor wife sits across the room while he carries on. It's pretty uncomfortable for her. She suffers deep humiliation; she prays that nobody will notice how Henry is cutting up, but she finds herself the center of her friends' attention, and she's well aware that after she drags her ancient wolf home from the fray there'll be plenty to say about how she ain't doing too good a job holding her man.

Arguing and pleading will get her exactly nowhere. The old man will say she's jealous because he's so popular. Of course she can try ridicule, a harsh but fairly efficient weapon against the male flirt; she can warn him that the cutie pies are laughing at him, and his own kids don't think he's such great stuff when he acts up like that. It may work, and then again it may not.

She might take the curse off the situation by reminding her husband that she knows he doesn't mean anything by it, and assuring him of her complete faith in his loyalty, but pointing out that others can only judge him by his behavior. She can mention how proud she's always been of his appearance, his charm, and his personality, and she may butter his ego up to the point where he doesn't need that extra apple polishing from outsiders. It's possible that he might recover some of his former dignity under this treatment.

Whatever she does, let her remember that all through this quest for fictitious youth her husband continues to love her. He'd be shocked if anyone hinted different. No matter how mortifying and humiliating the situation is, it's only a phase, and it must come to an end sometime. If she loves him enough, and if she's willing to wait, he'll come running to Momma like a scared kid, sooner or later. During this period of his life he's a very unhappy and uneasy and insecure guy, and he'll be mighty grateful to turn homewards and bask in her silent acceptance of him.

Let her be patient, trying as this period is, and together they can still enjoy what most married couples feel are the best years of all.

FUR-BEARING TROUT

I don't know anything that lends itself to exaggeration better than a fish story. Pulling the other fellow's leg has been the privilege—I might almost say the duty—of fishermen ever since Jonah got swallowed by that whale.

But I heard one the other day that kinda puts the kibosh on all other fish stories from here on in. I don't even want to hear any other fish stories. They'd be too tame.

Seems that in various trout streams scattered around different parts of the country they got fur-bearing trout swimming around in the

96

water. At least, that's according to the boys who like to tell fish stories—and who doesn't?

Fur-bearing trout have been reported in Colorado, in Michigan, in Maine, and in Pennsylvania, always along with some fantastic explanation of how they got that way—an explanation which gets worked over by the local wits until it's practically a three-decker novel.

For instance, here's the tale of how the fur-bearing trout of the Arkansas River of Colorado got to be fur-bearing:

Seems that the town of Leadville, Colorado, was founded about 1878, by a settlement of miners. That winter was so severe that the miners couldn't pack in any supplies from the outside, so all they had to eat was venison and fried potatoes. They ate so much venison and fried potatoes that the venison tallow caked in the roofs of their mouths to the extent that they couldn't taste their vittles. In fact some of them couldn't even get their mouths shut any more. This was a distressing condition, to say the least, so the miners hit upon the idea of wiring a bundle of pitch splinters on the top of a man's head and setting fire to it. The result was that the tallow melted and they got back their sense of taste, but nearly ninety-seven per cent of the miners in the camp had all their hair burned off so they were bald-headed.

Well, back East, folks heard about this fix the Leadville miners were in, and an enterprising hair-tonic salesman set out for Colorado with four gallon jugs of his product, which he guaranteed would grow hair on a china doorknob.

In the course of getting to Leadville he had to cross a trout stream on a foot log, and he slipped and dropped two of his jugs into the rapids, which whirled them straight into the Arkansas River.

Well, it wasn't more'n a couple of weeks before all the fishermen in those parts would go down to the river of a Saturday afternoon, stick a red-and-white pole in the riverbank, put on a white coat, wave a copy of the *Police Gazette* in one hand and a pair of scissors in the other, and yell "Next!" In a couple of minutes they had their limit of fine fur-bearing trout with full beards, who had leaped up onto the bank, each one with a fifty-cent piece stuck in his gills to pay for a shave and haircut. It was a mean trick.

Out in Leadville, they say that this kept up until the mill tailings from the mills muddied the water so much that the trout couldn't see the barber poles any more, and the fishermen had to go back to catching them with a bent pin and an angleworm.

DIARY OF AN INSTALLMENT BUYER

January 2. Bought an automobile today. Very easy terms. Very fine car, with handy cigar lighter on the dash. Ought to finish payment in eighteen months.

February 2. Paid installment due on car. Bought a radio set on easy terms. Fine set, and payments will be small and monthly.

March 10. A little late with payment on car this month, and will have to let the radio payment go over until April, as I bought a set of books and paid ten dollars down. Very fine books. Everybody should have this set of books.

April 12. Borrowed fifty dollars from the boss to meet payment on car. The radio man came to take away the set, but we put out the lights and weren't at home. The chump hung around all evening, so I couldn't see to read the books.

May 1. Borrowed a hundred dollars from Uncle Adolph to pay the fifty dollars I borrowed from the boss, and also to meet payment on the car. Got behind a little on the book payments, because I bought a piece of land in a new real estate development. This land ought to jump in value. Paid fifty dollars down.

July 15. Somehow I don't miss the radio set very much. And you can get all the books you want from the public library. The thing that hurts is that Uncle Adolph should be so hard-boiled with his own nephew. Of course, I told him I'd pay the hundred dollars July 1, but one can't do the impossible. Trying to arrange a character loan from the bank. If I can borrow two hundred and fifty dollars I can square up everything and have clear sailing.

July 16. Bank says I have no character. What a gang of pirates!

August 25. The garageman is holding the car for that repair bill. What right have they to hold the car? It doesn't belong to me.

September 1. It wasn't any use. I had to let the car go. Anyway, I'd rather have that piece of land. They've given me a month's grace on that. Real estate people have more heart, after all.

November 1. Well, they can have their old land. Good riddance. If I knew where to get thirty-five dollars to meet the payment on the victrola, I'd be all right. Bought a new automobile today, on the "pay out of income" basis.

November 15. Income stopped. Got the gate at the office. One has to look well when it's a job you're after, so I bought a new suit this afternoon. Five dollars down.

Anonymous

HOW A FLY FLIES

I read in the papers, just the other day, that at last they've found out how a fly flies. Flies have been flying around for something like fifty million years, but how they do it has always been a mystery to the boys until just recently. Seems that on October 16, 1947, up at the Museum of Natural History they showed a set of motion pictures that, for the first time, really enabled the scientists to study the flight of common houseflies. In the movies these flies were magnified seventy-five to a hundred times, and the boys ran the film off in very slow motion, so every detail could be clearly seen. The news account I saw said the pictures were so sensational and amazing that the audience burst into applause at several points.

Well, it takes all kinds of things to get a scientist's blood pressure up, and I suppose watching a fly fly is one of them, but I don't expect the average guy would get very stirred up about that deal. He's mostly interested in swatting the pesky things. However, my eyes kinda bugged out when I read a little further on that the experts from the Sperry Gyroscope Company were up there at the museum in full force, studying these movies to see how a fly maintains equilibrium in flight, a subject on which the company has spent a great deal of time in developing devices for the control of ships and of aircraft.

What they found out is that a fly beats its wings three hundred times a second, in an action similar to that by which a boat is sculled by a single oar. The trailing part of the wing flexes up and down. Furthermore, the movies showed something that hadn't been known before: a fly keeps its balance by a set of little beating rods, that move in the same rhythm, but in the opposite direction as the wings. The boys didn't know what a fly had these little rods for up till now, but the movies showed their purpose: to keep the fly balanced.

Dr. C. H. Curran, who's up at the museum in charge of insects and spiders, says that it was quite a job to take these close-ups of flies flying, because a fly is not particularly co-operative, and tends to be kinda camera-shy. He says it took about two years to select a group of fly actors and actresses who could be depended upon to fly at the proper moment. And then they had to resort to trick photography to show them in flight. Dr. Curran and the others rigged up little pieces of sticky transparent wax and suspended them in front of the camera, with a fly sitting on each one, and then photographed the action of their wings as they attempted to fly away. The experts from the Sperry Gyroscope Company went away well satisfied, and they hinted to the reporters that there were patents now pending on mechanical devices similar to that set of beating rods that keeps a fly in balance.

The old question of how a fly turns upside down to light on the ceiling remains unanswered, according to Dr. Curran. No pictures taken of that operation turned out to be successful, but the authorities are willing to guess how a fly accomplishes this action, which may seem the most ordinary thing in the world, if you've never thought about it, but which is really extremely complicated. A fly does this settling upside down on the ceiling deal by a half turn with a change of direction from the upright position, which is just what an airplane pilot does when he starts to make an Immelmann curve.

Seems, now they've started, the boys are going to do a lot more studying on this business of how a fly flies. It may sound like an inconsequential little thing, but if it's important enough to get the aviation experts stirred up, I guess we ought to know about it.

IN SPITE OF EVERYTHING—IT CAN WORK

I don't know what gets into these fuddy-duddies who predict dire misfortune for newlyweds, no matter what good auspices attend the marriage. Probably the calamity croakers read a book on psychology once and didn't stop to look up the big words. One of their favorite squawks is: "Of course that marriage is doomed from the start. Those two can't possibly get along, because they have conflicting temperaments."

Well, maybe they do have conflicting temperaments. We've been all over that side of the question already. But here's one cheery note in the whole exasperating question. Provided the marriage partners have a mature outlook on life and are both tolerant and understanding with each other and each other's foibles, there ain't no such thing as being temperamentally unsuited.

Of course, such a degree of maturity—mental, spiritual, and emotional maturity—may very well be lacking in young people. Probably the chief cause of failure in young marriages is the lack of maturity on the part of one or both partners. But actually, according to a recent bulletin of the American Institute of Family Relations, there are no particular combinations of temperament that are essential to success. Within the normal framework of human nature, almost any combination can succeed provided the couple know what the combination is, and recognize it as such, and are grown-up enough to compensate for the differences. Of course, unfortunate folks who fall in the categories studied by experts in the field of abnormal psychology have no business marrying at all, at least until they get themselves straightened out.

Dr. S. R. Laycock, president of the Canadian Federation of Home and School, has drawn up some yardsticks by which emotional maturity and the prospects of marital success can be measured:

1. The pair should be able to carry a reasonable load of emotional tension without blowing up.

2. They should have outgrown the childish habit of foolish fears and anxieties.

3. They should want to be treated, by each other and by the world, as equal partners engaged in the business of marriage and family life.

4. Previous to marriage, they should both have found constructive work that interests them.

5. They should be able to make up their own minds, and should be in the habit of doing so.

6. They should be able to assume responsibility, both for themselves and for others.

7. They should look their own faults, assets, and limitations in the eye.

8. They should maintain an open mind.

9. They should have a philosophy of life which enables them to come to terms with life's difficulties.

10. They should approach marriage with a wholesome attitude toward family life.

11. They must have a wholesome attitude toward sex adjustment for themselves, and they must understand the differing needs of the opposite sex.

12. They should have some training in the problems of child rearing.

THIS ANCESTOR BUSINESS

I've always kinda wondered about folks who take an exaggerated amount of interest in who your ancestors were, or what gang of people you sprung from, and recently I ran across a little yarn that points the moral. These folks who figure that if you go back to the year 900 you're some punkins and if you're just barely sure who your grandfather was you ain't exactly in the swim always seem a little odd to the rest of us.

Here's the yarn: an elderly society leader lived down South somewhere, and she was one of those blue-blooded gals who are sure that their veins flow with only the purest ink. Seems that her granddaughter went abroad to be "finished," as is the fashion with these highfalutin folks, and when the kid came home she had to make a report to Grandmamma about what she'd seen.

"I went to the Louvre every day I was in Paris, Grandmamma dear," she says, "and it was just wonderful. And I couldn't help noticing that the biggest crowd was always gathered before the portrait of Whistler's mother."

The old lady thought a minute. "That's odd," she says. "After all, she was only one of those McNeills from North Carolina."

It's funny how many folks feel that way about the background department. If you happen to have a name somebody tacked on you three hundred years ago, it's supposed to make a difference. Personally, I never could see it changed things much.

BEWARE OF MIXED MARRIAGES

You know what the psychologist boys say? They say "Beware of mixed marriages!" That's a mighty important consideration for anybody who's hearing wedding bells in the distance and wishing they'd come closer.

Now, I'm not going to go into the subject of marriage between two people of different races; that's another thing entirely. I'm talking about mixed marriages in the sense of a marriage in which great differences

102

exist between man and wife in the way of background and education and general culture.

Anybody with any sense knows that the more things people have in common, and the fewer differences between them, the more congenial they're likely to be. That's what being congenial means. And if congeniality is important in friendships and partnerships, think how essential it is in marriage! Even when two people are highly congenial, some little differences have to be adjusted between them. And when you add to these normal little differences a whole slew of fundamental differences of background and attitudes toward life and such, the sheer problems of adjustment are enough to make a marriage topple and come down crashing. And even if two people are sufficiently intelligent and sufficiently tolerant and sufficiently in love to bridge these differences and make the adjustment, they still find themselves with two sets of parents, and two sets of friends, and the differences multiply ad infinitum.

The various established marriage counseling services find that the greatest differences, and the most dangerous ways to mix a marriage, occur if the two parties have different personality traits. If John is stingy and Mary is a spendthrift, if John wants to sit by the fire and Mary has dancing feet and wants to go out every night, if John is neat and fussy and persnickety and Mary just has to walk through a room once to make it look as if a Kansas cyclone had struck it—well, that's a mixed marriage. Plenty mixed. It hasn't got too good a chance.

If there are fundamental differences of religion, you can have a dangerous mixture. If the philosophies of life of two people are deeply different, and if these two make a kind of fanatical issue out of it, and are utterly intolerant of the other person's deep-seated faith, then you get trouble right off, especially if there are children. There can be a very terrible kind of tug-of-war in a family about whether the kids are to be brought up in the particular church which the father or the mother attends. There are thousands and thousands of perfectly happy couples who have basic religious differences, but there are also thousands and thousands of couples who have gotten divorces after their religious differences made an issue between them. If both man and woman can develop a tolerant attitude toward the other party's particular religious bent, and if they can decide ahead of time how the children shall be raised, there's no reason why religious difference should be a bugbear to anybody. Of course, if you're the holier-than-thou kind of character who thinks that he and he alone has a monopoly

103

on salvation, you'd better find yourself somebody who is perfectly sub-missive, because you're going to try to convert the person you marry anyhow, and that way there'll be the least friction.

Differences of intelligence can make a mixed marriage. A wife can be somewhat less intelligent than her husband and they can still be per-fectly happy, but woe betide the marriage in which the wife is the considerably more intelligent partner! If a guy is a little on the stupid side, he'd better not marry a gal with a record-breaking I.Q., because, no matter how much she loves him, she'll start despising him after a while. But it just makes a man feel kind of big and masterful if he knows more than the little woman. If she looks up to him and depends on his every word, it'll work out. And even if she doesn't, she'll make him think she does, if she's a smart cooky.

Wide differences in formal education make a mixed marriage, but such differences are easily overcome if the two people have the same interests and attitudes. What with a library around every corner, and night schools and special courses in adult education and correspondence courses and educational movies and radio programs, formal education —the actual number of years you went to school—isn't so important. If you're a little lacking along those lines, you can catch up easy.

Differences in social and economic background can crop up and make trouble, but it's not likely, if both folks have any sense at all. Mothers usually urge their girls to marry "up" the social and economic scale, and to "make a good catch." On the other hand, a boy with no money, a lad who comes from the wrong side of the tracks, so to speak, can be regarded as a "good catch" if he's enterprising and tackles life and shows he can lick it. There's a lot more freedom, these days, about economic and social differences, especially since so many women have jobs before they marry.

Now there's one more fundamental difference, and that's the differ-ence in age. Generally speaking, it's advisable for the man to be at least the same age as the woman, or older, even considerably older, but not younger. This isn't a hard and fast rule, of course; there are plenty of exceptions. But cases when the woman is a great deal older than the man can easily head for trouble, because she's more a mother than a wife to him, and he's likely to stray toward somebody with his same more or less juvenile interests, for companionship. Remember that a woman is psychologically older and wiser than man at almost any age. And be-sides that, just plain common sense indicates that a woman who is getting along in years shouldn't marry a boy hardly old enough to need

104

a razor yet. For one thing, they'll come in for a lot of public ribbing and ridicule, and, for another, they aren't physically compatible, or psychologically compatible, and it don't seem to work out. On the other hand, the chances are better if it's the man who is a good deal older, especially if the girl is a serious type who enjoys his companionship and doesn't expect to spend every evening jitterbugging.

Now, all these problems of mixed marriages ought to be taken into consideration before folks apply for the license, because it's better to know what you're getting into before you get into it. Before marriage you're likely to gloss over differences that exist, differences that stick out like a sore thumb after the shine has worn off a little. We ought to face these things, and resolve them ahead of time, and we have to if we want our marriages to pan out.

THE BIGGEST ROSEBUSH IN THE WORLD

The solid citizens of Tombstone, Arizona, probably have plenty of things to be proud of, but I think, if I were one of them, I'd be sorta specially proud of that rosebush they've got out there.

It's the biggest rosebush in the world, and two years ago it was sixty years old. That rose tree, besides being a thing of beauty and a joy forever, sure has seen a lot of American history pass before its rosebuds. It was planted from a slip, in 1887, a slip sent by post all the way from Scotland to a girl who'd married in the Old Country and come out to the Wild West with her pioneer husband, a girl who wrote back to her folks that she was lonely for the sight of the white rosebush in the yard at home. So her folks cut this slip and posted it to her, all that way, in a time when mails were slow and none too safe, but by some miracle the rose slip still had life in it when the girl received it. She planted it and nourished it with loving care, and soon it was flourishing like Tombstone itself, the richest town between El Paso and San Francisco in those days, because of the silver mines in the hills all around. That rosebush has seen an awful lot of feudin' and fightin', and it's also seen Tombstone grow from a brawling mining capital into a health resort, from a place to die in with your boots on to a place to lose your sinus or arthritis or whatever you happen to have that sunshine can bake out of you.

The Tombstone rosebush blooms from the second week of April right around through Thanksgiving, and, as I said, it's the biggest one in the world. I suppose I'd rightly call it a tree. The trunk is more than forty inches around at the base, and the branches, spread over fifty posts, form an arbor nine feet high and fifty by fifty-five feet across. Nearly two hundred people can picnic in its shade. In a single season it bears hundreds of thousand of glistening fragrant white roses. That's a sight I'd really like to see.

Just in passing, here's the story of how Tombstone got its name. In 1877, ten years before that fabulous rosebush started out on its precarious journey across the ocean and the desert, a certain Edward Schieffelin, who was an Indian fighter attached to an army post in the Apache country, found daily riding with the scouting parties too dull. So he bought himself a prospector's outfit, and, with thirty dollars in his jeans—every cent he had in the world—he headed for the hills that stood, dim and purple and mysterious, behind the army post and beyond the San Pedro River. Officers and men laughed at him and said that all he'd find beyond those hills would be his tombstone. Those were the days when the fierce Apaches were on the warpath, and one lone man riding into the hills was just out looking for a none too easy death, minus his scalp. But the guy was lucky, and when he made his million-dollar strike in silver, he called the spot "Tombstone," in memory of those jeering men back at the post.

Ten years later Tombstone was a bustling mushroom of a silver town, by all accounts a pretty rough and crude and ugly place, and nothing green grew there and no one had time to stop a minute in the frantic search for silver ore to look for a scrap of beauty—no one, that is, until the lonely Scots bride wrote home and got a slip of her mother's white rosebush. Nobody in Tombstone ever thought to plant a flower before, but when the bush started growing and blossoming, folks came down from the mines to see something they hadn't seen in years—one little rosebush full of white bloom. The Tombstone rosebush became kind of a pet of the whole town, and today thousands of tourists make its shade a place of pilgrimage, year after year. That rosebush has kind of set Tombstone off from the other mining towns, and now that it's the biggest rosebush in the world, it's come to stand for the yearning for beauty in the hearts of men . . . a yearning that not even the lure of wealth can completely kill.

THE BEST YEARS OF YOUR LIFE

There are an awful lot of books in the bookstores and libraries today on the subject of how to get the most out of life after youth has passed. Maybe you've dipped into some of these tomes, and maybe you've found that some of them don't mean a thing to you, and others make a lot of sense, especially if you've worked yourself into that "over fifty" age bracket.

One book of this sort that I particularly like is *The Best Years* by Walter B. Pitkin. Walter Pitkin contends that "the best years" are the years over fifty, and he's out to prove it. I think you'll be kinda interested in what he says.

First, he says, what are the Best Years best for? Not for winning the hundred-yard dash or a twenty-round wrestling match. Not for singing in grand opera. Not for dancing in a ballet. Not for having children or working as a lifeguard on a bathing beach. Not for taking on any big new strenuous job requiring terrific physical stamina and hair-trigger thinking. The Best Years are best for living your own life —not a half life or a borrowed life, but the life that has always been latent in you.

Dr. Pitkin holds that having children and making a living are not life; they're functions of life. And he says that he, personally, would rather be a man of seventy nowadays than a youth in any earlier age of the world. Some time ago, you may remember, he brought out a book that became very popular, *Life Begins at Forty*. Now he says it can begin at fifty just as well, and he's got the figures to prove it.

Back in 1932 a baby at birth had a life expectancy of fifty-five years. Now, in the short space of seventeen years, the life expectancy of a newborn infant has been raised to close to seventy years, and the life insurance companies have actually had to revise their calculations. There are more old people now than ever before. Dr. Pitkin figures about seven million in this country are past seventy; in fifteen years there'll be around ten million, and within our own life span there may well be fifteen million oldsters, if things keep on the way they're going.

Fifteen years ago most workers were nothing but drudges. Six out of ten farm tasks were performed by hand. Today, with modern machinery, a farmer gets fifty per cent more work done in an hour than he used to, and some specialty farmers have doubled their output. It's a matter of using the best equipment in the best way, and the same thing has happened in other fields of work: factories, the building industry, and just about everything else you can name. Fewer and fewer workers can produce more and more goods. The boys got around to noticing that soon we would have a leisure problem on our hands; then the war came along and we didn't have that to worry about any more. But now things are back almost to normal, and work gets itself done quicker and more efficiently, and a guy can work hard when he's young and make his pile and then have a nice long time to enjoy the fruits of his labor, when formerly he had to keep plugging away until he was practically toppling into his own grave before he could stop and take a breather.

Fifteen years ago a guy who got pneumonia, say, in his thirties, didn't have much of a chance ever to get around to those Best Years Dr. Pitkin is going on about. Now they say, "Never mind, it's nothing serious—just pneumonia." Fifteen years ago there was no such thing as influenza vaccine, used today by doctors as a matter of course. And fifteen years ago, if you had your appendix out, you were there flat on your back in one of those high white beds for a full two weeks. Today they've got you on your feet along about the second day. A hospital is getting to be a kind of Fixit shop, and the time may well come when you walk in to get your appendix out like you walk into the dentist's office to get a tooth filled; it'll be a matter of half an hour or so.

Fifteen years ago nobody ever heard of the sulfa drugs, or penicillin, which the boys figure has added ten to forty years to millions of lives already, or streptomycin, or gramicidin, or a hundred other of the new wonder-working medicines. Nobody had yet hit on the method of curing stomach ulcers without drugs or an operation, and the doctors do it all the time now. And the word "cancer" pronounced over you was just the same as a death warrant. Today they're working on that, and almost miraculous reports are coming through about that dread disease, though the final research hasn't yet been done.

Then there's all the stuff you can do with this extra life that's been handed to you through the efforts of the scientists, with places you can go in fast airplanes, the television shows you can enjoy, the Technicolor movies which are being improved all the time, to mention just three. And the books and music and poetry and art which were always there, only folks didn't get enough time to enjoy them.

108

Back in 1932 a man had one chance in a hundred of making his pile and retiring at forty to live his own life. Of course, there actually are very few guys who do make their pile and retire, because they usually get kinda greedy along about the time they've made the amount of money they can reasonably expect to use up in a lifetime, and they just keep on going. Anyhow, back then, the statistics show that one guy in a hundred could make all he was gonna need and then pull out and take things easy after the age of forty. Today statistics show that one out of ten could, if he's a mind to. Dr. Pitkin says that when you boil it down men and women past fifty are not using more than one per cent of their Best Years the way they ought to, and that one per cent is confined almost exclusively to the richest and most highly trained one per cent of the people. He says that the vast majority of us "still linger in that dark, blustery, drunken world of the two-legged animal that laughs." And he says there ain't much excuse for it. We're working far too hard and far too long . . . and we're not making the best use of what we get for our labors.

Just the same, a normal man of sixty is younger, physically, mentally, and spiritually, than his great-grandfather was at forty. And a man whose capacities indicate that he is forty, no matter what his true age really is, has a whale of a lot of advantages over a kid of twenty. Maybe he can't run as fast, or hit as hard, but he's a better and gamer fighter, and he has the advantage of cool, steady judgment. He's a stabilized, smooth-running machine. That physical drive of early youth can be overestimated. I think it was Arthur Brisbane who was fond of remarking that maybe a young man is physically stronger than an old one—but the best prizefighter of twenty is no match for a young gorilla, either.

So there are some of the reasons why the Best Years can be the over-fifty years. More leisure, better health, less nervous strain, more things to do and places to see. We're enjoying life as none of our ancestors ever did. And as we get older, we won't look for a corner seat at the fireside; we'll be out giving the kids a glimpse of what it means to have fun.

RADEGUNDA OF POITIERS

I wish, sometime, one of the boys who knock out historical novels would go to work on the story of a gal named Radegunda, who lived back in the sixth century A.D. in northern France. Radegunda was quite a babe, any way you take her, and I'm kinda surprised nobody has made a novel out of her life. Maybe it's because not very much is known about her, but it seems to me there's the framework for a great story there.

Radegunda was captured in a forest in central Germany by the son of a French king. This was back in the days when western Europe was peopled by savage roving tribes who belonged, body and soul, to this or that feudal lord, and life was pretty sketchy and hazardous at best. Radegunda was only about twelve years old when this French prince caught her and tried to add her to his harem, but he soon found out he'd caught a Tartar, because the wild little girl would have no part of him. She must have been very attractive, or else this French prince was kinda intrigued by being turned down, because he locked her up to cool off, with full intentions of getting around to her later, when she'd calmed down a little.

While Radegunda was locked up a wandering priest came to this particular part of France, and the French prince—by the way, his name was Clothaire—captured him, too. Clothaire wasn't having any part of this newfangled religion called Christianity which the priest was handing out, but he sent the holy man in to talk to Radegunda, thinking that maybe that brotherly-love routine the priest tried on him would have some effect in taming her down.

And it did. Next time Clothaire visited his savage beauty he found her quiet and peaceable, and willing to marry him, if he'd promise to get rid of all his other wives and extracurricular girl friends, and if he'd agree to let her embrace this new religion the priest had been telling her about. Well, Clothaire was so crazy about her by this time that he sorta lost his head and agreed to everything she asked, and it wasn't long before he found out his mistake. Radegunda still wasn't having any part of him. She'd entered into the bargain for the sole purpose of doing good, according to the principles of her new religion, and doing good, in her book, had nothing to do with presiding over her husband's pagan revels and egging on his debauchery.

When Clothaire went into their room at night, it was always empty, because his queen was off on some errand of mercy. When he wanted to sit down to dinner, he had to wait, because, like as not, she was off taking care of some sick slave. If a priest or a scholar came to court, Radegunda ignored her husband entirely. Clothaire raged, and swore that he'd married a nun instead of a wife, but Radegunda said she'd laid down all the rules beforehand and he'd agreed, so he had no kick coming. Finally, in a fit of rage, Clothaire killed Radegunda's brother, and at that point the lady packed up and left his bed and board, and she got a nice little chunk of alimony settled on her, too, while she was at it.

With the money she got from Clothaire, she set up a monastery and hospital combined, just outside the city of Poitiers, the very first establishment of its kind anywhere in France. She took off her queenly gowns and put on a hair skirt and the plain woolen robes of a man, and she was recognized by the Church and ordained a deaconess. Now this hospital she established was a wonderful thing in those times. Radegunda knew nothing of surgery or medicine, except the simplest herb brews which every country woman knew, but she did know one thing, and that was bathing. In an age when bathing and personal cleanliness was considered a sign of worldliness, when mortification of the flesh was the path to a sinless life, Radegunda refused to believe that dirt ever did anybody any good. Maybe the saints and hermits went around crusted with dirt, but she didn't take to it. She wasn't afraid of any disease; she treated lepers and madmen and all the afflicted who came to her. The first thing she did was to strip her patients and then practically parboil them in a bath that lasted all day, and while they were soaking, she burned their soiled clothes and issued new, clean garments. She personally administered these baths, and, once the patient was clean, she kept him that way by prolonged soakings in warm water until he was either discharged as cured, or he died of whatever was the matter with him, or he up and left in disgust at being made to scrub himself all the time.

Well, it's easy to understand how Radegunda got a reputation as a miracle worker, as far as cures were concerned. In an age when bathing was frowned on, a few applications of soap and water cleared up any number of minor skin troubles; the long soaking took the aches and pains out of rheumatic joints, and, considering that prolonged immersion in water is one of the up-to-date methods for treating both infantile paralysis and insanity, nowadays, it was just as effective in Radegunda's time. Maybe she didn't know all the scientific ins and outs of this bathing deal, but she kept the boys at it, and they got well in droves. She lived out a long and useful life caring for the sick, and, in spite of the fact that, at the time, bodily cleanliness meant the defilement of the soul, she went down in history as a minor saint.

Late in her life Fortunatus, the most celebrated Latin poet of his time, fell desperately in love with Radegunda, but she didn't have much time for him, in a personal way. However, he settled down at the monastery, wrote poems to her, and, after he was convinced that she loved him for his mind alone, he became a priest, and, eventually, the Bishop of Poitiers. Fortunatus wrote an account of her life, which contains the only information we have about this brave and astonishing and unconventional woman. I think it's a good story . . . a lot better than some of these hoked-up melodramatic historical novels I've read lately.

LET'S EMPHASIZE FATHERHOOD

We've given a pretty thorough once-over to that stumbling block of marriage, the unrealistic and ridiculous attitude which, for want of a better term, we call "romantic love." But let's recall the subject for a moment, in the light of Philip Wylie's book, *Generation of Vipers,* which tossed a sting ray into the reading public not so long ago.

Wylie claims that the romantic idea of love and courtship has obscured the ideals of young motherhood, and it's done something even worse to the ideals of young fatherhood. It's wiped them out entirely. Of course, he takes a pretty dim view of the whole matter, but, according to him, nowadays the whole emotion of paternity begins and ends with the passing out of cigars after the birth of a son. Daughters don't even rate a five-cent stogie.

I think that, in spite of his pessimism, Mr. Wylie has a point when he says that one of the fundamental troubles with modern marriage is that nobody teaches fatherhood to prospective fathers. The emphasis, seen foggily through the misleading veils of romanticism, is all on motherhood. Father never has a chance to find out if he's good at the job or not.

I can't help thinking that it would be well-nigh impossible to teach a guy to be a father by getting him to attend classes or listen to cut-and-dried lectures. It seems to me that true fatherhood must come from experience, from observation, and from growing up with the kids from the day they're born. Nevertheless, I agree that after the birth of a child we have a tendency to lose sight of Pop entirely. He's at the office or the store all day, and at night he collapses into his easy chair, moans about what a tough day he had, and sinks into a semicoma, secure from eager young questions and implorings to tell stories or play games. Or, if he's the kind of a guy who comes home all full of bounce and

112

stuff and eager to go places, he plows through his supper, takes a quick shave, and he's playing bridge or off bowling with the boys before the kids have a chance to take a gander at the strange man in the house and learn if he's really their daddy or not.

He probably has time for a quick hello all around, but that's about all. There's no opportunity for discussion of problems, no time for play, no time for that most beautiful and all too brief period, the children's hour. If Father does stay at home, he's either half asleep or entertaining his friends, and the kids are hustled off to bed before the company arrives. That kind of father is just the man who fights with Momma, as far as the youngsters are concerned.

As a result, the children must have substitutes: movies, the radio in its more terrifying aspects, and comic books. Parents often feel that camp is a fine substitute for fatherhood and motherhood in the summer, especially if the camp is expensive enough to make them feel that they're really giving their small fry some wonderful advantage, which is, of course, just another example of the way we believe that if a thing costs a lot it must be good. In almost every case a summer camp is a lazy parent's excuse for shirking his personal responsibilities and getting the kids off his hands for anywhere from two weeks to two months without putting himself out further than writing the check to pay for it. If he really wants to dodge his responsibilities completely, he can stick the youngsters in boarding school for nine months out of the year, and then he really only has to have them underfoot about ten days at Christmas and Easter. Of course, they may not recognize him at their rare meetings with him, but that's hardly his fault—they're away at school all the time, and anything they learn that don't exactly please him must be the school's fault.

Mr. Wylie holds that the modern father is so derelict of his duty and ignorant of his privileges as a father that he's both unwilling and unable to accept the general responsibility of fatherhood at all. Of course, such a broad statement can't possibly apply to all fathers, but why not look about you and do a little checking up on your own hook?

How many men do you know in your own town or community, even on your own block, who give vital chunks of their energy, time, money, and creative effort to being real fathers? How many of them take an active interest in their local school boards and parent-teachers' associations with intelligent vigilance? How many of them take an active part in the solution to one of our most stringent problems—juvenile delinquency? You'll find, unfortunately, that not many of them do.

113

However, you can't put the blame entirely on the men. Don't forget that the wimmenfolk are half responsible for what goes on. If they assume the same attitude the old man does, if their social activities and games and parties are more interesting and absorbing than their home life, then you have a home built on shifting sands. It's bad enough for one marriage partner to flitter through life, but if both do, the marital relations will ultimately result in either separation or divorce. And the children are shuttlecocks in the marital badminton game. They're banged back and forth until their senses of reasoning and proportion are dull and distorted.

If the home is the foundation of the nation, and yes, of human society itself, then a lot of us had better begin making real homes and real families. The good life is far from a pleasure hunt. If you want to be happy, you've got to pursue true happiness, not that devil-mirage pleasure. The measure of a really happy person is his ability to be tough with himself and tender with those he loves.

THE GLISTENERS

There are a lot of funny deals going on deep in the heart of the ocean that we land animals never get to know about, or, if we do, we probably don't understand much about them. One of these deals is phosphorescence, that cold, light greenish-yellow glimmer we sometimes see following the wake of a ship. It's actually caused by millions of tiny sea animals who are disturbed by the passage of the ship and give out with that mysterious glow.

Some creatures light up—I really mean *light*—when they're in love. Everybody's seen fireflies carrying a torch, and, believe me, that's exactly what they're doing. But the weirdest angle anything has on this lighting-up-and-carrying-a-torch deal has to do with a sea worm, technically called the palolo, which swarms by the millions in tropic waters, only nobody ever sees one, except on just one certain day, once a year —the day the palolos fall in love.

In fact, they're so regular about it that in the South Sea Islands the natives declare an annual holiday and feast on the date the palolos exhibit their sex in Technicolor.

What happens is something like this: a palolo is built in detachable

114

sections, something like the way a railway train is hitched together. And on the day set for mating the end of the palolo which contains the reproductive organs, as well as the mouth and stomach, unhooks from the rest of the worm and floats to the surface, glowing like a neon light. The female of the species glows more brightly than the male, by the way.

These worm segments all unhook and start glowing at once, exactly fifty minutes after sunset on the night after the first full moon in October. Boy meets girl on the surface of the ocean, which within a few minutes is so thick with palolos that you can't see any water; it's just a heaving, solid mass of billions upon billions of brightly glowing sea worms carrying the torch for each other.

Now it took the naturalists some time to figure out that this amazing phenomenon of an ocean chock-full of leaping worm fragments glowing like Broadway on a Saturday night is really the worm's courtship. When they first saw it, they just didn't know what it was. But the natives of the South Sea Islands were smarter than the naturalists on this point. They've always recognized the seemingly miraculous appearance of the palolos as a love dance, and they go into orgiastic ecstasies of their own when the worms swarm to the surface.

As a matter of fact, the natives believe that a feast of these worms will insure their own fertility for the coming year, and men, women, and children rush into the water with baskets of coconut fiber, scooping up the assembled multitude, which they boil and eat in great quantity. This mess of boiled worms wouldn't be appetizing to the ordinary palate, as it looks like chopped-up seaweed, and it smells, and tastes, very fishy. But the natives go for it in a big way, both because they like the taste of it and because it's supposed to guarantee the potency of the men and the fertility of the women.

And it's a funny thing, but the sharks and barracudas and other man-eating fish that infest these waters swim right in where the natives are busy scooping up the palolos, and these sharks and barracudas and such like the palolos so much better than they do the humans that they pay no attention to the natives whatsoever. It's one time when natives can go into shark territory with impunity. And why should the sharks bother them? A shark can get a bite of human flesh any day in the week, but the feast of the palolos comes only once a year.

This phenomenon of the appearance of the palolos takes place at several spots in the ocean: around the South Seas, on the night after the first full moon in October; westward to the Gilbert Islands they swarm up in June and July; and in the Malay Straits they pick the second and third nights after the full moon in March and again in April. The natives call them "the glisteners." They appear as far north as Japan, flooding the seas in November with their eerie, unearthly light. And they've got cousins, a smaller, less spectacular breed, who populate the Atlantic Ocean, but with nothing like the spectacular effect of the palolos in the South Seas. "The rising," as it's called, of "the glisteners" is a pyrotechnical extravaganza on a tremendous scale that would turn Hollywood green with envy. It's one of those wonders of the world that I hope I live long enough to get around to see, someday.

AND A DOG RUNS OUT AND BARKS

It's kinda hard to find anything new to say about Christmas. Seems like we've got the true significance of the birthday of Christ so packaged up in red ribbon and cellophane and popcorn balls that we've pretty near lost sight of what started this whole business of Santa Claus and plum pudding in the first place. Sure, we go to church Christmas morning . . . at least, a good many of us do. But even while we're there, the kids are thinking about the presents, and Mother is thinking about the stuffing for the roast goose, and Father is worrying about what the whole shebang is going to cost when the bills come in on January second.

Bruce Barton, whose writings I've referred to before in this book, once wrote a Christmas editorial which I think kinda covers the whole situation, and at the same time manages to say something fresh and new about it. The whole editorial is too long to reproduce here, but I'm going to pick out a few highlights, and then, when you get a chance, you read the whole thing for yourself in Bruce Barton's book, *It's a Good Old World.*

Seems that when Barton was about thirty-five or so, and was commuting some distance between home and office, there came a winter evening when he felt like a good long brisk walk, so he got off the train a couple of stations away from home and set off across the hills. After a while a little snow began falling and it turned really chilly and the wind was sharp, and just as he passed a lighted house by the side of the road a little dog ran out and barked at him.

116

And, just as the dog ran out, he remembered a long, chilly road, along which he used to tramp delivering newspapers more than twenty years before. It was two miles out and two miles back, through the winter dark, and the kid used to wonder what kind of hearts the newspaper publishers had, to issue big heavy supplements of advertising in the papers every Saturday night. He figured those publishers never had been newsboys who had to travel a paper route in the winter.

And there was one house in particular where the kid had to deliver papers and where he hated to go, because there were two big dogs in that yard that used to run out and bark and snap at him. At the time, the dogs were bigger than he was, and the space between his knickers, tight around his knees, and his ankles, seemed destined to become dog's meat. And the owner of the house where the dogs were used to stand and laugh at him, because he thought that the sight of a little newsboy harried by two big dogs was comical. Brue Barton says that he never forgot the owner of those dogs.

But what he remembered, that snowy evening when the little dog ran out as he was walking home, was, not the owner of the two dogs, but the guy who lived in the house next door to those dogs and their owner. Seems that one particular evening the road seemed darker than usual to the kid, and the snow came down heavier, and the papers weighed him down more than ever, and the route was longer. And that night the dogs snapped and growled and barked more than before. But when the kid stepped onto the porch of the house next door, suddenly the door opened and a big jolly-faced man stood smiling in the lamplight.

"Hello," says the big guy. "I've been watching for you. Do you know what night this is?"

"Yessir, says the kid. "It's the night before Christmas."

"And here's something from Santa Claus," said the man, and he opened his hand, and there was a big round shiny silver dollar.

Bruce Barton says that he can't remember that man's name; he's never laid eyes on him again since the paper-route days. But on this particular evening, when he was around thirty-five, walking home through the snow, he got kind of a warm feeling around his heart, thinking about that man. He could see just how he looked, standing there in the doorway with the light behind him, holding out that silver dollar to the cold, frightened kid. And Barton fell to thinking that now he was grown up, just about as big as that man had been, and just about as old.

117

And he thought about how he looked to the kid who delivers his papers, and whether he turned out to be the kind of a man who was always too busy to be kind, or whether he was the kind of a man that a scared kid would sort of like to run into, on a dark night when it's cold and the route is long, and the burden heavy, and a dog runs out and barks.

I guess I don't have to sort the moral out of that little tale for you. It's the kind that holds something for everybody.

MORE ABOUT ANCESTORS

I think it was Upton Sinclair, in one of his speeches, who gave out with the yarn about the tramp who was nonchalantly strolling one day through the woods on the estate belonging to the Duke of Norfolk.

The duke was out strolling too, so of course he was kinda curious about why this tramp was strolling about on the ducal property as care-free as a thistledown, so before he called for the sheriff, he thought he'd ask what made the guy so unconcerned about it.

"Look here, my man," says the duke, "do you know you're trespassing on my property?"

"Well," says the tramp, "I ain't got no property of my own, so I hafta walk on somebody's. And, by the way, how come this is your land, any-how? Where'd you get it?"

"Why, I got it from my ancestors," says the duke. "Scads of it, as far as you can see in any direction. You couldn't ride over it all on horse-back in a whole day. I own it all."

"Where'd your ancestors get it from?" asked the tramp.

"From their ancestors, of course."

"And where did those ancestors get it from? Those ancestors of your ancestors?"

"Well, I guess they fought for it," says the duke.

"Okay," says the tramp, pulling off his coat. "Let's you and me fight for it, and start all over again."

Seems like a lot of folks, including some countries, have the same idea.

I BELIEVE

Here's a credo which I think you'll like. As a rule, credos are written by great philosophers, prophets, or poets, but this one is a little different. This credo was written down by one of the great businessmen of today, John D. Rockefeller, Jr., a man who has made a science of philanthropy and who has done an enormous amount of good with the vast fortunes which he inherited and which he has made by his own initiative. When a prince of philanthropy and good works says something, it's worth listening to. You see, John D. Rockefeller, Jr., is one of those intelligent guys who consider the possession of great wealth a public responsibility and a public trust. Here's what he has to say in his credo, which he calls "I Believe":

"I believe in the dignity of labor, whether with head or hand; that the world owes no man a living but that it owes every man an opportunity to earn a living.

"I believe in the supreme worth of the individual and in his right to life, liberty and the pursuit of happiness.

"I believe that truth and justice are fundamental to an enduring social order.

"I believe in the sacredness of a promise, that a man's word should be as good as his bond; that character—not wealth or power or position—is of supreme worth.

"I believe that every right implies a responsibility; every opportunity, an obligation; every possession, a duty.

"I believe that law was made for man, and not man for the law; that government is the servant of the people and not their master.

"I believe that thrift is essential to well-ordered living and that economy is a prime requisite to a sound financial structure, whether in government, business or personal affairs.

"I believe that the rendering of useful service is the common duty of mankind and that only in the purifying fire of sacrifice is the dross of selfishness consumed and the greatness of the human soul set free.

"I believe in an all-wise and all-loving God, named by whatever name, and that the individual's highest fulfillment, greatest happiness,

119

and widest usefulness are to be found in living in harmony with His will.

"I believe that love is the greatest thing in the world; that it alone can overcome hate; that right can and will triumph over might."

I think you could look around quite a spell and not find a better credo, not only of Americanism, but of manliness and humanity. Maybe you've seen it before, in anthologies, but it's a good one to remember.

DON'TS FOR PARENTS

Don't say: "You're too young to understand."

Don't frighten your child with threats of what *Father* will do when he comes home.

Don't "bawl out" your child in front of his friend or the neighbors, for some little mistake.

Don't tell your child everything he does is terrible. Encourage him, instead.

Don't make promises unless they can be kept.

Don't push your child socially or scholastically.

Don't turn on the radio or get in an argument when your child is doing homework.

Don't laugh at your child's ideas or you will lose his confidence.

Don't be a killjoy or a wet blanket in the home.

Don't choose all your daughter's clothes—help her choose them.

Don't make an older child take younger ones along every time he goes somewhere.

Don't keep your children at home all the time—how do you think they will learn social behavior?

Don't worry so much about what your daughter does at the dance, or about your son's participation in sport.

Don't set a hard and fast time limit—it's horribly embarrassing to have to be the first to break up every party.

Don't veto all your child's suggestions without investigating them.

Don't be rude to your child or tease him.

Anonymous

MARRIAGE AND THE INJURED VETERAN

One of the knotty problems confronting us nowadays is the question of marriage for injured war veterans. In World War II, which lasted some forty-four months, casualties of one sort or another touched one million men; approximately three hundred thousand lives were lost, and something over fifteen thousand veterans lost an arm or a leg or suffered even more serious debilities. This figure of one million casualties includes the whole gamut, from the most severe to the lightest injuries, and it takes in both mental and physical damage wrought by the war.

Well now, you've got approximately one million young men who've gone through just about the most terrible experience possible to mankind. Now they're back home, don't they have a right to a normal life, to marriage, and a home, and children, just like anybody else? You bet they have. They deserve it more than most people realize. But marriage to an injured man isn't always too easy for the girl, no matter how much she loves him, and it isn't always too easy for the man either. It depends upon strong, stable character even more than ordinary marriage does.

Here is a problem that the psychologists have gone to work on in earnest, and it looks as if the boys have come up with some real sound reasoning, instead of that fancy mental doodling that seems to take up so much time among the brain mechanics. Dr. Clifford Adams, the psychologist who specializes in marriage problems, has done a lot of work in this field, and he's found out some mighty interesting facts that help to answer this pressing question of marriage for the injured veteran.

Dr. Adams took a poll of young women, most of whom were engaged to servicemen, on the question of just exactly what injuries would they consider so serious that marriage with a returned veteran was out of the question. And there were only two injuries, according to this poll, that would cause a girl to break an engagement or refuse a marriage proposal, even if she were desperately in love with the guy. The first of these injuries was the complete loss of sexual potency, and the second was mental unbalance requiring institutional confinement. And even these didn't faze some of the gals; they said they'd wait for the guy to get cured. The loss of an arm or a leg, or even both arms or legs, didn't

121

scare them off, if the limbs could be replaced artificially. The gals had all heard about the progress made nowadays in rehabilitating amputees; many had seen the amazing results with their own eyes, and they'd lost their fears about marrying men with such injuries. Also, blindness and deafness, scars and burns requiring plastic surgery, recurrent malaria and similar troubles were all things the little ladies could take in their stride. They didn't even mind general permanent bad health, especially those gals who were already engaged to servicemen. They'd take on just about anything except those two I first mentioned: impotence and mental unbalance. And even those can be overcome; impotence due to psychological causes is usually curable, and mental unbalance may be only a matter of rest and treatment.

Dr. Adams lays down a set of four rules for the girl who plans to marry an injured veteran, and these rules apply not only to serious and permanent injuries but to psychological casualties as trivial as slight nervousness and inability to settle down in a groove the minute the guy gets out of uniform. I think these rules make a lot of sense.

1. No girl should marry a veteran because of pity. It should be for love.

2. No veteran should hesitate to marry just because he has a defect, providing the two love each other, one of them (preferably he) can make a living, and providing they have discussed the handicap and both understand its nature and limitations.

3. They should give themselves a waiting period, just as any other two people who have been separated should do, for a period of about six months before marrying.

4. They must remember that few people, war or no war, are one hundred per cent perfect. Under usual conditions, eighteen per cent of our working population has either a physical defect or a chronic disease. Of our war handicapped, more than eighty per cent can be placed, by careful selection of jobs, in work where they can be happy and just as efficient as they would be without the handicap. And the remaining twenty per cent can be helped along the road to health and happiness and useful living once more. At least, most of them can. So much for that.

Yes, the consensus is that the injured veteran is a pretty good marriage risk. He's not for a flighty dame who wants all the frills and feathers and furbelows of life and who isn't grown up enough to shoulder her half of her man's problems. And a flighty dame is not for him. He's way beyond her.

But, remember, among the injured war veterans there are a few—
and we are fortunate that the percentage is no larger—who have been
rendered no longer fit for normal life. The mentally unbalanced who
are incurable are certainly among these. It's pretty grim to think that
some of our young men have nothing to look forward to but life in a
veterans' hospital, but that's the case and there's no getting around it.

And remember, too, that there are always a certain number of young
single men who are bad marriage risks to start with. They never ought
to marry, whether they're returned veterans, former 4-Fs, or what have
you, just as there are a certain number of women who aren't psychologically suited for a little vine-covered cottage and its attendant joys
and sorrows. The best criterion for marriage to an injured veteran is,
would you marry the guy if he weren't injured? Because, if you
wouldn't, your marriage to him is based on shifting sands, the same
sands that shipwreck a hundred other marriages every week. Go into
the thing with your eyes open, and, so long as you do, he will, too.

THE ELBERFELD HORSES

Have you heard anybody saying lately, "My brother talks to horses"?
Because, if you do, just ask if the horse said anything back.

Now everybody who has ever been around a horse, or a dog, or a
cat, or any other tame, affectionate animal knows that animals pretty
near can speak. You know if Fido is worried or hungry or has a thorn
in his paw, and you know when he's telling you he loves you. His heart
just about bursts with affection while he washes your face with his
tongue, and his tail thumps and wags until you expect he'll wear it out.

But in all the annals of clever beasts there's just one instance—
thoroughly investigated by famous scientists, some of whom are still
living—in which animals actually talked. That instance is the Elberfeld
Horses.

Now I wasn't there, and I didn't see it, and it's just as unbelievable
to me as it is to you, but a whole group of trained scientific bigwigs
investigated the Elberfeld Horses over a long period of time and came
up with the conclusion that these horses could reason, could answer
questions intelligently, and could do complicated sums faster and more
accurately than the mathematicians who came to study them.

123

The reason they're called the Elberfeld Horses is that they were trained in a place named Elberfeld, in Germany, by a man named Karl Krall, who was a wealthy manufacturer. After Krall discovered the talents of his remarkable beasts, he gave up his business and devoted all his time and his money to their care and development. All this happened about the turn of the century.

Krall liked horses, and he'd heard about animals who had been trained to count by tapping their hoofs on a board. In fact, he'd seen such "counting horses" on exhibition in Berlin and other big cities. So, just for the heck of it, he tried to train one of his horses to talk—that is, to tap out numbers on a board. He'd call out "Three" and sure enough, the horse rapped three times with his hoof. "Five" . . . and he got five raps. "Seven" . . . "Ten" . . . the horse rapped back the right number of raps every time.

So Krall took another step. He taught the horse to do simple addition; he'd call out "Two and four" and he'd get six raps in answer. Of course, all this took practically all of Krall's time; that's why he had to give up his manufacturing business.

Well, Krall finally got so fascinated by his experiments that he came to believe his horses could do just about anything. One horse in particular, a big Arabian stallion named Muhamed, learned to do the whole multiplication table. And so Krall wasn't too surprised, one morning, when Muhamed rapped out some higher mathematics which Krall hadn't even taught him. The horse was doing sums in square and cube root, something a lot of smart people can't do with a pencil and paper. Muhamed didn't have anything but his head and his hoofs.

So Krall started calling in the experts. Muhamed played right up to them; they tried every possible way to trick him; they gave him mathematical problems that would crack the brains of a wizard, but Muhamed came through every time. And some of the other horses were pretty near as good, though they couldn't do sums as complicated as those Muhamed never missed on.

Finally Krall invented a numbered alphabetical chart for the horses' use, and after a couple of workouts Muhamed and the others were right in there with the goods. They could now spell out words with raps, according to the place of each letter in the alphabet: one rap for A, two raps for B, three for C, and so on.

It's said that the scientists and professors investigating the Elberfeld Horses had a breathless time keeping up with the rain of blows, and the horses would sometimes stop and wait with magnificent condescension for the humans to catch up with them. It must have been quite a sight: graybeards from every big university in the world clustered in a stable listening to horses rapping out their remarks!

Krall, their owner, welcomed any tests and any test conditions. The horses performed equally well if he was present or absent. Finally, he bought a blind horse and trained it, just to prove that he wasn't giving any visual high signs to his animals.

Krall died during the First World War; his animals were dispersed, and, to this day, nobody else has ever succeeded in getting a horse any farther along than the stage tricks and circus maneuvers which everybody has seen.

Maybe it's just as well. I wouldn't like to go out to the barn knowing that if I said to Old Dobbin, "What's the fourth root of seven million eight hundred ninety thousand four hundred eighty-one?" he'd come back with a snappy "Fifty-three" before I got the words out of my mouth. I'd feel too queer, hitching him up to a plow, or a surrey with a fringe on top. It'd be downright embarrassing, if you've got your girl out for a ride and the horse turned around and said, "Look, Bub. I hate to tell you this, but your technique's all wrong. If I'd been sitting on that seat beside you, you'd have been walking home by now."

If this is just a lot of horsefeathers to you, you can look it up. It's all written there for you, in any number of impressive and weighty books. And don't ask me what's good in the second at Saratoga. Just ask one of the horses.

BRINGING UP FATHER

So much advice has been given to fathers about how to treat their children that perhaps a little advice would be in order to children about how to manage Father.

1. *Study your father.* Look him over and think him over.

2. *Be patient with him.* He is probably doing the best he can according to his lights.

3. *Sympathize with him.* He is growing old, and someday, as you will find out, growing old is no joke.

4. *Respect your father.* Never seem to disregard his opinion. When he speaks, listen.

5. *Be polite to him.* There is no place where courtesy counts for more than toward your father.

6. *Flatter him.* Say things you think will please him. There is no one whose good opinion a father values so much as his son's.

7. *Be affectionate with him.* If he makes it difficult for you to do this, then be as affectionate as you can.

8. *Do not argue with him.* He may not know as much as you do, but some day you will be forty yourself and then you will not know as much as you do now.

9. *Do not contradict him.* Well-bred people do not contradict each other flatly.

10. *Help him.* Remember that while you are a colt and frisking in the pasture, Father is a pack horse and the load sometimes becomes burdensome.

11. *Never show that he hurts your feelings.* He probably will hurt them, but do not let him see it.

Finally, remember that you are playing for high stakes—to win a father. You will never have but one father and when you lose him you cannot find another.

Anonymous

WHEN THEY TRIED TO BURN DOWN NEW YORK

It's really surprising what crackpot ideas people will get sometimes. It's bad enough when just one guy at a time gets a screwball notion, but when he manages to infect a few of his friends with it, then you've got anything from a minor crime wave to a world-wide war. It's a lot of fun to read history and try to dope out the spots where just one or two loopy jerks got a big idea and tried to pull a nation, or the planet, apart.

One of the nuttiest notions I ever read about was the plot to burn down New York City, back in the year 1864. Here's what happened.

Around the fifteenth of November of that year there was a hilarious crowd in the streets of New York, celebrating the fact that the War between the States was going well for the North and Sherman had just burned Atlanta. There were parades, and guys were dashing out of the newspaper offices with handbills, distributing them to the crowds, and a real whoop-and-holler time was had by all.

Now in that crowd there were two guys, young fellows, by the names of Bob Martin and Johnny Hedley, who weren't having a good time at all. They were Southern sympathizers; and what's more, they were sore at the world and didn't care who knew it. Bob Martin looked down the street at the wooden buildings of New York, and he said: "I'd like to burn this rat's nest right down to the ground. I wonder how much those people would cheer then?" And he stood there and thought about it a minute, and then his friend Johnny Hedley turned to him and said: "Why not?"

So Bob Martin, who'd been a colonel in the Confederate Army, and Johnny Hedley, who'd served under him, scared up six other Confederate officers who, like themselves, had slipped up North to see what they could do to keep things lively for the Union Army, and they devised a very simple plan to burn down New York City. It was so simple that only a genius—or a prime nut—could have thought of it. Of course, if they'd been geniuses, they probably would have seen the one flaw that was just as simple as the plan itself.

First they got themselves some Greek fire, which is an easily ignited mixture of phosphorus and carbon bisulphate. They were sure they'd thought of everything, because Greek fire will even burn under water.

On the morning of November twenty-fifth Johnny Hedley took a suitcase of tinder and paper and Greek fire and went out to the old Astor House, where he registered for a room, deposited his suitcase, and went about his business. Simultaneously, on that same day, the seven other men went each to one of the leading hotels, made his preparations, and lit out for his next assignment. The idea was to start eight serious fires in the eight biggest hotels in the city, by heaping the bed in the room with everything that would burn, piling on tinder and papers, dumping a bottle of Greek fire on the whole thing, lighting it, and then shutting the door and getting out quick before anything amiss was discovered. After the hotel fires were started, each man had a further task: Hedley was to ignite the hay barges in the river; another man was to burn the Metropolitan Theater, another Barnum's Museum, and so on. With sixteen bad fires going great guns in a town built entirely of inflammable buildings, the conspirators ought to be about to beat it and report mission accomplished in short order.

But it didn't work that way, for a very simple reason. Greek fire may burn under water, but no fire will burn without oxygen. Those tightly closed hotel rooms smoldered and went out in short order, leaving nothing but some barely scorched furniture. The sight-seeing crowds at Barnum's Museum and the theaters and other spots put the flames out in record time with scarcely any damage at all, and the only thing

127

that burned was a few hay barges in the river, which were in the open air and not of any great value after all. All the conspirators except one slipped away and got over the Canadian border, and that one was trapped by his own abortive bonfire and found himself at the end of a rope a few months later.

And that was the end of an apparently sensible but practically impossible idea. The boys couldn't burn down New York with closed-in fires any more than they could boil a kettle without opening the draft on a stove. It's a beautiful example of a big idea that nobody bothered to think through to its logical conclusion.

ROMANCE CAN WRECK YOU

From time to time I've turned to the writings of Dr. Paul Popenoe, the eminent psychologist and marriage expert, for authoritative word on marital problems that have come to my attention. Something Dr. Popenoe had to say on that much overworked subject, Romance with a capital R, has stuck in my mind for a good many years, and I think it's just as good today as it was when he wrote it back ten years or so ago.

Dr. Popenoe said that Romance with a capital R gets the blame for more things than you can shake a stick at. For instance, there's the wealthy, bored young lady who elopes with the taxi driver or the ranch hand or the band leader. Not that we have anything against band leaders and taxi drivers and ranch hands, who are as likely to be good guys as anybody, but the combination of bored and well-fixed debutante or divorcee and a Joe who works with his hands and figures all the angles just don't pan out. Everything is pretty as huckleberries and cream on a pink plate to start with, but it seldom stays that way. So the gal, who of course had no idea what she wanted in the first place, repents and blames Romance. Same thing goes with those creaky would-be Don Juans who leave the wife and half-grown kids for some cutie-pie with pretty ankles. Both he and the now disillusioned Bedelia who just X-ed out her experiment with the ranch hand will justify themselves by saying that they consider Romance necessary to their lives. Of course, they probably couldn't give you a definition of Romance if they tried, but they'll sling the word at you.

Now this plea of Romance can't be laughed off lightly, because anything with such a compelling force has to have substance back of it. Dr. Popenoe says this substance, in almost every case of this kind, is just plain self-love. You're in love with yourself. You say that love is mysterious, and just happens like lightning striking. Nuts to your friends, relatives, public opinion, and responsibilities. It's nobody's business but your own. It may end any time, and there's nothing to do about it when it goes, but of course the old dead fires may be relit from another torch, quite unexpectedly, and then it's off with the old and on with the new, and the only difference is that you've stopped loving one guy and started loving another, the way you might suddenly change your taste for flavors in ice cream. You may try to excuse or explain yourself by saying that you're "in love with love," but that's just another way of saying that you're in love with yourself.

Dr. Popenoe said that this overly romantic attitude shows that the person who has it is actually an emotional infant. Nobody is more in love with himself than a baby. All a baby asks is satisfaction of his own needs and gratification of his own whims, and he is blandly unconscious of the sacrifices others make to meet his requirements. Unfortunately our pulp magazines, rankly sentimental movies, billboard posters, and sticky popular songs keep these runners after Romance from ever growing up. They remain in a constant state of syrupy befuddlement. The boys who mess around with psychology call this state "Romantic Infantilism."

The search for Romance with a capital R is an effort to escape the monotony which makes people without inner resources so uncomfortable. Monotony and boredom increase the natural desire for new enjoyment, and these unfortunate and Romance-blinded men and women see wondrous visions even in the most unpromising surroundings. It's a matter of wishful thinking. That big husky ranch hand wasn't the person the little heiress really saw, but a pure and simple creation of her imagination. Neither was the middle-aged businessman really in love with the little cutie. They both fell for daydreams which they themselves created. And sometimes, I'm sure, the tragic figures are the husky lad and the little cutie who can't quite realize why they're tossed over as soon as the newness wears off, and the heiress and the businessman find new enthusiasms.

Of course, there is a legitimate escape—in fact, many, many legitimate escapes—from monotony, and most adults devote a certain amount of time to finding these ways of escape and to enjoying them, once found. As a matter of fact, the psychologists say that we should

129

devote considerably more time to it than we do. Sports, reading, music, handicraft, hobbies of all kinds, photography, modeling, riding horseback cross country, or fishing by a quiet stream, knitting or working puzzles—these are normal, healthy, and reasonably profitable outlets from boredom which indicate a mature mind and a mature emotional equipment. Brooding, self-imposed "loneliness," which is, of course, only another term for self-love and self-pity, and incongruous romantic experiments which are based on daydreams and which turn into nightmares reveal us as immature and emotional infants.

Here are a few suggestions to remedy an overly romantic attitude toward life, in case you happen to be unfortunate enough to be suffering from one, or you know somebody who is:

1. Acquire a more accurate knowledge of human nature.

2. Find some method of self-expression. If you need a temporary boost, go shopping. Stay within your budget, but scrimp on something else to buy one bang-up new hat, the kind you've always dreamed of but never dared wear. You'll be surprised what it does for your spirits.

3. Shift the furniture around. If you've always wanted to try the davenport near the window, and paint the kitchen table red, go ahead and do it. Occasionally neighbors pool their pictures, ornaments, and books together, and form a "lending library" so that everyone can rearrange their living room once a month or so.

4. Find variety in your recreation. An unsocial life can stagnate. Drop out of your boring circle and form a new one. Ditch force of habit and dodge inertia.

5. Find a variety of intellectual stimuli. Most of us have a tendency to go to lectures on subjects of which we approve in advance. Try going to a lecture on a subject you disapprove of. A pacifist lecture would benefit a belligerent militarist and vice versa. We need more variety, in both mental and physical exercise. Everyone has a right to a creative outlet, but it's a good idea to get rid of the notion that we must all be professionals. The boy or girl who has a small talent for music or art need not make money out of it, but he or she can find lifelong release from monotony.

6. Strip away the infantile elements attached to Romance with a capital R. Look for satisfying and long-lasting emotional experiences that enrich your life. They are the true substance of Romance that emotional babies search for and never find.

7. Keep your eyes open for Romance, whether you're nineteen or ninety, but don't buy any gold bricks.

A QUESTION OF TACT

There have been a lot of definitions of tact, but I think this little yarn is a honey.

It seems that a careless depositor received a letter from a bank manager returning a check with that all too familiar N.S.F. (Not Sufficient Funds) rubber-stamped across it. And here is how the bank manager's letter read:

DEAR MR. SO-AND-SO:

Your personal account at your bank has returned your check given to us a few days ago, with a notation, Not Sufficient Funds. We are very sorry indeed that your bank is in such dire financial straits, and does not have sufficient money on hand to honor this small check. We realize that the situation may be due to poor management on their part, but, on the other hand, they may be very good friends of yours and deserving of your continued patronage and assistance.

Doubtless you will wish to give them some much needed advice, and possibly you may also wish to save them further embarrassment by depositing some more money.

So, we are putting the check through again as soon as you return it to us, and we trust that by the time it reaches them, you will have had an opportunity to adjust this particular difficulty for them.

Of course, most banks that I've had anything to do with don't seem to operate along those lines, although I've seen the time when I wished they would. But anyway, that's what I call being real tactful and diplomatic.

ON NEEDLING PEOPLE

There's a very peculiar thing that people get to doing to one another after they've lived together for some time. It's commonest among husbands and wives, but sometimes children do it to their parents and parents do it to their children. The psychologists have several fancy terms for it, but in plain speech it's known as needling someone into doing a thing that he'll probably be ashamed of, and then holding it over his head forever afterwards.

Now this needling is a very ugly business, but an awful lot of it goes on, and for the most part the person who does the needling isn't aware he or she is doing it and hasn't the faintest idea of the unconscious reasons for such actions, and probably would be horrified at the whole notion.

The way it usually works is this: a woman hits on some little thing that her husband is kind of sensitive about. Maybe he's beginning to get bald, or he's got some funny little habit of speech, or some mild phobia like being afraid of thunderstorms. A guy who's very hard-boiled about everything else can turn weak as water in a thunderstorm, if that's the particular thing he has a phobia about. So his wife gets onto this, and at every possible opportunity she keeps rubbing it in. She teases him about it; she scolds as if it were some terrible sin; she holds him up to ridicule in front of his friends. Probably she isn't even conscious that she's harping on this particular thing. But if she keeps it up long enough, one bright day, all of a sudden for no reason at all, according to *her* story, her husband hauls off and bops her one and swears something awful. She just can't imagine what got into Henry. Of course, what got into him was that needling business, maybe just one little phrase said over and over for the past umpteen years until Henry couldn't take it any more. Now this needling isn't limited to the gals; men do it, too. I know a perfectly nice, dignified woman who broke a broomstick over her husband's head not long ago because for fifteen years he'd customarily referred to her as the "ball and chain" and somewhere along about the second week of the third month after their fifteenth wedding anniversary he said it just once too often.

The boys who mess around with psychology have dug into this needling business, and they've found out that the person who does the needling really does know, unconsciously, that sooner or later the victim will blow up. There are several reasons why a needler may provoke her life partner to violence.

In a few cases needling is due to a distorted sex impulse. The woman can't really enjoy married life unless her husband beats her up once in a while; she gets a morbid sort of thrill out of being punished or mistreated, and since her husband is a nice quiet guy who behaves in too gentlemanly a way to suit her, she has to goad him until he gets into a blind rage before he'll lay a hand on her. Sometimes you'll hear women confess, in a coy sort of way, that their husbands spank them if they get out of line. What actually goes with that is that they're really getting a forbidden thrill out of being spanked or abused, and they unconsciously connect the excitement of a quarrel and the consequent spanking with sex impulses not otherwise aroused.

Then, some people needle one another as a sort of moral blackmail. If you can get an otherwise peaceable guy to forget his manners and strike you, he's going to be so mortally ashamed of it that you've got a club to swing over his head for the rest of his days. Or a man may smooth the path for his wife to have a mild little flirtation with his best friend, and ever after he's got a sweet little bone he can pick with her any time he feels like it.

And another thing, if you feel that you've been in the wrong about something, nothing salves your conscience so completely as to find that the person you've wronged has done something really bad to you, and one way to get him to do something bad is to needle him into it. Children do that sort of thing with "dares" all the time. It's a sure sign of emotional immaturity if it carries over into adult life and you start trying it on the man, or the woman, you married.

So if you find yourself saying a thing over and over, sort of rubbing a raw surface with some slick little phrase, just stop it. Everybody does it now and then, but most people stop before the danger point, because they're adult enough to wake up and get wise to themselves. If you don't stop needling, you're just asking for what you'll get, because there's a point when even a mouse will put on boxing gloves.

THE TALKING SCARF

There's a creepy little tale concerning a red woolen scarf that seems too weird to be true. Nevertheless, it stood up under the investigation of a lot of experts, and they couldn't explain it, but they had to acknowledge that it happened. I'm throwing this in just to remind us all not to be too cocksure about the evidence of our eyes and ears.

It seems that on March 2, 1914, an eighty-two-year-old man named Etienne Lerasle left his cottage in a small town in France and took a walk into the neighboring woods. As it was a warm day for that time of year, he didn't bother to wear the long red woolen scarf he'd kept his

133

head wrapped in all winter. Old Lerasle never came back from that walk, and, when the townsfolk searched for him, they couldn't find a trace. A posse of twenty-four people searched night and day; they dragged the ponds and pools, but as far as they were concerned, the old man seemed to have turned into thin air.

About sixteen days after this mysterious disappearance the Paris police were called in, and they couldn't find him either.

And now the creepy part of the story comes in. A woman in Paris, who claimed to have some sort of psychic powers, was given the red woolen scarf Lerasle left behind, that spring morning when he did the vanishing act. This woman had never heard of the old man, she'd never been to the village where he lived, and when she was handed the scarf nobody told her anything about it.

No sooner did she have it in her hands than she started talking. She said she could see a sort of mental picture of an old man, very much stooped over, who was full of aches and pains and who decided that his usefulness was over and he'd go out in the woods and lose himself and die there, so he wouldn't be a burden to himself or anybody else any longer. She described in detail the striped shirt he wore, the way he carried his stick, the road he took out of the village, and the buildings he passed on the way.

The searchers, all excited over these revelations, which were accurate in every detail, went out and looked again in the direction she told them, but no soap. They didn't find a thing.

So a few days later they came back and she held the red woolen scarf in her hands again, and she traced the old man's progress a little farther, through the woods to a great rock. Well, everybody was puzzled by the mention of a rock in a part of the country where rocks are never found. But a day or two afterwards, the woman cleared that up, too. She said old Lerasle lay down to die by the moss-covered stump of a big tree, and that she'd mistaken the stump for a rock in her previous vision. She said the stump was beside a horseshoe-shaped pond; she gave exact directions for finding the body: the pond was so many miles from the village, the stump so many feet from the pond, and so forth, and so it was. The old man's strength had held out longer than anybody thought, and the body was several miles away from the village, where nobody had thought to look.

Now there is no question of a crime. The old man was absolutely alone when he died, and examination proved he died a natural death. So what goes with a thing like that? Were all the pathetic details sort of spiritually fingerprinted into the red woolen scarf the old man left behind, or what? There are some things that just can't be explained, or perhaps we should say, understood. Either we don't know all the angles, or we misinterpret the facts, but logical explanation breaks down when confronted by them.

IT ISN'T THE CHURCH; IT'S YOU

It isn't the preacher's flowery prayer, or the way the choir sings,
Or the size of the coin your neighbor gives, or the help your brother brings.
It isn't the size of your favorite church or the cost of your favorite pew,
Or the style of the clothes the members wear; for it isn't the church,
                                        it's *you*.

It isn't the way the work is done, or the way the money is spent,
Or whether the doctrine suits your taste; or whether there's some that's sent.
It isn't the kind of creed they love, or peculiar things they do.
Or whether the doctrine suits your taste; for it isn't the church,
                                        it's *you*.

For a chain is as strong as the weakest link, and it breaks with a heavy load,
But a church that is *full* of the links that *pull* can level the roughest road.
If you get in tune with the Master's will with your heart and your labors, too,
You will love your church, though it has its faults; for it isn't the church;
                                        it's *you*.

                                        Anonymous

YOU CAN RUIN HIS CHANCES!

You've heard that behind every successful man there stands a woman, a wife or mother, maybe a sister or a sweetheart, but anyhow, some woman who loves him and believes in him, and is responsible for making him into the success that he is. Well, maybe behind every man who is a failure there stands a woman. Perhaps she loves him, too, but perhaps, also, she's responsible for making him into a failure. The extent to which a wife can influence her husband's career is a subject which

135

hasn't been dug into too deeply by the boys who mess around with psychology, but it seems to me that it ought to be. It's pretty vital, not only to the individual, but to our whole culture and civilization. Nowadays we can't afford failures.

For instance, a nagging, whiny wife can take all the fight out of a man. She can make him so discouraged that he just crawls off in a corner and curls up and won't make any effort at all. He'll even quit just for spite, just to show her that he's through trying.

An aggressive, pushing wife can actually "take things into her own hands"—at least, that's what she calls it—and go to the boss, or the boss's wife, demanding a raise or a better job for her man. That sort of stuff only gets a man into trouble, especially as the woman who employs these tactics is likely to be argumentative and she never knows when she's gone too far.

A wife who henpecks can turn her husband into an office joke. "Hank jumps when Mary cracks the whip." "Hank has to ask Mary what clothes he is to wear." "Hank probably won't turn up to the meeting. He'll have to find out if Mary will let him." There's one in every office, and that's a fine kind of a reputation for a guy to get when he's trying to act like he knew the ropes!

An extravagant wife can work a man into his grave and make him long for the peace that cometh after. The husband of an extravagant woman always looks shabby; he can't afford a new suit, even if it's important for him to make a good appearance in order to keep his job. He's the guy who goes without lunch, or eats a hurried sandwich brought from home—and he probably had to make it himself, at that. He never reads a book or sees a movie; he's too tired and too broke for anything but a glance at the paper—after the little woman has cut all the interesting bargain ads out of it. His mind gets as dull and tired as his body, and as undernourished. It's a rare guy who can force himself to develop in order to keep up with his wife's spendthrift ways. Maybe a few millionaires have been made that way, but it's sure a tough row to hoe.

A wife who loads a man with home details and domestic errands "to be attended to without fail before you come home tonight" is no bargain either. A guy shouldn't be expected to tend to the milk bill, argue with the coal dealer, and buy the little woman's bobby pins on office time. It not only distracts him, but the boss takes a very dim view of such nonsense. If you can't, for some real good reason, tend to those things yourself, get Hank to do them on his day off.

136

A squabbling, complaining wife can take up all a man's resting time with her wails, and make a Sunday afternoon at home far more tiring than a tough day's work on the job.

And a social butterfly is poor wife material, too. A gal who has to entertain, or be entertained, every evening can actually cut into a man's sleeping time, by insisting on late hours, and can drive him to physical and nervous exhaustion. Maybe she says that she has to sit at home all day alone: she's entitled to a little life and fun when he gets home. Well, if she flaxed around a little, and didn't do so much sitting, she might be healthily tired too. Not only does a social butterfly sap away a man's very life, but she's disagreeable about it while she does. She pouts and acts hurt when he has to work or get some rest.

Well, that's a general idea of the harm wives can do, good, ordinary, well-meaning women who love their husbands and wouldn't harm them for the world. I'm not even mentioning the harm that can be done by a jealous woman, or an alcoholic, or an unfaithful wife. On the other hand, a steady gal who believes in her husband and really helps, who is a partner as well as a wife, who can adapt herself to new and un-congenial surroundings if he will benefit, who urges him to improve himself without letting him know it—that woman is a pearl beyond price. Any guy who's got one of those can count himself blessed. He sure picked good when he picked her out.

HEAVEN VIA KNOXVILLE

Guess it's about time to throw in the yarn about the old guy, and come to think of it, he was pretty old; about ninety-seven and a half on the record books.

Seems that Grandpa had never gone what he called "an overnight piece" from his birthplace in the Appalachian Valley, never, not even once. So, after church one Sunday, he waited to talk to the mountain preacher, and he got the reverend to one side, and, stroking his beard thoughtfully, he said: "Parson, I don't reckon I'll ever get to do no traveling, till I'm a spirit. But," he said, "I've allus had a hankering to see a big town, and I wish you'd just mention casually to the Lord that, while I'm on my way to heaven, I'd like it powerful well if I could make a little detour down around Knoxville."

OLD FOLKS IN LOVE

I don't know why it is so many people give out with a silly snicker if you so much as mention anybody over twenty-one who's fallen in love. The popular idea seems to be that love—"that kind of love," anyhow—is only for the very young. And I think there's something a little cockeyed about that notion. I think an older person needs love and companionship and being fussed over just as much as a young one, and old folks don't necessarily need this love and companionship and fussing over from their children and their grandchildren. In fact, they don't necessarily get it from them, either. But they need it, just the same. And there's nothing wrong with their having it.

Now I'm not talking about those ancient juveniles who chase after kids a quarter of their age and make those May-December marriages that get in the headlines twice: once when they happen, and once when the old goat either dies of heart trouble or ends up in the divorce court. Very little that's good comes out of those deals. Once in a while they succeed, but the boys who mess around with psychology say that they're just on the border line between normal and abnormal psychology. The younger partner in such a marriage is looking for security, quite possibly in the form of an insurance policy that's going to come due before long, and the older partner is just trying to prove something.

I'm talking about older folks who've lived the most part of their lives, and who find themselves at loose ends in their sixties and seventies, and who meet somebody they really like and are attracted to, maybe somebody they've known for years, who's approximately their own age and who has the same interests, and they fall in love and get married and live happily for ten or fifteen or twenty or thirty years. Now what's wrong with that?

Maybe it is kind of a shock to hear that Grandma just eloped with old Colonel Widdershins, who's been a friend of the family for the last fifty years, but it don't prove that either one of them is some sort of a biological freak. In fact, it just goes to prove that both of them are unusually charming and attractive people who don't have to depend on physical allurements to make a member of the opposite sex want to spend the balance of a lifetime with them. And, believe me, the older folks are a lot more choosy than the young ones, so dear old Grandma must be pretty good. But a whole lot of folks look askance at a deal like that, calling it impossible and ridiculous and even indecent, and they go around saying, "There's no fool like an old fool." And that shouldn't be.

For one thing, according to the psychologists, youth is a bad time to fall in love. Of course, young marriages are necessary, as a matter of race survival if for no other reason, but young folks confuse sex and love so thoroughly that it's a wonder as many marriages turn out well as they do. As it is, one out of three go on the rocks. But age and experience seem to help. Second marriages usually are happier than first ones. Statistics show that widows and widowers who marry are pretty unlikely to get divorces. Either they have more sense about picking a mate in the first place, or they're better able to adjust themselves after marriage.

And for another thing, the older person has more leisure time to enjoy a courtship. There are no critical parents and no financial pressures, such as are on the necks of a young couple just starting out in life. Older folks are less impetuous and emotional and uncertain, and they haven't got half the problems of the very young. They're not likely to be jealous and they've got their tempers under control. Sex is neither a mystery nor a bugaboo. They're more interested in companionship and common interests. They've got just about everything to make for a well-adjusted, happy marriage.

Now of course some people never ought to marry at all, because they can't adjust themselves to the likes and dislikes of the other party. And those people shouldn't marry when they're old, just as they shouldn't marry when they're young. They aren't cut out for marriage. But for the normal, healthy, adaptable older person who's still young in mind and heart, there's no deadline on love and courtship and a happy married life.

There's a very beautiful tribute to mature love by the English poet, Stephen Phillips. It's not too well known, but it ought to be. I wish every older person who's lucky enough to be in love and to be loved back could have a copy of this:

. . . We two
On the low earth shall prosper hand in hand
In the odors of the open field
And I shall rest beside him in the night,
And fearful from some dream shall touch his hand
Secure; or at some festival we two

Will wander through the lighted city streets;
And in the crowd I'll take his arm and feel
Him closer for the press. So shall we live,
And though the first sweet glow of love
Pass off, there shall succeed a faithful peace;
Beautiful friendship tried by the sun and wind,
Durable from the daily dust of life.
Then, though we must grow old, we shall grow old
Together, and he shall not greatly miss
My bloom faded, and waning light of eyes
Too deeply gazed in ever to grow dim.
Nor shall we murmur at, nor much regret
The years that gently bend us to the ground.
But we shall sit with luminous holy smiles,
Endeared by many griefs, by many a jest,
And customs of sweet living side by side.
Last, we shall descend into the natural ground,
Still like old friends, glad to have met, and leave
Behind a wholesome memory upon the earth.

IF YOU ARE WELL BRED

You will be kind.
You will not use slang.
You will try to make others happy.
You will never indulge in ill-natured gossip.
You will never forget the respect due to age.
You will not swagger or boast of your achievements.
You will think of others before you think of yourself.
You will not measure your civility by people's bank accounts.
You will be scrupulous in regard for the rights of others.
You will not forget engagements, promises, obligations of any kind.
You will never make fun of the peculiarities of others.

You will never, in any circumstances, cause pain to another if you can
help it.

You will not think good intentions compensate for rude or gruff manners.

You will be as agreeable to your social inferiors as to your equals and
superiors.

You will not have two sets of manners; one for company and one for
home use.

You will never remind a cripple of his deformity or probe the sore spot of a sensitive soul.

You will not attract attention by either your loud talk or laughter or show your egotism by trying to monopolize conversation.

Anonymous

SALAD AND THE REV. SYDNEY SMITH

There's a famous line of poetry that gets kicked around an awful lot. You meet up with it almost any place, and it's one of those lines that you always think you know the author of, but you just ain't sure. I wasn't sure myself, until I looked it up. It's that line "Fate cannot harm me,—I have dined today." Of all things, it was written by a clergyman. Now there's nothing wrong with a clergyman liking to eat, same as the rest of us. Eating is a mighty popular habit. But it don't do to make gluttons of ourselves. It especially don't do for a clergyman to gourmandize; it just don't look nice. And as a matter of fact the Rev. Sydney Smith could probably have risen as high in the Church as any mortal could, if he hadn't been so preoccupied with food. He wrote so much, and so wittily, about this food hobby of his that the Church fathers took kind of a dim view of him as a pastor; they gave him the worst parishes and never advanced him any at all. He really queered his chances for sure in an essay in which he remarked that his idea of heaven was eating pâté de foie gras to the sound of trumpets. The bishop didn't like that one bit, and you've got to admit that for a man of God to come out with a statement like that was kinda tactless, to say the least.

One of the things the Rev. Smith had a passion for was strawberries. He is said to have remarked: "Doubtless God could have made a better berry, but doubtless he never did." And he wrote in one of his letters: "What is real piety? What is true attachment to the Church? How are these fine feelings best shown? The answer is plain: by sending strawberries to a clergyman. Thank you very much."

You can't exactly blame the Church of England, back in the beginning of the nineteenth century, for kinda tromping on statements like that. But the Rev. Smith went right on eating, and liking it, and writing about it.

Here's what he wrote about pheasant: "If there is a pure and ele-

141

vated pleasure in this world it is roast pheasant and bread sauce. Barnyard fowls are good enough for dissenters, but for the real churchman, the pheasant, only the pheasant."

So you could expect a guy like that to write "Fate cannot harm me,—I have dined today." The line occurs in some rhymes he wrote called *Receipt for a Salad*. It's kind of a curious old rhyme. I like salad myself, and I certainly like dressing on it, because without dressing it's sorta like chomping away on the front lawn. But something tells me that the Rev. Sydney Smith's recipe is just a bad waste of good materials. Here goes:

To make this condiment your poet begs
The pounded yellow of two hard-boiled eggs;
Two boiled potatoes, passed through kitchen sieve,
Smoothness and softness to the salad give.
Let onion atoms lurk within the bowl,
And, half suspected, animate the whole.
Of mordant mustard add a single spoon,
Distrust the condiment that bites so soon;
But deem it not, thou man of herbs, a fault
To add a double quantity of salt.
Four times the spoon with oil of Lucca crown,
And twice with vinegar procured from town;
And, lastly, o'er the flavored compound toss
A magic whisper of anchovy sauce.
Oh, green and glorious! Oh, herbaceous treat!
'Twould tempt a dying anchorite to eat;
Back to the world he'd turn his fleeting soul,
And plunge his fingers in the salad bowl.
Serenely full, the epicure would say,
"Fate cannot harm me,—I have dined today."

Nothing could get Sydney Smith down, neither the heat of official disapproval nor the dog days of August. Once when a parishioner remarked on the extreme heat of a sticky summer day he agreed gently. "Yes, it is very hot. Let us both take off our flesh and sit in the garden in our bones!"

"NEVERS" IN MANAGING CHILDREN

I found a good list of "nevers" for managing the kids in Marion Hurst's book, *The 1-2-3 of Homemaking*. I think you'll get an idea out of this list. You're probably covering all these points anyhow, but there might be an angle you've missed.

1. Never leave a small child alone in the house, even though asleep.

2. Never frighten children or threaten them to get them to do as you wish.

3. Never nag. Tell them what to do and see that they do it. Avoid unnecessary commands.

4. Never raise your voice in speaking to young ones. Wait until you get the kid's attention, then speak firmly and quietly.

5. Never show favoritism among the kids, regardless of age or appeal.

6. Never compare children, either favorably or unfavorably.

7. Never make a promise, either of reward or punishment, that you can't keep.

8. Never deliberately tell a child a lie. You have to set an example of truthfulness, if you want the kids to be truthful.

9. Never make accusations against a child if you are not sure.

10. Never blame a child for mistakes or accidents.

11. Never talk about a child to others in the presence of the child.

THE GUY IN THE GLASS

When you get what you want in your struggle for self,
 And the world makes you king for a day,
Then go to your mirror and look at yourself,
 To see what that guy has to say.

For it isn't your father or mother or wife
 Whose judgment upon you must pass;

The fellow whose verdict counts most in your life,
 Is the guy staring back from the glass.

He's the man you must please, never mind all the rest,
 For he's with you clear up to the end;
And you've passed your most difficult, dangerous test,
 If the man in the glass is your friend.

You may be like another and "chisel" a plum
 And think you're a wonderful guy;
But the man in the glass says you're only a bum,
 If you can't look him straight in the eye.

You can fool the whole world down the pathway of years,
 And get pats on the back as you pass;
But your final reward will be heartaches and tears,
 If you've cheated the guy in the glass.

Dale Wimbrow

SEX DIFFERENCES IN GROWTH

Anybody who's been around kids even a little has noticed that a fifteen-year-old girl seems a whole lot older, physically and mentally, than a boy the same age. Compared to the boy, she's a mature young lady, and he's just a gangly puppy who doesn't know where to park his feet and elbows, and he can't come through a door without slamming it and then falling over the hall carpet. Around that age, boys seem awful unfinished, and mothers look at them and then at the girls in the family, who are neat and quiet and poised and act all grown up, and these mothers kinda wonder if Sonny isn't a little backward or something. Sometimes he seems like a man, and ten minutes later you'd think he was three years old again.

As a matter of fact, that's about the size of it. A girl does all her growing at once, and it's kind of smooth and even. In five years, between the ages of ten and fifteen, the average girl grows as tall as she's ever going to be; the soft cartilage of her baby joints sets and hardens into an adult's, and the entire machinery of sex is set in order for her future life. With most girls, all this process of growing is comparatively easy, and they shift from childish to womanly interests and habits without too much stress and strain on all concerned.

But boys take as much as nine or ten years to grow up, and some things about them grow much faster than others. The apparatus of sex starts growing in a boy around his tenth year, and matures very rapidly, while the rest of his body takes a whole lot longer. Seems as if a boy sorta grows by fits and starts. Girls do most of their growing between their twelfth and thirteenth years, and a boy doesn't start getting real tall until he's around fourteen, two years behind the gals. And he grows, and keeps on growing, until he's close to twenty. And he's got a lot farther to go. The average man is about five inches taller than the average woman, according to the statistics. A boy doesn't cut his permanent teeth until late, either; a girl is usually all through with growing teeth, except for her wisdom teeth, by the time she's around twelve. A boy has to mess around with his for a year or two more. The soft bones in a girl's wrists harden when she is about thirteen; and in a boy's when he's about seventeen. A girl loses her puppy fat, puts on the curves where she wants them, and has a nice trim little figure at the age of fifteen; a boy is likely to stay too skinny or too fat until he's maybe eighteen or nineteen. And he has to put up with his voice changing, too. Girls' voices change, but it isn't so noticeable. And boys blush more, and longer, and harder than girls.

So there you've got a critter that's spending maybe ten years being neither fish, flesh, or fowl. Some of his organs and glands and such are all grown up; some are just in a babyish state yet. It's pull and haul all the way, while parts of his body are racing to catch up with other parts. No wonder he falls over his own feet and can't go through a room without making it look as if a Kansas cyclone had just struck it. No wonder he talks like a wise old man one minute and next minute comes out with something so dumb you start wondering if that time he got dropped on his head at the age of two didn't arrest his development, right there. But don't worry. He'll come out all right, once he catches up with himself. Just take comfort in the fact that your young daughter will get the business of growing up over with in short order, and be reasonably neat and quiet while she's at it. Life is a lot harder on boys.

145

GREAT FEASTS

Every once in a while we read in the papers about some clam-eating or pie-eating contest in which a lot of guys lay away an incredible amount of goods. And of course you all remember about the kind and quantity of food Henry VIII would consider suitable just for a light snack.

Well, Henry wasn't the only King of England who dug into the groceries with a kinda heavy hand. One of the early British kings, whose name was Albinus, and who was in the king business way back in the days of the Roman occupation of Britain, could sure lay away plenty. At one dinner he ate one hundred peaches, fifty large green figs, ten melons, and three hundred oysters before he decided he'd had enough and staggered away to sleep it off.

William the Conqueror was a heavy eater, too, but his appetite was nothing to that of his son Rufus. Rufus spent a fortune of his subjects' money to build a great banquet hall solely for his own use. It was two hundred and seventy feet long and seventy-four feet wide, with not a pillar in it to interfere with the waiters and servants hurrying to him with their trays of food, and the ceiling was made out of wood, to hold and send back the fine odors of the spices and roast meats. When his guests exclaimed at the size of the room, Rufus snorted that it was nothing, and as soon as he could squeeze more money out of the countryfolk he was going to build one so big that this one would look like a clothes closet in comparison. However, Rufe died of excesses before he got around to it.

Richard II regularly, every day, wined and dined ten thousand people. It took two thousand cooks and as many servingmen to take care of the lot.

But the top-off feast of all time, not excepting the fabulous Roman banquets, was a feast given back in the fourteenth century by Edward the Black Prince for the new Archbishop of York. You have to remember that, in those times, Church and State were practically synonymous, that enormous church feasts were the customary thing, and that the monasteries themselves served as luxury hotels, the only ones of the time, where any traveler was welcome to stop and make himself at home. Carousing was the order of the day, but so was limitless gen-

146

erosity. All the poor in town were invited to a church feast. In addition, the bishops distributed food freely from their private stores. The Archbishop of Canterbury fed five thousand poor beggars daily, and great numbers of invalids in their homes, and he gave a loaf of good bread to anybody who asked for it.

But to get back to this feast to end all feasts that the Black Prince threw for the Archbishop of York: it's still known to historians as "The Great Feast." It was prepared for approximately a thousand invited guests, but countless thousands of needy folks gathered around the castle and took the leavings. Here, from a contemporary account, is a partial list of the food prepared and consumed: one hundred and four oxen, six wild bulls, one thousand sheep, three hundred and four calves, three hundred and four hogs, four hundred swans, two thousand geese, one thousand capons, two thousand suckling pigs, four hundred plover, three hundred dozen quail, one hundred and four peacocks, four thousand ducks, two hundred and four cranes, two hundred and four young goats, two thousand spring chickens, four thousand pigeons, four thousand rabbits, two thousand eight hundred small birds such as pheasants and woodcocks, five hundred deer, four thousand cold pasties of venison, one thousand dishes of fancy jelly, four thousand cold tarts, three thousand cold custards and three thousand hot custards, fifteen hundred hot venison pasties, six hundred and eight fishes, twelve porpoises, and three thousand dishes of plain jelly.

Such a feast lasted hours and hours, while musicians played and jugglers entertained between courses. Every dish had to be tasted by the court taster, because in those days it wasn't too unusual for a bit of poison to be added as extra flavoring. Then everybody waited to see if poison showed up, and when it didn't the boys dug in.

And another feature was the way the food was arranged, on vast trays carried at arms' length by the waiters. Much of the food was made into fancy figures and set pieces called "subtleties," and a procession of these subtleties was carried round and round the room for everybody to admire. They were fantastic creations and the assembled multitude applauded and cheered as each new one appeared. The crowning piece of this particular feast was a huge set piece consisting of a lifelike statue of the archbishop molded in almond paste, seated upon a golden throne and surrounded by almond-paste statues of his patron saints and fellow bishops. At his feet almond-paste knights challenged one another to battle on a field of green aspic jelly, and angels with spun-sugar wings were suspended over the piece.

Of course, a thing like that was meant to be admired rather than eaten, and it wouldn't have been considered the proper thing to do to take a bite out of it in passing.

Today, when the world is in need of food, such extravagance seems sinful. But feasts like these brought quantities of free food to untold numbers of poor folk, besides providing them with that equally important food which is romance and splendor and magnificence in an otherwise dull and dreary life. At all events, nothing was wasted, which is more than we can say of modern times, when waste actually creates and supplements want. The uneaten victuals that are dumped into the garbage cans of the bigger and swankier New York hotels every day make these feasts look mighty thrifty by comparison.

THE MILD NEUROSIS AND THE NERVOUS BREAKDOWN

Sometimes I get mighty tired of hearing so many people described as neurotic. "Neurotic" is a word we use much too loosely without thinking about its real meaning. We have a habit of tossing words around that way. A while back, when everybody was reading Freudian psychology, the word "complex" was bandied about in the same fashion. This or that person was described as okay except for a "complex"—inferiority, superiority, or some other kind. As a result, lots of people developed complexes they wouldn't have had if they'd never heard the term. And now we talk about neurotics.

According to the boys who mess around with psychology, a neurosis is a sickness of the self, a disease of the personality. And everybody alive has a touch of it, just as everybody sometimes has a touch of physical illness, a backache or headache or a cold. But you wouldn't call a person with the accepted average of three colds a year, which is about what everybody catches, a chronic invalid. With most of us, the particular neurosis we've got is so mild that we live and work effectively and enjoy life, and go on for years on end never knowing we're neurotic unless somebody tells us. A certain amount of feelings of withdrawal or depression combined with spurts of go-getting energy are common to almost all of us. It's normal to depend on our friends for praise and attention, to fight for our rights and get upset if our toes are trampled on, and to want occasional periods of being completely alone. In the mentally balanced person these desires are healthy and reasonable. In the true neurotic the balance is lost.

Every day the neurotic is faced with evidence that he's not the person he thinks he is. But he can't admit his inward failings to his friends or family, so he has to find excuses and try to shift the blame for his actions to someone else. He never makes an error of judgment, according to him; he's always the victim of a cheat.

The neurotic can't live a full and happy life because he's always at war with himself. Nevertheless, he can be cured. He may seek the help of a trained psychiatrist, or, through real courage and honesty, he may be able to cure himself and to move back into a healthy relationship with his fellow man. However the cure is effected, he has to face facts, quit lying to himself, tackle the problem head on, and see what can be done.

Of course, a neurosis, even a mild one, isn't particularly good for you. But, on the other hand, don't let anybody call you neurotic because you occasionally "get in a mood" about something. Most neuroses start in early childhood, and unless they develop to the point where they interfere with your health and happiness, they're not worth fussing about.

On the other hand, a real nervous breakdown is no joke. It's a definite illness, just as much as a contagious disease is an illness. Its roots lie in fear, and there are thousands of causes for fear—financial worries, loss of a job or a loved one, to mention only three. A nervous breakdown stems from these fears, and it may also have some physical ailment at its base.

Suppose you take a guy who has a little nagging fear of being a failure. He's had it since he was a child and possibly it developed because at home somebody was always pointing out that he looked an awful lot like Uncle Hank, who was a nice, lovable, old, broken-down bum. Everybody liked Uncle Hank, but he was the type who'd never been able to keep a job and didn't much care. So—let's face it—this guy grew up with a neurosis. His fear of being a failure never bothered him much, but it was there all the time, at the back of his brain.

Then let's say that our hero is kinda getting along in life, and there's an economy wave at the office and a few guys are let go. Nobody even looks crosswise at him, but he gets a notion that he's in line for the ax. He starts a vicious circle of negative thoughts to the effect that he could never get another job and the boss won't give him a recommendation

149

and he's too old to start over again. And, while he's worrying about it, he develops some physical illness. It needn't be much. A touch of indigestion will do it. Right there you've got a picture of a guy all set for a nervous breakdown.

One of his first symptoms will be an intolerance to noise. Actually, having a nervous breakdown means that his tolerance to everything connected with life has passed the limit of comfort. Mentally and physically, he's oversensitive. The squeak of a door sounds as loud as a steam whistle, and a loud crash will cause him to scream and hold his head.

Two more unpleasant things happen in rapid succession: he loses his ability to sleep and he begins indulging in long periods of self-analysis of his health. Doubtless these two distressing conditions aggravate each other, because no human being can feel well after a succession of sleepless nights. An experiment was conducted recently to find out what happens to man's body and mind when he's kept awake over a period of time, and, as I remember, four or five completely sleepless twenty-four-hour periods were all that we can take. Imagine, then, the bad effects of sleepless weeks, or even months. And I don't mean the "sleeplessness" that you go on about at great length if you wake up for fifteen minutes in the wee small hours and then make a long yarn at the breakfast table about how you never closed your eyes all night. The sleeplessness of a nervous breakdown is very real and very total.

The fear and frustration, combined with some ailment, usually a minor one, cause the nervous collapse. The nervous collapse causes the victim to lie awake night after night. As he lies awake he tries to figure out why he can't sleep. And as he figures, he becomes conscious of his heartbeats and the rhythm of his breathing.

Now there just ain't a human being alive, with the possible exception of the experienced Yogis, who can concentrate on the two bodily functions of heart and lungs without causing irregularity and even serious disturbances. The least the guy can expect is a rise in his heart rate and an unpleasant breathlessness. Any normal person can experience the same thing if he wants to be in for an uncomfortable few minutes, before he realizes that he's just hearing things he never noticed before. Lie in bed, particularly on your left side with your left wrist under the pillow, so that you can really hear the pound of your heart, and concentrate on listening to it and to the rate of your breathing for about five minutes. You can scare yourself half to death.

About the time that our lad with the nervous breakdown begins listening to himself and his normal heartbeat, breathing, internal rumblings, and so forth, he decides that all the doctors he's been to are crazy. None of their diagnoses pleases him, and he makes up his mind that they know from nothing. They're all wrong and he's right; he's got a mysterious ailment that nobody is smart enough to analyze. That's the way he wants it, and he coddles his "sickness" to him, refusing to recognize that it could easily be cured if he'd only co-operate. He's now a finished product of a long training in negative thinking. Many factors have contributed to his frustration, like a snowball picking up extra snow and growing bigger and bigger. In addition to his original fear, he's acquired hates and jealousies and disappointments he never gave a nod to before. Mentally he's running around in circles until he's dizzier than a hoot owl in a high wind. He is like a hypnotist who has performed a miracle of autosuggestion and can't bring himself out of it, because he's blocked himself off from the roots of his own neurosis. He refuses to recognize the original fears that sent him off on his mental wild-goose chase.

Like most problems that take a long time to build up, a nervous breakdown takes a long period of brooding, worrying, and general unorganized fussy thinking. However, it's brought on by some sudden outside influence, such as our guy seeing other men discharged from the office and wondering when his time would come. What's more, even the product and pattern is of the victim's own making and design; he's stuck with it until some constructive outside influence comes along and knocks him loose from it. That outside influence must re-educate and reprocess the sufferer so that he regains his mental stability.

I've spent some time going into this distinction between the mild neuroses that everybody has and the unreasonable, uncontrolled fears and frustrations that cause a nervous breakdown. It's pretty important to know the difference, and to realize that you're not going into a mental nose dive just because you get kinda worked up about something once in a while. Even though you're beset by troubles and worries, if you think of life as a good and healthy thing, you'll have life and health. Try to keep a carefree attitude about your personal troubles. If you're mentally strong enough, you can stop the process of fear and frustration wherever you choose. You can have a mental house cleaning, all by yourself, when some worry seems to be getting the best of you, or you can wait until you're the finished product, and then call in outside help and have a nice expensive breakdown for yourself.

151

And another thing: some people have the odd idea that just because somebody has had a nervous breakdown, he's going to be kinda on the peculiar side for the rest of his life. 'Tain't so, any more than a car with a flat tire won't run properly any more when the tire is changed. You can have a breakdown and be as good as ever, probably even better, afterwards. But why get one in the first place?

SOMETIME

Sometime, when all life's lessons have been learned,
And sun and stars forevermore have set,
The things which our weak judgments here have spurned—
The things o'er which we grieved with lashes wet—
Will flash before us, out of life's dark night,
As stars shine most in deeper tints of blue;
And we shall see how all God's plans were right,
And how what seemed reproof was love most true.

And we shall see how, while we frown and sigh,
God's plans go on as best for you and me;
How, when we called, He heeded not our cry,
Because His wisdom to the end could see.
And even as wise parents disallow
Too much of sweet to craving babyhood,
So God, perhaps, is keeping from us now
Life's sweetest things because it seemeth good.

And if, sometimes, commingled with life's wine,
We find the wormwood and rebel and shirk,
Be sure a wiser hand than yours or mine
Pours out this potion for our lips to drink.
And if some friend we love is lying low,
Where human kisses cannot reach his face,
Oh, do not blame the loving Father so,
But wear your sorrow with obedient grace!

And you shall shortly know that lengthened breath
Is not the sweetest gift God sends His friend,
And that sometimes the sable pall of death
Conceals the fairest boon His love can send.

152

If we could push ajar the gates of life
And stand within and all God's workings see
We could interpret all this doubt and strife,
And for each mystery could find a key!

But not today. Then be content, dear heart!
God's plans, like lilies, pure and white unfold,
We must not tear the close-shut leaves apart,
Time will reveal the calyxes of gold.
And if, through patient toil, we reach the goal
Where tired feet with sandals loose my rest,
When we shall clearly know and understand,
I think that we will say, "God knew the best!"

Anonymous

FEARS

For persons assailed by irrational fears:

1. Don't exaggerate your own importance. You are exaggerating it if you are sensitive and timid.

2. Don't care too much about what other people think of you. They are only human.

3. Don't think you can attain happiness simply by seeking it directly. If you try to give it to others you will find that this thing we call happiness has an amazing elasticity. It will come bounding back to you.

4. Don't be constantly thinking about your health. Just make sure you live a hygienic life in sanitary surroundings.

5. Don't be afraid of fear. Just remember that it is part of nature's apparatus to stimulate in you the impulse to survive, and is useful as a protection from real and present dangers.

Since your fears are centered in yourself, you can control them to a large degree by devoting yourself to things outside yourself.

AND THEY DID EAT

Behold! The lodge lodgeth together and they eat. The club clubbeth together and they eat. The businessmen take counsel together and they eat. The church hath a social and they eat. The young people elect officers and they eat. And even when the missionary society meeteth together they eat. But this latter is a good cause because they eat in remembrance of the poor heathen who have not much to eat.

Behold! Hath man's brains gone to his stomach, and doth he no longer regard intellectual dainties? Canst thou no longer call an assembly or get together a quorum, or even a "Baker's Dozen," except thou holdest up the baker's dainties as a bait? Can it be that the day cometh when, to get a crowd at a prayer meeting, the preacher must serve a six-course supper with the benediction?

Yea, verily, thou hast heard of the child races of the world. But behold it nigh thee, even at the door. For as one calleth unto a child and sayeth, "Come hither, little one, and I will give thee a cooky," even so must thou say to his grown-up papa and mama, "Assemble ye together and we will serve refreshments." And lo, they come like sheep into a pen.

Anonymous

MY MOTHER

You'd expect that only some great poet could write a perfect tribute to his mother, and a lot of great poets have, but somehow the tributes come out sorta flowery and overly sentimental, and when you get through reading them you don't quite believe them. Seems like the guy sat down and said to himself, "Well, now, I gotta write something about Mom, and it better be good, or I won't dare show my face around the old home town any more," and then he writes something about Mom and the whole thing is so forced and deliberate that you know just what was in his mind while he was doing it.

Personally, I don't go much for these hoked-up tributes to Mom, and all the Mommas I know feel purely embarrassed by them, because Mommas usually have pretty keen insight and know what's up, and

154

they'd rather have just plain love, uncluttered by fancy rhyme schemes. However, there's one tribute to a mother, his own mother, written by a guy who was a plain, forthright man with no nonsense about him, and I think every mother would like it. The man who wrote it happened to be John Quincy Adams, the sixth President of the United States, but when he sat down to write his little piece, he was just anybody's son talking about his mother, whom he loved and respected very much.

"There is not a virtue that can abide in the female heart that was not an ornament of hers. She had been fifty-four years the delight of my father's heart, the sweetener of all his toils, the comforter of all his sorrows, the sharer and heightener of all his joys. It was but the last time what I saw my father . . . that he told me, in all his struggles and in all his sorrows, the affection and cheering encouragement of his wife had been his never-failing support, without which he was sure he should never have lived through them.

"Never have I known another human being the perpetual object of whose life was so unremittingly to do good. It was a necessity of her nature. Yet so unostentatious, so unconscious even of her own excellence that even the objects of her kindness often knew not whence it came. She had seen the world—its glories without being dazzled; its vices and follies without being infected by them. She suffered often and severely from fits of long and painful sickness, always with calm and resignation. . . . She was always cheerful, never frivolous; she had neither gall nor guile.

"Her attention to the domestic economy of her family was unrivaled—rising with the dawn, and superintending the household concerns with indefatigable and all-foreseeing care. She had a warm and lively relish for literature, for social conversation, for whatever was interesting in the occurrences of the time, and even in political affairs. She had been, during the war of our Revolution, an ardent patriot, and the earliest lesson of unbounded devotion to the cause of their country, that her children received, was from her. She had the most delicate sense of propriety of conduct, but nothing uncharitable, nothing bitter. Her price was indeed above rubies."

That's what one son, back in the early days of our country, thought about his mother. I guess a lot of sons think the same, most of them, in fact, only they ain't got the right words to say it with, or even if they have the words, it comes out all fancied up and prettified, and not real true. I like what old John Quincy Adams had to say, and I kinda think you mothers will, too.

155

LADY ASTOR'S GAG

Someday if you want to prove which sex is vainer, the male or the female, try something that Lady Astor once worked at a large formal dinner party. It seems that she remarked, at this shindig, that men were far vainer than women, and she met with a lot of stormy opposition, so she said that she was ready to substantiate her opinion.

She proceeded to steer the conversation around to men's fashions, and then, when everybody had forgotten her original statement, she said in a very loud voice that it was such a pity that the most intelligent and important men attached the least importance to the way they dressed.

"Right at this table," she said, "the most cultivated man I know is wearing the most clumsily knotted tie."

So, just like somebody shot off a gun, every man in the room put his hand up to his tie to straighten it.

I DON'T KNOW

I wonder how many times you've been given a wrong steer by somebody who refused to say three harmless little words: "I don't know"? I wonder how many hours, or minutes, you've wasted, and how much embarrassment you've suffered, because some dopey guy couldn't or wouldn't bring himself to say those three words?

Few people know enough to say "I don't know." Most of us have a weird idea that saying it displays ignorance, when actually it shows a considerable amount of knowledge, not to mention honest common sense. It wouldn't hurt us to remember that Socrates, the wisest man of his time, proved that he knew more than anybody else in Athens by acknowledging that he knew so little. Socrates taught by asking questions instead of by answering them, and in all his lifetime of question asking he found very few pupils who were willing and able to say "I don't know," although most of them should have.

Now why is it that people hate to say "I don't know"? It's certainly easier to say it than to give a botched-up and incorrect answer, and then, later, to find out that you're confronted with the embarrassing necessity of admitting that you didn't know what you were talking about.

If you don't understand, let's say, symphonic music, why not say so? Why not admit that not only you don't understand it, but you don't even like the stuff, and maybe you don't like it because you don't know anything about it? Maybe you'll shock some lovers of classical music, but it's no crime if you prefer Johnny Mercer to Johann Sebastian Bach. That's nothing against you, and no sign that you're inferior in any way. If you don't happen to know anything about polo, or stamp collecting, or Duncan Phyfe furniture, or what goes in the Balkans, why not say "I don't know"? You may learn something interesting if you're willing to listen. If you've never heard of Picasso, why then, just admit it. Don't try to fake your way through. In the first place, you'll get caught at it, sure as shootin', and in the second place, if you keep your own tater trap shut after that simple "I don't know," you'll hear some information which, stored away, will keep you from having to say "I don't know" the next time the same subject comes up.

The famous poet and philosopher, Goethe, was looked up to and admired wherever he went, and he said the secret of why everybody liked him was that he was always asking questions. He spent a lot of his time talking to carpenters and masons and farmers and bootmakers and peddlers, and he learned something from everybody he met. Needless to say, when he talked to all these people, they listened, too, because he never said anything unless he was sure of his facts. They learned from him, just as he learned from them, and he said "I don't know" whenever necessary.

It's a mark of the intelligent person to be able to say "I don't know." No matter how many facts you have at the tip of your tongue, somebody, sooner or later, is bound to bring up some question to which you don't know the answer. After all, everybody is ignorant, but only on different subjects. It makes sense to be honest about it.

I remember a yarn about a lady who was at one of those literary teas the boys get up every once in a while, and at this tea she was being asked a lot of questions. Now, as it happened, this particular gal didn't know sickem about literature, but she was bound nobody was going to find out, one way or another, so when one guy turned to her and asked her if she liked Scott, she said, "Er, yes." And he said, "Well, what of his do you like most?" And she said, "I believe, of everything, I like his Emulsion the best."

Don't feel ashamed to say "I don't know." Feel ashamed only if you're ashamed to say it.

AS I GROW OLD

God keep my heart attuned to laughter
When youth is done,
When all the days are grey days, coming after
The warmth, the sun.
God keep me then from bitterness, from grieving,
When life seems cold;
God keep me loving and believing
As I grow old.

Anonymous

HOW WE DEVELOP FEARS

One of the worst things about fear is the mystery that surrounds it. Every detective-story fan knows that. It's the suspense and mystery that send the icy ripples down your spine and the hackles rising along your neck. Mystery and suspense are all very well in a detective story, but in real life they just ain't good for people. They're the wicked little pair that build up a troublesome, unpleasant, but only momentary feeling of discomfort into a real neurotic fear. You're actually not afraid of the thing, but of your feeling of the fear.

I don't think there's anybody going today who's dug deeper into the study of fear as a mental and physical illness than Dr. Edward Spencer Cowles. His book, *Don't Be Afraid,* certainly strips neurotic fears of their suspense and mystery, and leaves them exposed for exactly what they are: nasty little evils that we can, and do, get rid of, once we're able to face them squarely.

Dr. Cowles's theory is extremely simple, so simple that most of the experts skipped over it because it didn't seem as if a thing as easy as that could account for all the complicated whingdings the human mind and body can get into. He says that fear is founded in fatigue. First you get overtired, then you start worrying about things, then your physical sensations of weariness and your mental worries gang up on you and you develop neurotic fears, and the neurotic fears work on your physical well-being and undermine your health, keep you from sleeping, spoil your appetite; you get more and more overtired from not sleeping and eating right, and by the time you're real good and sick and just about ready to order out the coffin and a nice bunch of lilies, some doctor or other comes along and yanks out your appendix or something—your appendix is probably due to be yanked about now, because it's in a bad way on account of how you've been abusing your innards—and you feel a whole lot better when you get out of the hospital. In fact, you're okay. Well, granted your appendix had to come out, you had two weeks of real good care and rest and nourishing food getting over it, didn't you? And people made a fuss over you and old friends you hadn't heard from in ages came around or sent flowers? But mostly, you rested. You got over, or almost over, that fatigue which gave you the neurotic fear, which in turn got your innards all churned up. So now you're all square with the world, at least for a while, until you get chronically overtired again. Then you'll worry yourself into getting something else out of whack inside—your heart or your liver or your gizzard—and you can keep this up for quite a spell. But not indefinitely. There's a limit to the things the doctors can whittle on.

Well, that theory of Dr. Cowles's kinda makes sense to me. There are a lot of sick, complaining people who actually shouldn't be sick at all. Of course, the theory don't cover everything. You don't catch measles because you have a neurotic fear, although being overtired can lower your resistance to infection. You don't break a leg through fear, but you may be so fatigued that you get careless. So you see this fatigue-fear-illness cycle has a pretty broad application after all, although Dr. Cowles's purpose is to apply it to common ailments such as stomach trouble, heart trouble—things that are definitely brought on through weariness and worry, through not eating and sleeping right. And if you can avoid trouble before it starts, you've not only saved a lot of wear and tear on yourself, but on your pocketbook, too, and that's something to give a nod to, nowadays.

TEN THINGS I WISH I HAD KNOWN BEFORE I WAS TWENTY-ONE

1. What I was going to do for a living . . . exactly what my lifework would be.
2. That my health after thirty depended in a large degree on what I put in my stomach before I was twenty-one.
3. How to take care of money.
4. The commercial asset of being neatly and sensibly dressed.
5. That habits are mighty hard to change after you're twenty-one.
6. That worth-while things require time, patience, and work.
7. That the world would give me just about what I deserved.
8. That a thorough education not only pays better wages than hard labor . . . but it brings the best of everything else.
9. The value of absolute truthfulness in everything.
10. That my parents weren't old fogies after all.

Anonymous

HOW TO GET OVER WORRIES

Worry is our national habit. Sometimes we worry with good reason, but a lot of our worries are completely without substance, and it's a good idea to get rid of them before they clutter up our lives to such an extent that they hamper every movement, every free idea, every impulse. That kind of worry can make your breakdown get nervous in short order.

Ever read David Seabury's book, *How to Worry Successfully?* It's got a lot of ideas that would come in handy for the chronic worrier. For instance, there's Dr. Seabury's analysis of worry and anger. He, and some of the other boys who mess around with psychology and behaviorism, say that worry and anger are very closely connected.

For instance, if you get mad at somebody and go into a silent brooding rage about it, instead of blowing up and letting off steam and getting it over with, every time you see the guy you got mad at you'll get mad all over again, in a quiet way that nags at your nerves. You go into a slow burn if the guy's name is even mentioned, or if you see

160

somebody wearing the same kind of necktie he does, or walking with his characteristic walk or using a phrase he uses. After a while, if this guy is somebody you have to see a lot of, if he's in the same office with you, or if he's your next-door neighbor or an in-law or one of your own relatives, you'll work this slow burn into a first-class worry, all by your little self, without even knowing it. Seabury says that much worry is only anger in disguise, a sullen brooding which we're kind of ashamed of, so we rationalize it into what we think is necessary pondering. Restrained anger poisons mind, body, and spirit, and we'd be better off yielding to a few outbursts than simmering away in a cauldron of bitterness.

Suppose, for instance, you're sore at your next-door neighbor because his dog barks at night and ruins your sleep. You can't go over and punch him in the nose, because otherwise he's a good egg—if he'd only shut that dog up. You like dogs in general, so you don't take it out on the pooch, and you don't report it to the police because you don't want to get your name dragged into anything, so night after night you lie there sleepless, getting mad at your neighbor.

Well, a guy can get used to about anything, so after a long time you get used to the dog barking. You don't even hear it any more. But you've set up a chain of worry reactions toward that neighbor. You may find that you worry about his health, or the way he keeps his yard, or how he's doing in his job. You compensate for not doing anything about your very natural anger and annoyance over the barking dog by worrying about the guy in general. Everything about him is wrong. You get so you wish he'd drop dead, or else you go a step farther and get terribly sorry for him and concerned about him, but whatever you do, he's on your mind entirely too much. And worry breeds worry, so pretty soon you're worrying about things that have absolutely no connection with that guy who owns the barking dog. You worry about your own health, and whether the milkman will leave the right number of bottles, and who is going to be elected mayor next year. But it all goes back to that first worry that started up because you were mad and didn't blow off steam. And, what's more, mere blowing off steam isn't quite enough. After you've worked off your mad—and remember, the danger in anger lies in our unwise use of it, not in the emotion itself—you've got to go out and do something constructive to correct the thing that made you angry in the first place.

Dr. Seabury says that if you hold your peeves in, you become sick. Years pass but repressed anger remains. Keep your mind free of irritation. Never let it collect. If you have troubles, set a little time aside for yourself to get your irritations out of your system. Here's what he recommends doing:

1. Get a punching bag, or a pillow, and let your feelings out on it, or take a walk and whack stones with a stick.

2. Sit down and write a letter to whoever angered you. Tell him just what you think. Then tear it up and burn it. Don't send it, whatever you do.

3. Go into a room alone and talk it out. Cuss if you feel like it, and talk just as if you were face to face with the guy who did you dirt. But don't go out and hunt him up and tell it to him directly, or you'll end up with something really worth worrying about.

4. Lie down quietly, flat on your back for half an hour, and relax.

5. Then get up and tend to your trouble with intelligence. You will know exactly what to do.

Now, those are the five steps Dr. Seabury says will save you from making an unholy show of yourself and getting into all kinds of trouble and acting stupid and developing a worry complex and ending up with absolutely nothing accomplished except getting yourself into a mental tizzy that you may have to spend a lot of time and money getting out of. I think it makes sense.

LINES FOR TOM BRENEMAN

When we must die, how good it is to die
As in mid-battle, with our battle-gear
Still bright upon our backs, our battle-cry
Still ringing in the ear.

Even so you passed, upon your lips a jest,
O warrior for joy and hearty laughter;
Surely some quip, your last and merriest,
Rocks Heaven to the rafter!

And now God rest you, friend, who by your art
Of sweet and simple goodness served us well;
Your golden laughter heals the lonely heart;
God rest you, Tom! Farewell!

Joseph Auslander

FAT IS A PSYCHOLOGICAL DISORDER

There was a pretty interesting talk given up at the New York Academy of Medicine a while ago by Dr. Hilde Bruch, who's on the staff of the Department of Psychiatry at Columbia University.

Dr. Bruch came out with the idea that fat people are fat because of some kind of psychological whingding they've gone into, without even knowing it.

Now, this doesn't mean people who are just pleasingly plump. Dr. Bruch is talking about folks, men, women, and children, who are grotesquely fat and can't seem to do anything about it. Up until now, the doctors have laid this fat to glandular disorders, but Dr. Bruch says that's all wrong. His idea is that folks who are fat may also have glandular troubles, but that's not what lays on those heavy pads of unwanted and unlovely flesh.

"If one learns to understand fat people more thoroughly," Dr. Bruch says, "it appears that their tremendous size, which they so loudly bemoan, is not without a positive emotional meaning for them. Physical size and bulkiness convey a feeling of strength, safety, and power to the timid fat child.

"Heavy layers of fat seem to act as protective walls against an outer world which the fat person often experiences as unfriendly and threatening. Many fat young girls, though outwardly very concerned about not getting married, nevertheless persist in remaining fat because it is a protection against men and sex and the responsibilities of adult womanhood which they dread even more than the disgrace of being fat."

Dr. Bruch says this fatness gets on people when, in plain language, they eat too much. He uses a lot of medical terms to explain this, but that's what it boils down to. The average guy eats just about as much food as he works off energy, and the thing is balanced so that he stays about the same weight all the time. And if he cuts down on his activity, and don't burn up so much energy, then his appetite sorta goes into a decline. But if he cuts down on his activity, and goes right on eating, then he gets fat. And, if he has any little psychological bugbear waiting around to pounce on him, his appetite will increase and increase,

163

and food will become more and more important to him. It finally has an exaggerated emotional value that has nothing to do with the normal pleasant enjoyment of your groceries because they taste good and dinner is a happy social affair. These psychological fat people get to be secret eaters, just like some alcoholics are secret drinkers. They can't do without their food; they can't even cut down a little bit.

"Food stands for love, security, and satisfaction," says Dr. Bruch. "On the other hand, muscular activity and social contacts are associated with the concept of danger, threat, and insecurity.

"Fat can be traced to a family setting characteristic of it. The typical obese family is usually small. Often it is the youngest child, or an only child, who is fat."

He goes on to say that fat is most likely to occur in families where Mama has the say, and Papa is kinda on the henpecked side. Mama has a particularly close hold on the children; she lives out her own dreams and frustrations in their lives, and she tries to realize, for them, all the luxuries and the idleness which she feels life has deprived her of. So she overfeeds them and stuffs them with tidbits and does everything for them and waits on them hand and foot. Well, the result is that they grow up feeling that the world is a dangerous place from which Mama will protect them, and Mama doesn't really mean a loving, kind person to them any more—she means food. Just food. Because that's what she's stood for, all along. And when finally they're pushed out of the nest into this alien, hostile world they've been protected from, eating is their only known source of comfort and satisfaction. They're timid folk, scared of the opposite sex, and they never adjust to normal life.

"The fat grownup," says Dr. Bruch, "like the fat child, is emotionally immature, passively dependent, and helpless in meeting the problems of life. He seeks comfort in overeating in the face of failure and frustrating experiences." That's just about the size of it. If he skids and bumps his nose on a disappointment, he goes out and stuffs himself on food, sort of the way a drunk goes out and gets fried.

Dr. Bruch says that it ought to be the easiest thing on earth to lose fat, but it ain't, because fat people simply will not stick to diets and they will not take exercise. They may swear up and down that they will; they may protest that they'd do anything to get rid of their fat, but actually, they'll do anything to keep it. Of course, they aren't consciously aware of this desire to keep their fat, but it's a lot stronger than any desire they have to get thin. Give up their security and their comfort and their soft lazy ease just to get thin and energetic? Don't be stupid!

Well, now, these are Dr. Bruch's ideas, not mine. But I think it's an interesting angle on being overweight. In these times when we're being urged to whittle down on some foods because so many folks in the world are starving, it might be a good thing to remember that, by whittling down, we're helping ourselves as well as helping others. If you're a little bit on the roly-poly side, that don't mean nuthin'. Maybe you're just good-natured and have a healthy fondness for your food. But if you're one of these five-by-fives, just a hard block of solid fat trundling around, and your feet hurt and you're short of breath all the time, think it over. Maybe you haven't really wanted to get thin, up to now, no matter what you've tried. If that's the case, Dr. Bruch thinks you might talk it over with a psychiatrist and find out if you've got a botheration, deep down inside; some fear or some frustration that's keeping you walled up in a protecting prison of unnecessary flesh. Because, if that's what's wrong, you can get rid of it, if you only try.

REASONS FOR BELIEVING IN PRAYER

Here's a statement by Dr. Daniel A. Poling, the famous preacher, about why he believes in prayer.

"I believe in prayer because a personal God would inevitably wish personal contact with His children. Prayer is part of that contact.

"I believe in prayer because prayer has produced results. Some people say there is nothing in it . . . that only means that they, themselves, have found nothing. A blind man will say he does not see a mountain. An unsuccessful prospector will declare there is no gold in such and such a stream. But the mountain and the gold are both there.

"I believe in prayer because it gets results, for me and for others. I believe in prayer because, whatever a man's estate, prayer will enrich his life, give him a finer, truer character, a surer hold on his career, a poise and a peace for sorrow, a confidence in difficulty, and at last the unquenchable hope of immortality.

"Prayer for me has never stopped the sun. Prayer for me has never changed God; but it has done more—it has changed me."

MIDDLE-AGE FEARS

There's one thing that we're all gonna go through if we live long enough, sure as death and taxes, and that's the period somewhere between the age of forty and fifty in women and fifty-five to sixty-five in men which we commonly call the "change of life." This "change of life" is not well understood by the average public, and it ought to be. The average guy in his late fifties feels kinda cross; he's got something the matter with him but he ain't exactly sick, and as far as change of life is concerned, he's heard of it in connection with women but as far as he's concerned it never occurs to him. He don't even know men get it. The average gal in her middle forties has been dreading the change of life ever since she was old enough to know about such things, and now she just knows she's beginning to get it and it's gonna be awful because she feels perfectly horrible. And both of them are scared to death (1) that they're losing their mind, (2) that they'll make fools of themselves in public by extreme flushing, fainting, dizzy spells, and nausea, and (3) that they'll lose all sex attractiveness and sex potency, and their partner in marriage will look to greener pastures and all joy and love is gone henceforth from their lives.

Well, none of those things are about to happen. If you want to really know what goes on in the mind and body of both man and woman during this difficult time, read Dr. Edward Spencer Cowles's book, *Don't Be Afraid*. I've mentioned this book before. Dr. Cowles is just about tops in his field of behavioristic psychology, and he has something some of the other scientific brain mechanics don't have: the warm human touch. If you read his book you'll see that he ain't just writing down facts and figures from charts; he's writing about you and your problems and telling you not to be afraid, and when he gets through you just ain't afraid any more! You can't be, because there's nothing to fear; there never was anything, except your own exaggerated fear of fear.

Now, about this change-of-life deal, here's what Dr. Cowles says: the human body actually undergoes two changes, one in the teens, when the boy changes into a man and the girl into a woman. We call this period adolescence, but it's actually a change of life, a lot more

166

severe, physically speaking, than the one that comes later, only generally speaking we take it a lot easier because there's no shadow of fear over it. It's a change in voice, a change in personality, a change of physique, a change in the entire glandular structure, and, finally, a change in sex development. You notice that the change in sex development is just one part of the over-all job.

Well, most of the fears, the nervousness and melancholia of the middle-aged change of life, stem from a misunderstanding about the sex changes during that time. Actually these sex changes are only a part of the picture. In women they're more spectacular, because a woman loses her power of childbearing at this point, but that's the only thing she loses. Her enthusiasm for living, her capacity to give and to receive love, remain exactly the same; in fact, may even be increased, and Dr. Cowles says there's no reason why women should not live a rich and satisfying life right up to their last days on earth. Both men and women go through other changes; the hair begins to gray, fine lines appear in the skin, and the glandular system pulls some fast ones understood only by doctors. Along with these changes come the personality changes, as noticeable as the ones of adolescence, and just as unexpected, sometimes.

Now, during this period, if there is great fear present, both men and women go through something called "involutional melancholia." Even when there is little or no fear, it's a time when every now and then you get a few days when you don't care if school keeps or not. With fear present, you get something with all the symptoms of true melancholia. A guy don't know what's the matter, but he feels all loused up, and he gets scared. So one morning he wakes up feeling as if a banshee was sitting on his chest, he walks the floor, he agonizes over everything, his sleep is assailed by dreams that defy description of their horror, like seeing his wife hacked to pieces before his eyes. That's a real common one. He wakes, and can't realize it was just a dream. His mental misery is indescribable; he conjures up all the sins of his past, even childish misdeeds, and they make him seem like a monster, and he gets suspicious of everybody, believing that the people around him know his guilt. He imagines he is being spied on, that his letters are being opened, that people are following him, that enemies are hiding in the closet, that the police are coming after him. The only escape is that tempting window over there; the only solution is suicide. That's a thumbnail sketch of the state a guy can get into through involutional melancholia.

167

But there's one good thing about it: you can get over it. It differs from true melancholia in that it is not simply an exhaustion of the nerve-cell energy, it's an effort of adjustment on the part of every cell in the body during this period of change of life. Dr. Cowles calls it a "metabolic toxic disorder," which just means that your whole system is poisoned. You'll live. It's not hereditary. It won't repeat itself. Once passed, it cannot return.

The treatment is probably the most delicate the physician is called upon to carry out. It requires tact, profound understanding of the particular case, and a lot of knowledge about the glandular system. Equipped with these, a competent doctor can carry the patient through without this violent emotional suffering in which the original nervousness and bodily sensation and fear magnified and multiplied itself into a thousand plaguing demons.

So just take it for granted that during the change of life both men and women are going to be in some degree irritable, indecisive; they can't make up their minds as readily as they used to; they're more touchy and sensitive to imaginary slights, and they tend to be just a bit suspicious. All these can be minimized if you have a clear picture of them and understand the cause. You, too, can get through the change of life without anything but slight inconvenience, or you can get yourself a mess of fears and fear neuroses that make you act like a candidate for a nut farm. You can really hurt yourself, maybe totally, like with that jumping-out-of-the-window deal, into the bargain. The thing to remember is, change of life is a metabolic process that occurs in all men and all women; it is sometimes accompanied by involutional melancholia, especially if you're scared, and this melancholia can be quickly and safely cured, and no hereditary tendencies can be attached to it. You won't go crazy during it, even if there is a record of insanity in your family. But before you get to that age when this thing will sneak up on it, read some good book like Dr. Cowles's *Don't Be Afraid,* so you'll know what the deal is, and then, if it gets kinda out of hand, go to a real good doctor for help. And remember, it's just as natural as that earlier change from boy to man or girl to woman, and, no matter what old wives' tales you've heard, after it's all over, even during it, you can enjoy life to the full.

FOUR LESSONS FROM HISTORY

When Charles A. Beard, the eminent historian, was asked if he could condense into one short book the lessons taught by history, he replied that he could do it in these four sentences:

"1. Whom the gods would destroy, they first make mad with power.

"2. The mills of the gods grind slowly, but exceedingly small.

"3. The bee fertilizes the flower it robs.

"4. When it is dark enough, one can see the stars."

SIX KINDS OF MEMORY

Did you know we've got six kinds of memory? I didn't; I always thought memory was memory, and that's all there was to it. But the boys who mess around with psychology say we've got six kinds: each one separate and distinct and useful in a way different from the other five.

For instance, we have recognition memory. This one is kinda hard to define. It's a sort of vague, over-all type of memory that enables us to find our way around the streets because we recognize certain trees or buildings or shop windows without consciously knowing they're there at all. You probably couldn't describe in detail everything you see on a certain street in your town, but once you walk down that street, you know right where you are and you turn off on the right corner, and so forth. Same thing with situations and events. Something comes up, and you dimly recall that you acted so-and-so in a situation that's kinda like this one, and things turned out all right, so you do the same thing again. That's recognition memory. Without it we'd be as helpless as blind kittens, even more so, because at least blind kittens always know where their mama is.

Then there's incidental memory. That's all the stuff you learn without really meaning to; you just kinda latch onto it as it flows by you. If you read over a meaningless string of a hundred words several times, without any attempt to remember them, you'll be able to write down about eleven per cent of them correctly afterwards. If you go to the theater, you'll remember the show you saw, and you'll also remember something about the people you sat near, and whether the seat you had was comfortable or not, and what the lobby of the theater looked like. The show was the important thing, but all these other memories just stuck to you accidentally. Incidental memory is an indicator of general alertness, and to it belong all the little anecdotes and incidents, the spice and variety of life. Things would be pretty dull without it.

Immediate memory is the kind of memory we have for telephone numbers, names, and addresses that we use once and never again, and so forth. It's extremely important to remember a telephone number long enough to give it to the operator, or to remember an address long enough to get to it, but there's no point in cluttering up your brain with every telephone number you've ever called. Some folks mistakenly think that remembering such things is a mark of a "good" memory, but it isn't. The psychologists say it's a mark of efficiency to be able to forget unnecessary things.

This immediate memory gets better and better in children until they reach maturity, and then it stays about the same way for the rest of your life. For instance, a child of three can repeat three numbers after hearing them once; you say, "Four, six, eight," and he'll say, "Four, six, eight," right back. He won't remember it an hour later, but he can repeat it after you. A child of ten can repeat six numbers, and at eighteen he can repeat eight, and get them right, and that's about as far as the average immediate memory ever gets. It's as far as it needs to. It just seems to cover the ground it's called on for, and that's all.

Then there's such a thing as memory for limited recall. This is for things that we need to remember for limited periods of time, and that are utterly useless after that time has passed. Teachers dislike this sort of memory when it's used to cram for examinations, because they hate to think that they've spent a whole term talking about something and a kid who has paid no attention can cram at the last minute and get as high marks as the ones who paid attention all the time. Nevertheless, memory for limited recall is very useful if you ever have to learn a part for a play. It's the memory actors use all the time. We memorize poems, enjoy them for a while, and then they fade out and other poems take their place. When we move to a new town, or even a new neighborhood, or when we take a new job, we make a whole new set of friends and acquaintances who, to some extent, dull the memory of the last set of folks we knew, and next time we move, we make still another set. When you were a kid, you knew the birthdays of most of your classmates. Now you know the birthdays of most of your intimate friends, and the people you work closely with, but you've forgotten those of your classmates. That's memory for limited recall. It may work for a week, or for several years, but eventually the memories fade out as they cease to be useful, and others take their places.

Then there's memory for permanent use. This is just what it says it is. These memories are part of you, just like parts of your body. You learn your own name; you learn that fire burns; you learn that Columbus discovered America. People don't even have to think about this kind of memory; they just have it. It's a combination of the things we learn by experience and the things we learn in school, and it's very useful and necessary, but it's probably less trouble to us than all the other kinds of memory put together. This is the memory that starts slipping a little sometimes when people get real old, or if they have been sick a long time.

Then, lastly, there's memory for problem solving. A lot of the things we memorize for permanent use are never used exactly in the form in which they are memorized. This memory is the tool by which we solve life's problems. We learn the rules of arithmetic in school, not because we are going to do arithmetic all our lives, but because every once in a while we have to know that two and two make four, and x is equal to a plus b. We learn rules of grammar, but we don't all turn out to be grammarians. We learn a vast stock of principles and facts which we apply in later life, and the extent to which we retain and apply these facts and principles in solving our problems is a good indication of how smart we are.

PRAYER OF ANY HUSBAND

I guess the nearest thing to heaven on earth that we know is a happy marriage, where husband and wife are perfectly mated, and admire each other's virtues and forgive each other's faults. We all have faults, and we must learn to bear and forbear, because nobody is perfect. There's no such thing as a paragon of perfection, short of being dead or being an impossible prig. If you're human you have faults, and you make mistakes, just like the next guy. But love kinda brings out the best in us. If we stay in love we'll always be at our best.

I ran across a little poem that I think you'll like. It's called *Prayer of Any Husband:*

Lord, may there be no moment in her life
When she regrets that she became my wife,
And keep her dear eyes just a trifle blind
To my defects, and to my failings kind!

Help me to do the utmost that I can
To prove myself her measure of a man,
But, if I often fail as mortals may,
Grant that she never sees my feet of clay!

And let her make allowance—now and then—
That we are only grown-up boys, we men,
So, loving all our children, she will see
Sometimes, a remnant of the child in me!

Since years must bring to all their load of care,
Let us together every burden bear,
And when Death beckons one its path along,
May not the two of us be parted long!

Anonymous

IMAGINATION IN CHILDREN

If you've ever been around children much, you know that there never was a normal healthy kid who didn't give his imagination a real good workout morning, noon, and night. In fact, the more normal and healthy Junior is, the more nonsense you're going to have to put up with in the way of his lively imagination and the trouble it can get him, and you, into. A listless kid with no imagination to speak of needs to be trotted off to a doctor to find out what's wrong with him. The medicos say nowadays that the "good" child who never gets into mischief or tells tall tales or gives Momma any worries is just the kid she ought to worry about.

But if Junior's imagination is running riot of late, if he's fascinated by wild and woolly adventures, especially the bloodthirsty ones, and if

172

he's just shaved the cat with Pop's electric razor and dug a pirate cave under the back porch and painted a skull and crossbones over it, if he whoops through the house, letting out Tarzan yells and swinging from the chandeliers—don't worry. He'll get over it. And, to tell the truth, you started him off on this violent career, you know; you're the one who did it. Because back when he was two or three years old you encouraged him to use his imagination. You told him bedtime stories, and you applauded whatever he said, and you pointed out the wonders of this and the wonders of that; you took him to the zoo and showed him all the strange animals and you had a Christmas tree for him covered with magical lights and presents appeared like miracles; you probably took him to movies, and he heard the radio—a voice coming out of a box when there's no person in the room. Now that's all as it should be; just about everything in his babyhood was set up to make his imagination grow by leaps and bounds, and now he's around eight or nine you suddenly clamp down and try to stop what's started, and started good. And you can't do it. If you make him quit playing Tarzan, he may mind you when you're looking, but inside of him he'll still be swinging through the jungles and evading the enemy. Incidentally, the enemy may very well be you, especially if you accompany your little lecture on being a gentleman by whapping him a couple of times. Just hang onto yourself and he'll get it out of his system.

What you can and should do, however, to help Junior along, and, incidentally, to help your own nerves, is to start early teaching him what is reality and what is fantasy. Don't start when he's just a baby, because then everything in the world is magic to him. His idea of the world, you know, is entirely different from yours. A very young child just hasn't yet had the experience or developed the judgment to distinguish between what's real and what isn't. Sometime around four or five years old he starts learning about what's good and what's bad, wholesome and unwholesome, and what behavior is acceptable and what isn't. First, he has to test everything. There's that trying period when he puts everything in his mouth, for instance. Then he has to learn how to touch things, and how to climb, and how to fit words to meanings, and why a ripe apple is good and a green one don't promote anything but a stomach-ache. And all during this period of experimentation and learning you're feeding him rhymes about the cow that jumped over the moon and Little Jack Horner who messed up a plum pie. What do you expect?

A kid has quite a lot of growing up to do before words like "death," "stealing," "lying," and so forth mean anything to him. Such words are just noises until personal experience or the emotional attitudes of adults give them a significance which a child can accept. But as soon as he can accept these more or less abstract concepts, you've got to get with it and show him what is reality, and what is just fantasy, a story in a book or a whopper he dreamed up and came rushing in to tell you. You can tell which is which right off; any mother can, but don't just glare at him and snap out, "That's a lie . . . and you know it!" If he says there's a three-headed dragon in the back yard ask him if he's sure, and suggest that you both go out and look at it together. Like as not it's a garter snake, or a crooked stick, or old Fido fixed up with a leftover Hallowe'en mask tied around his ears.

Well, in the natural course of events, Junior's imagination will calm down. He'll cease taking an exaggerated interest in blood-and-thunder stories and take to something more appropriate and adapted to his higher emotional and intellectual level. After all, he only gets out of those lurid yarns the excitement that a healthy child needs; most of it is way over his head, and will be ignored or forgotten almost at once.

So don't worry if your pride and joy peppers his conversation with weird references to gangsters, international spies, monsters on the moon, and such. As long as he talks about them, and knows what's real everyday living and what's made up, he's all right, and so will you be, provided you survive. And you will survive, even though you think you can't at the time. You'll get a few gray hairs . . . but that's what parents are for.

IN MEMORIAM

They are not dead, our sons who fell in glory,
Who gave their lives for FREEDOM and for TRUTH;
We shall grow old but never *their* great story,
Never their gallant youth.

In an eternal April set apart,
Their memory forever green shall grow;
In some bright secret meadow of the heart
Where never falls the snow.

Joseph Auslander

174

WHY GEORGE SAND DRESSED LIKE A MAN

Curiosity about the private lives of famous people seems to be part of human nature. That's what keeps all those movie magazines going, not to mention a whole host of biographers who are always digging up startling facts about Cleopatra or George Washington or Queen Elizabeth or old Ben Franklin. And it's really fascinating to consider famous private lives in the light of modern psychology, especially the lives of people who were considered, in their time, as pretty queer customers, on account of some funny little foibles they had that weren't just like the habits of their next-door neighbors.

For instance, you take the great French novelist, George Sand. Nobody even bothers with her right name—Madame Aurore Dudevant. She's just known by her writing name, George Sand. Well, now, why did she prefer to go down in history with a man's name? And why on earth did she customarily wear trousers, in an age when anything less modest than a hoopskirt was considered positively indecent?

The biographers have taken a crack at George Sand from time to time, but they never got very far before the psychological boys came along and found out what made her like that. The best the biographers could offer was that either she dressed like a man to shock people and attract attention, or she was a very masculine type of woman with a masculine attitude toward her own sex.

The biographers were unjust to George Sand in coming to those conclusions. The truth of the matter is that she was all woman. George Sand was just about as feminine as a woman can get. She had a husband and several children, and a whole host of admirers. She was extremely attractive to men, though she was far from pretty. She always had a lot of men around her, and she mothered them and fussed over them and loved them, and they sat at her feet and adored her.

But, far from trying to attract women to her by her masculine dress, and her man's name, she actually disliked women intensely and avoided them as much as possible. That's the point the biographers missed, and the psychologists dug up. She didn't like women, and she didn't have any women around her. And she preferred masculine clothes because hoopskirts and bonnets reminded her that she herself was a woman, which, in her peculiar make-up, was a very poor sort of critter to be. She wasn't showing off; she just didn't like anything to do with the female of the species.

Now, how she got that way is a very interesting story. Her father, Maurice Dupin, was the great-grandson of the Polish king, Frederick Augustus. And his mother, an extremely aristocratic old lady, never let him forget it for a minute. There was royal blood in Maurice's veins, and he was supposed to act accordingly. But he forgot himself one time, and got out from under Momma's eye, and married a woman named Sophie. Sophie didn't even have a family name. She was just Sophie. And she was no better than she ought to be, either. She was a completely uneducated woman, extremely coarse in her tastes and habits, and before Maurice married her, she already had several illegitimate children.

Well, after old Madame Dupin got over the conniption fit she threw, and you can't exactly blame her for throwing one, she couldn't very well accept Sophie as a fit wife for Maurice, but she could try to extend a decent influence over their children. So when little Aurore was born, there was a very terrible tug of war over her. Her grandmother wanted her to grow up as a well-educated, well-behaved young lady, and her mother didn't know what education meant, and, as for behavior, Sophie's behavior is best left unmentioned.

The poor kid was between the devil and the deep blue sea. Everything one woman stood for was exactly opposite from the other, and there was a dreadful scene going on all the time. But little Aurore loved both women, only she loved her mother the most, because anything went, with her, and around Madame Dupin, Aurore had to mind her Ps and Qs.

And then, when Aurore was ten years old, her mother ran away and went back to the streets of Paris, to the companionship of other women who weren't choosy about marrying the men they stayed with. And from that day forth, Aurore became George Sand.

She hated her mother for abandoning her; she hated her mother's shameful way of life, and yet she felt that somehow she ought to justify her mother's right to live as she pleased.

And so all the heroines of George Sand's novels are womanly, sweet, and maternal, like the mother she was deprived of in real life. And George Sand herself put on men's clothes as a sort of defiant gesture to the world that women could do anything men could. Men were not despised for being promiscuous. Why should women be? In a way,

George Sand was the first woman to stand up for equal rights and women's suffrage, but, in another way, wearing men's clothing kept the hated frills and bonnets and petticoats out of sight—the pretty feminine lures poor Sophie used in the Paris streets. George Sand could beat men on their own ground. The most famous men of France flocked around her, and she didn't need any ruffles and laces to catch their eyes, either.

So that's what the psychologist boys found out about George Sand. It's a pathetic little story: the pitched battle of mother and grandmother, the weak, aristocratic father who stood aside and let them fight over a helpless child, Sophie's return to the streets, and finally, the aging, dumpy, homely woman, George Sand, who had the love of poets and musicians—Chopin and Alfred de Musset and Balzac, just to mention three—the woman who never knew happiness, even in her own children, and who is chiefly remembered today because, unlike her next-door neighbors, she wore pants.

NINE DANGEROUS CHARACTERS

I always get interested in lists people make of things, especially lists that help people to live happier and more useful lives.

Let's turn again to Dr. Clifford R. Adams, the psychologist and marriage problem specialist, who has made a list that really intrigues me. He's catalogued the nine characters that, in his judgment, can make a flop out of any marriage. These are nine types of people to steer clear of when you're thinking about getting married.

First, there's the jealous individual who watches you like a hawk, no matter how you tread the straight and narrow path. He wants to know where you've been, where you're going, everything you ever did and everybody you ever knew before you met him, and what you've been thinking about for the past ten minutes thrown in for good measure. Dr. Adams figures that jealousy causes at least one out of every five quarrels between man and wife, and it's awful hard to keep in love with a jealous man—or a jealous woman. You lose your respect for such a life partner, and you can't ever, ever be yourself and act natural around the house. You're under suspicion . . . every second.

Then there's the mate who wants to improve you. That's pretty hard

177

to take, too. Don't ever marry anybody and then start changing him around, soon as the vows are said. And don't let anybody try to do it to you, either. You can usually see the signs coming on before it's too late.

The nervous husband, or wife, is no bargain either. Marriage won't cure emotional instability, and it may make a neurotic person even more frustrated and jittery. And nobody has a right to inflict personal troubles and nervous worries on anybody else.

Avoid the bird with money on the brain, by all means. Couples quarrel five times as much over money as over an important issue like rearing the children. The "root of all evil" isn't lack of money, but mismanagement of what you already have. Wives complain that their husbands are too tight, husbands howl about extravagance. If you're either stingy or spendthrift, you're a bad bet in the marriage market.

Then there's the alibi artist—keep away from him, or her. No woman really believes those farfetched tales of sitting up with a sick friend. You know how the yarn goes. She says, "Who was he?" And he says, "I dunno. He was too sick to tell me." A routine like that can get the little woman mad as a bear with a sore head in no time flat.

Also, no man, according to Dr. Adams, ever gets used to repeated excuses for late meals, unmade beds, missing buttons, and such. It's not the lateness or the untidiness or the inconvenience he resents. It's the constant excuses and alibis.

The escapist, who drowns his sorrows, takes refuge in daydreams, or employs any and every possible dodge to get away from reality isn't a reliable life partner either. And marriage never cured dipsomania, or any other mania, for that matter. The escapist needs a psychologist, not a wedding ring.

A person who is chronically disorderly in his habits can be hard to live with. Of course, there's such a thing as being so neat that it makes everybody uncomfortable, but, on the other hand, if the gal makes a nice home, there's some justification in her complaint if her husband turns it into a pigsty. And vice versa: a man has a right to expect a reasonably neat household and a woman who takes some pride in her appearance.

The mate with relatives clinging close as barnacles can lead to in-law trouble. That spells good for nobody. If you're thinking of getting married, look over your prospective family in its entirety. If your sweetheart hates his relatives, that's a danger signal that something is wrong. But if he can't spend an hour out of their sight—boy, that's courting plenty of headaches. And that goes for women, too. The gal who's tied to Mama's apron strings is likely to stay that way. I'm not referring now to a healthy respect and a world of love for your relatives, but if you just can't get along without them for a little while now and then, you'd better stick to them altogether and forget anybody else exists. Otherwise someone is going to have a broken heart.

And last but not least, there's the chronic flirt. Anybody who has to indulge in a lot of shallow, pointless flirtations that never get anywhere will be poor husband or wife material. Dr. Adams accuses the flirt of being incapable of genuine love, and of causing at least a quarter of all divorces. So if you're any one of three corners of a triangle . . . watch yourself. Maybe it's you that's causing the trouble.

ARE YOU SPOILING THEM?

Here's a little problem that you may have been wrestling with lately:

You go in the store with Junior, aged four and a half, and while you're buying the stuff you want, the kid roots around until something catches his eye, and when he's in the middle of that "Mommy, buy me this!" routine, getting red in the face and yanking on your skirt, Mrs. McGillicuddy from across the street comes in the store and just when Junior gets to the screaming and kicking point she remarks snootily that, after all, he *is* getting awfully spoiled. Then you buy the thing, to shut him up, and the old cat goes on to say that of course he acts that way, if you get him whatever he wants. The implication is that you're teaching him to misbehave.

Or Aunt Nettie says that it's a funny thing, when she's baby-sitting Junior when you go out in the evening, he goes to bed like a little lamb, but she's noticed that you practically have to drag him upstairs by the hair, and it takes two hours to get him settled down and asleep. Or Grandma cracks wise to the effect that he eats his prunes for supper over at her house, but for you he eats cholocate cake, or nothing. You spoil him, that's all; and he knows he can get away with it.

By the time Mrs. McGillicuddy and Aunt Nettie and Grandma get through with you, you feel limp as a dishrag, and you suspect yourself of being some kind of an unnatural monster who's out to ruin the character of a sweet innocent little child and turn him into a brat. You start

179

thinking you, his own mother, aren't good for the kid. Now, what about that?

Let's admit, right off, that some mothers really do spoil their children, and this makes the kids unpleasant now and unhappy later, when they find out the world just ain't ready to accept them and their big idea of their own importance, and roll out the red carpet for them the way they think it ought to.

But what most people don't realize is that even thoroughly unspoiled children inevitably will act spoiled around their mothers. If they've got even the least little streak of wanting to get their own way—and who hasn't?—they'll show it to Momma. Especially when somebody is there. Especially when company's around. And why Junior picks out company days to act bratty in is very simple. He's jealous and he wants everybody to know that he has first claim on you. When you're alone with him, he acts like a little angel; he's happy with the love and companionship he's getting. But just let a third person come around and he turns into a little tarantula. Likewise, he can be contented as a doodlebug alone with Aunt Nettie when she's baby-sitting him, but if she's around when you're putting him between the sheets, it's another story entirely.

Now the boys who mess around with psychology have figured this one out pretty good. They say that a baby isn't born loving. He has to learn how to love, both wisely and well. From the very first they seem to know they need love, but it takes a little while to know how to give it. A baby's love ain't very considerate, as you've probably noticed when the kid yells loudest and longest the day you have a headache; and when you've got a cake in the oven, that's the time two-year-olds always practice hurdle-jumping in the kitchen, and right in the middle of washday you've got to stop and play cat's cradle or Little Sister acts like she don't you any more. That inconsiderateness is just something they have to learn to get rid of, and they will, usually around about five or six years old, when they realize that Momma can get tired, too, and sometimes her back aches, and she's ashamed to have them act up before an audience. The boys say that up to five or six it's nothing to worry about if the kids act spoiled. In fact, if they didn't, once in a while, it's a sign that they haven't really been loved enough. You are absolutely indispensable to the kid until he's around five; every bit of comfort and love and safety he knows comes from you and the other members of his family. But the most important one is you. After all, Daddy goes off to work, but you're there all the time and you're the one he turns to when he wants something. At five or six he begins getting wider interests, starts going to school, and you aren't so essential any more.

But there are several things you can do when Junior is still a baby that'll keep the spoiled-child business down to a minimum. If you're clever enough, you'll get plenty of compliments on raising the kids without spoiling them one bit—which you know in your heart ain't quite true—but it's music to a mother's ear. Here are some suggestions the psychologists have figured out:

1. Have fun with the kids. Devote some time exclusively to companionship with them, playing, telling stories, and so forth. Then, when you're busy with your own affairs that they can't share, they'll understand that a good time is coming, when you finish your work. And see that the kids distinguish between work and play—your work and your play. A walk to the store to get the groceries may be fun, but it's primarily a business trip and should be done in a businesslike manner. A walk to the park to feed the squirrels is something else again.

2. In handling matters of routine, bedtime, meals, baths, and so forth, make them fun but be as impersonal about them as possible. That "do it because you love Momma" deal may work, temporarily, but it ain't gonna make for the formation of good lifetime habits, and even worse is "Mother won't love you unless you do it!" That's really bad for the kid; it sets up all sorts of insecure feelings and resentments, and it's a downhill road to temper tantrums.

3. Act as if you expected the kid to grow up a little every day in independence, self-control, and initiative. When he makes mistakes, tell him they happen in the best-regulated families, and try to show him how to do better next time. You don't get anywhere telling him Momma's feelings are hurt because he broke the cream pitcher. Show him how to set it down on the table so it won't get knocked off next time.

4. Teach him consideration for other people. Real small babies can start learning to take real pleasure in doing things for others. A two-year-old can fetch your slippers or the paper, and a three-year-old can pour out milk for the kitten, if it's in a little jug that's easy to handle.

5. See that the kid has plenty of opportunities for constructive play, for making things, block buildings, doll clothes, stories, and songs. Constructive play builds independence, self-respect, and honesty in facing and overcoming difficulties.

6. Don't pay attention to him just for your own emotional satisfaction, either to make him appreciate you more or to shut him up because

you can't stand his noise any longer. Think for his own good, not for yours.

And remember, it's unusual, almost abnormal, for a child to be really spoiled after the age of six years old. If he is, it's your fault. But it ain't fatal. Being spoiled is one of the easiest habits in the world to break, provided you start in early.

HEARSAY

In every town, in every street,
In nearly every house you meet
A little imp, who wriggles in
With half a sneer and half a grin,
And climbs upon your rocking chair,
Or creeps upon you anywhere;
And when he gets you very near,
Just whispers something in your ear—
Some rumor of another's shame,
And "Little Hearsay" is his name.
He never really claims to know—
He's only heard that it is so;
And then he whispers it to you,
So you will go and whisper, too.
For if enough is passed along
The rumor, even though it's wrong—
If John tells Henry, Henry—Joe,
And Joe tells Mary, Mary—Flo,
And Flo tells Mildred, Mildred—Ruth,
It very soon may pass for truth.

You understand, this little elf,
He doesn't say he knows himself,
He doesn't claim it's really true—
He only whispers it to you,
Because he knows you'll go and tell
Some other whisperer as well;
And so before the setting sun
He gets the devil's mischief done,
And there is less of joy and good
Around your little neighborhood.

Look out for "Hearsay!" when he sneaks
Inside the house—when slander speaks
Just ask the proof in every case;
Just ask the name and date and place;
And if he says he only heard,
Declare you don't believe a word,
And tell him you will not repeat
The silly chatter of the street—
However gossips smile and smirk,
Refuse to do their devil's work.

Anonymous

WE ARE ALL ONE PEOPLE

We hear an awful lot today about the necessity for racial and religious
tolerance among ourselves, right here in our own country, where, believe me, there are prejudices at work that you aren't even aware of,
because if you were, I know you'd get out and do something about
them. This piece is a statement by an Indian chief, by the name of
Hiamovi, who was operating out among the Cheyenne and Dakota
Indians around the turn of the century, and he sent this message as a
sort of open letter.

I know this is about Indians, which may seem remote to you, but it
sure applies to a lot of situations that crop up every day in connection
with racial and religious differences. So I'd like you to read it with that
in mind. I'm sorry that I have to shorten it up some. Incidentally, you'll
notice that it sounds like a poem. Here it is:

*A message from Hiamovi, High Chief of the Cheyennes and Dakotas,
to the Great Chief in Washington, and to the Chiefs of Peoples across
the Great Water:*

"Long ago the Great Mystery caused this land to be, and made the
Indians to live in this land. . . . Then came strangers from across the
Great Water. No land had they; we gave them of our land. No food
had they; we gave them of our corn. The strangers are become many
and they fill the whole country. They dig gold—from my mountains.
They build houses—of the trees of my forests. They rear cities—of my
stones and rocks. They make fine garments—from the hides and wool
of animals that eat my grass.

183

"And when I think upon this I know that it is right, even thus. In the heart of the Great Mystery it was meant that stranger visitors—my friends across the Great Water—should come to my land; that I should bid them welcome; that all men should sit down with me and eat together of my corn. It was meant by the Great Mystery that the Indian should give to all peoples.

"But the white man has never known the Indian. It is thus: there are two roads, the white man's road, and the Indian's road. Neither traveler knows the road of the other. Thus ever it has been.

"I want all white men to read and learn how the Indians lived and thought in the olden time. . . . When I think, I know that it is in the mind of the Great Mystery that white men and Indians who fought together should now be one people.

"There are birds of many colors—red, blue, green, yellow—yet it is all one bird. There are horses of many colors—brown, black, yellow, white—yet it is all one horse. So cattle, so all living things—animals, flowers, trees. So men: in this land where once were only Indians are now men of every color—white, black, yellow, red—yet all one people. That this should come to pass was in the heart of the Great Mystery. It is right thus. And there shall be peace."

I kinda like that. I think old Hiamovi had a lot on the ball—a lot more than some of the rest of us.

RULES FOR SUCCESS

Baron Rothschild, the famous financial wizard, had a set of rules for success that every enterprising young man could paste in his hat, the day he steps into his first job. I think maybe you'll get an idea out of them. This is what the old baron said:

"Carefully examine every detail of your business.

"Be prompt in everything.

"Take time to consider, then decide quickly.

"Dare to go forward.

"Bear your troubles patiently.

"Maintain your integrity as a sacred thing.

"Never tell business lies.

"Make no useless acquaintances.

184

"Never try to appear something more than you are.

"Pay your debts promptly.

"Learn how to risk your money at the right time.

"Shun strong liquor.

"Employ your time well.

"Do not reckon upon chance.

"Be polite to everybody.

"Never be discouraged.

"Work hard and you will succeed."

HOW TO INVITE TROUBLE

You know, if you happen to be over fifty, there are a number of cute little ways you can invite trouble so that your last half century won't be half as pleasant as your first. In his recent book, *Aging Successfully,* Dr. George Lawton, who's one of the few real authorities on the problems of aging, spends a whole chapter on ways to invite trouble after fifty.

Dr. Lawton says that one of the best ways is to get a wonderful cook. If you have an artist cook whose gifts simply cannot be neglected, you can wreck your health and develop your waistline, and you may turn into one of those unhappy, lonely old people to whom eating is their only real enjoyment.

Another way to invite trouble is to make complete rest the only cure for fatigue. Of course an old person gets physically tired quicker than a youngster, but the tiredness of the old is not so much a result of excessive physical exertion as it is of relentless emotional conflict or dissatisfaction with the dull monotony of life. Many older people blame fatigue for their lack of accomplishment. The cure for it is a purpose for every day and an escape from boredom and a general straightening out of the person's fears and inner conflicts.

Then you can invite trouble after fifty by using sedatives to get to sleep. You get worried and frightened because you wake earlier and earlier, as you get older and older. Well, this isn't anything to get upset about; as you get older you need less sleep, but sometimes it's hard to fill in those early morning hours when the rest of the household is snoring away. Whatever you do, don't take sleeping pills. It's better to get right up, if you don't like reading or writing in bed, and find yourself a good book or write letters or listen to the early radio programs. You might even start writing the story of your life. Some perfectly healthy normal old people go to bed at eleven and are wide awake at two in the morning. Well, it won't hurt them a speck, but fuming and fussing in the dark and then resorting to sedatives will. Older people may want to supplement a short night's sleep with a catnap in the afternoon . . . although many do not even care for this.

Another way to invite trouble and drive away your friends is to start reliving your past in public. It can make you an awful bore. If you've had an exceptionally full and interesting life, you may want to write your autobiography; it will be treasured by your family and there's one chance in a million that you'll get on the best-seller list. But don't let everything you talk about hinge on the past. Disraeli talked about our "anecdotage" and Burges Johnson, in his *As Much as I Dare,* noted: "In the late sixties, a man may begin to remember too much out loud."

Another "don't" is: don't concentrate on your place in history. Some older folks seem to think they're kind of an animated footnote in a prospective chronicle of their town and time. They get indignant if another oldster is prominently mentioned in the local paper. Some ancient folks get so strongly conscious of being about to enter into the Hall of Fame that, to all intents and purposes, they've already passed on.

Don't become a refugee from maturity, decide that old age is a prison, and try to escape from it by trying to beat the young folks on their own ground. The philosophers say that the only way to avoid old age is to die young, and nobody wants to do that, so we should try to accept the fact we've been living for quite a spell.

Don't postpone the preparation for maturity. To grow old gracefully, you ought to know something about what it's like to be old, before you actually get there.

Don't believe that age means birthdays instead of "aliveness." It is the eager mind which participates in all that is happening about it, and this mind may be nine or ninety. You can be twenty, too, and still be insensitive to beauty, incapable of thought, and indifferent to the rights of others. Some folks, the lucky ones, as they grow older become more active in their thinking, their feeling, and their friendships, more responsive to ideas and people's needs.

Then, another way to invite trouble is to concentrate on the prolongation of life. There isn't much we can do about living longer, as individuals, but we know that we, as a nation, will live longer than our ancestors, and our children will live longer than we will. How long we live isn't so important as how long we can enjoy an active, useful existence. Mere empty living just for the sake of outlasting everybody else isn't much to look forward to.

If you really want to make yourself miserable, brood over your illnesses, real or imaginary, and talk about them all the time and compare them with your friends' troubles. You'll have more troubles than friends! And another way to make yourself unhappy is to make a daily study of your face in the mirror, and take a minute inventory of every wrinkle and count each fallen hair.

Don't succumb to that greatest temptation of old age, self-pity. And don't convince yourself that boredom is inevitable. If you keep saying, "I'm bored," you soon will be. And don't blame all the shortcomings of old age on illness or fatigue or neglect. That's just seeking a scapegoat for unhappiness.

You can invite trouble after fifty by becoming a bank hater. Plenty of old people keep their fortune in a cooky jar or under the mattress; they lose their money through fire, theft, or forgetfulness. You read about such tragedies every day. Loose cash belongs in a bank, and no place else. And aging people should figure that maybe their judgment isn't quite as good as it once was. Banks have reliable trust departments for just such cases. Don't give your money to a relative or a friend to manage for you; let the bank do it. And don't believe that just having money solves the old-age problem. It sure helps, but it's no substitute for the ability to get along with yourself and with others. A pension doesn't guarantee that you will have emotional, social, and recreational activities when you get old.

Don't be afraid to be venturesome and take a chance and strike out in some new interesting activity. But at the same time, don't specialize in the kind of chance taking that involves crossing the streets against the traffic lights. A young, agile person may possibly get away with it, but after fifty, no matter how young you feel, you ought to obey certain rules of caution. For instance, you're just as safe a driver or maybe safer now than you were ten years ago, at normal speeds, but you're not as safe at high speeds.

And don't demand honor and respect just because you are old. You'll get it if you are worthy of it; you'll probably get it anyway, but honor and respect given to a complaining, argumentative, whiny old party can't be much satisfaction. Just be yourself, and you'll not only get honor and respect: you'll get love, which counts even more.

187

TWELVE ESSENTIALS OF A SUCCESSFUL SALESMAN

A successful salesman must have . . .

> The curiosity of a cat;
> The tenacity of a bulldog;
> The brashness of a Charles McCarthy;
> The determination of a cab driver;
> The diplomacy of a wayward husband;
> The patience of a self-sacrificing wife;
> The deductive powers of a Sherlock Holmes;
> The persuasiveness of a job-hunting politician;
> The enthusiasm of a radio announcer;
> The good humor of an idiot;
> The self-assurance of a college graduate;
> The tireless persistence of a bill collector.

> Anonymous

TEN HINTS ON AGING SUCCESSFULLY

Here is a list of ten useful hints for those of us who ain't quite so young as we used to be. I think this list of hints makes sense, and again we must credit Dr. George Lawton for making it. I think I'm going to keep this in my notebook to look over when I feel age sorta sneaking up on me in the years to come. Here it is:

1. Admit that you are growing older.

2. Remember that age brings good things as well as bad.

3. If anybody says you're too old, come back with a snappy "Too old for what?" You're not too old to modify an attitude or a habit, acquire a skill, render a service, keep up to date, create something beautiful, or try out a new idea.

4. A long life is its own reward. Do not expect homage *only* because you are old and have seen and suffered and survived much.

5. As opportunities for self-expression in your work or family lessen, realize than the human imagination does not grow old, and find your creative outlets in hobbies, the arts, and community services.

6. Don't act as if you expected people to feel sorry for you. Pity cannot replace love and approval, but it can crowd those two out. More essential than a home of one's own is a life of one's own, without dependence on children or relatives for entertainment, companionship, or emotional support.

7. Learning is a form of living. The older man or woman should acquire some new knowledge each year. As physical pleasures diminish, and the main daily problem is how to hold our bodies together, we must cultivate more and more the pleasures of the mind and our other inner resources.

8. Realize that maturity is most valued for the knowledge of strategy, not for strength or speed. Look at the older doctor or lawyer, the craftsman, the political leader, the artist in living.

9. As replacements for old friends, continually make new ones. The most devoted couple does not know when one of them, carrying on alone, will need the companionship of friends.

10. There is only one ultimate peace. Until then, there is no escape from struggle or the problems of maturity. Always we need a tomorrow, goals to strive for and present activities that go on. Seventeen centuries ago a Greek philosopher wrote: "Employment is nature's best physician and is essential to human happiness." Ever necessary is: "A plan, a task—and freedom."

NOBODY KNOWS BUT MOTHER

Nobody knows of the work it makes
To keep the home together;
Nobody knows of the steps it takes,
Nobody knows—but Mother.

Nobody listens to childish woes,
Which kisses only smother;
Nobody's pained by naughty blows,
Nobody—only Mother.

Nobody knows of the sleepless care,
Bestowed on baby brother;
Nobody knows of the tender prayer,
Nobody—only Mother.

Nobody knows of the lessons taught
Of loving one another;
Nobody knows of the patience sought,
Nobody—only Mother.

Nobody knows of the anxious fears,
Lest darlings may not weather
The storm of life in after years,
Nobody knows—but Mother.

Nobody kneels at the throne above
To thank the Heavenly Father
For that sweetest gift—a mother's love;
Nobody can—but Mother.

Anonymous

THE NEW COMMANDMENTS

If you read any books at all, you've probably read a book called *Peace of Mind*. It came out in 1946, and it's been a top best seller ever since.

Peace of Mind is a mighty good book. It was written by Dr. Joshua Loth Liebman, who was a rabbi in Boston. But Dr. Liebman didn't write *Peace of Mind* just for people of the Jewish faith; it's a thoughtful attempt to interpret religion—all religions, and man's crying need for something to believe in—in the light of modern science, especially in the light of practical, applied psychology. Just about everybody can get something out of Dr. Liebman's book. I guess you might say its immediate, and immense, popularity just goes to show how much people want peace of mind, these days.

At the very end of the book is a set of commandments to those who strive for peace of mind for themselves. These commandments are in no way intended to take the place of the eternal Ten in the Bible, or even to supplement them; these are simple working rules which apply to our mental and emotional attitude toward everyday life. Dr. Liebman couched them in biblical language for the very obvious reason that they're easy to remember, that way. I think maybe you'll get something out of them. He calls them "the commandments of a new morality." I've shortened them up a bit.

1. Thou shalt not be afraid of thy hidden impulses.

2. Thou shalt learn to respect thyself and then thou wilt love thy neighbor as thyself.

3. Thou shalt transcend inner anxiety, recognizing thy true competence and courage.

4. Thou shalt stand undismayed in the presence of grief. Thou shalt make no detour around sorrow, but shall live through it, and win dominion over it.

5. Thou shalt eternally respect the truth, and tell it with kindness and also with firmness to all of thy associates, to the young child as well as to thy brother, and through truth shalt thou find healing and salvation.

6. Thou shalt reject all flight from freedom, all escape from maturity, as unworthy of thy person. Thou shall seek together with thy brothers a kingdom of mature equality.

7. Thou shalt not make God the scapegoat for thy emotional wounds. Thou shalt commune freely with Him, who is the source of truth, and the giver of peace.

THE CONNECTICUT BLUE LAWS

Every once in a while you hear the term "blue laws" mentioned, usually to mean, loosely speaking, any law or regulation which is puritanical to the point of being ridiculous. You know, there are a lot of kinda foolish bits of local legislation in every community. If you dig back far enough in the city or state records, you'll find laws that are never enforced nowadays, but that are there on the books because nobody has bothered to take them off. Every once in a while the boys have a legal house cleaning and get rid of a slew of these foolish and unnecessary laws, but then a new crop builds up after a while in the books for somebody to get rid of later on.

The original "blue laws" were a set of statutes laid down by the early colonists in New Haven long before there was a United States; in fact, back in 1673. They were based on the principles laid down by the Rev. Thomas Hooker more than twenty years before, and they were a deep dark blue. Of course, they weren't quite as bad as the codes drawn up by Samuel Peters in 1781. He was the guy who decided that it was a punishable offense for any woman to kiss her child on a Sunday. However, the Peters laws were not constitutional in the state of Connecticut, and the original "blue laws" were. Old Thomas Hooker still believed that the Church was the State. He leaned very heavy on biblical authority, quoting chapter and verse, and the lawmakers who followed him drew the laws up accordingly. In those days you sure had to watch your step if you wanted to live in New Haven.

There were fifteen offenses for which the punishment was death. These included blasphemy, idolatry, witchcraft, willful murder by poison, stealing or selling another man, or bearing false witness. If a child of over sixteen cursed or struck his parents, that called for the death penalty, too, unless it could be proved that the parents were so cruel that the child was forced to defend his own life. A disobedient son could be brought to court and, upon the parent's testimony that the boy "is stubborn and rebellious, and will not obey their voice and chastisement, but lives in sundry notorious crimes, such a son shall be put to death."

Curiously enough, there were heavy punishments exacted of anyone caught abusing dumb animals, and, in contrast to that law about putting a rebellious son to death, these laws against cruelty to animals are surprisingly just, and almost exactly anticipate the A.S.P.C.A.

The Connecticut laws were supposed to apply only to "Christians, and Christians so-called," which might seem to offer a little loophole in that you could claim to be a heretic and maybe get away with it. But that didn't work, because heretics were guilty of everything in the book from the word "go." They were condemned without a hearing and that's all there was to it. "A Quaker, Ranter, Adamite or other notorious Heretick" was kind of an expensive guest to have in your house; it could cost you five pounds a day, as long as he stayed there, if the town fathers heard of it. If you even stopped and talked to a "Heretick" on the streets, there was a fine of twenty shillings, straight off. A "Heretick" was subject to being thrown into jail without specific charges, and kept there, any time the sheriff could catch him, or he could be stripped of his goods and clothing and banished from the colony, and that wasn't exactly healthy, with nothing but a wilderness full of Indians in the offing. Just to have any Quaker literature in your possession made you liable to a fine of ten shillings. For some reason, the colonists in Connecticut bore down especially heavy on Quakers.

If you spoke contemptuously of the preacher or his sermon, you had to stand two hours openly on a stool four feet high on the next public meeting day with a sign around your neck on which was written in large letters, "An open and obstinate contemner of God's Holy ordinances." If you stayed away from church services just once, you were up before the magistrate, but fast, and it cost you five shillings. And if you told a lie, and it was found out, you paid ten shillings or sat in the public stocks for three hours.

If you worked on Sunday, or played, or even went out of the house except to go to church, there was another five shillings, right off the bat. Education was chiefly a matter of learning the Scriptures, and of course learning the Scriptures is a mighty good thing, and never hurt anybody. Only the Connecticut lawmakers kinda bore down on book larnin' going any farther than that. There was only one college in America in 1673, Harvard, so very few boys, and, of course, none of the gals, ever got past grammar school. Every settlement of fifty householders had to provide a schoolmaster for the kids in the settlement. Of course, they paid the teachers as little as possible, same as today, but at least they had teachers, after a fashion.

Now it seems amazing that a people would come to a new land seeking political and religious freedom, and then hamstring themselves with such a set of laws, and start yapping their heads off about "Hereticks," which, of course, were all the rest of the folks in the world who didn't worship just the same way they did. However, compared with the laws they left behind them in Europe, where the theft of a loaf of bread could mean death or life imprisonment, the Connecticut blue laws were actually lenient. They were a start toward government by and for the people, and it took a lot of courage to lay them down. Back in Europe, if you poached for rabbits on a lord's property, you could die a very lingering and unattractive death, but in Connecticut as long as you minded your own business, sent the kids to school, and showed proper respect for the preacher, they let you pretty much alone. And that was a big step forward in the world of lawmaking.

THE SECOND MARRIAGE

Here are some notes on a subject which I hope you'll find real interesting. It's kind of a delicate question, but one that a lot of women have to face in the course of their lives. They've had a very wonderful married life, and they've had friends who have lost their husbands and remarried, and they always felt that those friends maybe didn't care deeply, or how could they be happy again after losing their husbands? How could they find a new life and a new love? But now Henry's gone and after the shock of grief has become kinda dulled, life seems awful empty and lonesome, and those lonely years stretching away into the future are almost more than an already broken heart can face. Maybe those friends who were widowed and who married again weren't so callous and heartless after all.

Well, of course, how a gal feels about this question of whether or not she should latch onto a second husband is decided pretty much by what kind of a marriage she had the first time. If the first marriage was unusually happy, it's reasonable to suppose that she's now even better equipped by experience to pick herself off a man who can make her just as happy or even happier than she was the first time. If the first guy she had was no bargain, maybe she'll have better luck this time; at least, she's been warned what not to look for in a husband. On the other hand, a very happy marriage may make her reluctant to take a chance on something that couldn't ever be more than second best, and an unhappy one may scare her off the marrying idea entirely. And still other gals, no matter what kind of an experience with married life they've had, kinda dust their hands and declare that once was enough; they've been through that, good, bad or indifferent, and now they're ready to try something else, so they go on and carve out a career for themselves and that's that.

Now, I'm not gonna stick my neck out and recommend what any gal should do under the circumstances, and I certainly ain't here to tell her how to get another man if she decides she wants one. She'll know how to go about that from instinct, just like she got the first one, only now that she ain't got the first flush of youth to help her, she may have to act a little smarter about it than she did back then. But here are a few little ideas I'll toss out at random.

The question is, actually, now that Henry's gone: does she miss Henry or does she just miss being married? If she was still head over heels in love with Hank right up to the day he went over the Great Divide, she's missing Henry, and that's for sure. If she was married to the guy twenty-odd years and she knows all the little details of how he liked things and what made him cross and what made him bust out grinning, and if now it don't seem worth while getting up a nice hot meal because there's nobody to eat it, she's missing being married. With most folks it's probably a combination of both, and since very few marriages are perfect, the gal is perfectly justified to scare up somebody to eat those apple pies she's yearning to bake, and chances are he'll turn out pretty much like Hank did, after all.

Obviously it don't make sense to go looking for another guy exactly like the first one. He ain't to be found, and even if he was, the gal wouldn't feel quite the same way about him. A second marriage in no way "takes the place" of the first marriage. Most folks seem to have a mistaken idea about this. What our gal wants is not another Hank. She probably wouldn't even recognize him if she found him, and if that's what she looks for she'll end up with a guy who has those same beautiful blue eyes Hank had, and he's about as tall and he kinda walks like him, but what she's overlooked in her excitement about finding this duplicate of a guy who was a perfectly satisfactory husband is that the new fella has a disposition like a nest of mad bumblebees and she's gonna have to split her own kindling and polish her own floors from here on in. Don't look for outward resemblances to a lost mate. You took a chance that Hank would be sweet and ever-loving; and it was your good luck that he turned out that way. Better look twice at that nice Joe down the street with the steady look in his eye and the steadier job. Second marriages are oftener than not much, much happier than first ones, mainly because they are made with due consideration and the parties involved are older, more tolerant of one another, and they don't let their feelings get to the boiling point over every little thing.

What a gal ought to look for in remarriage is a combination of companionship, compatibility, and reasonable financial security. Under no circumstances should she marry for that security alone. If she does, she'll be just as miserable as the proverbial girl in a gilded cage, and she'll be wanting out in short order. On the other hand, she shouldn't let her loneliness and emotional confusion drive her into the arms of a guy who knows she has a little legacy and plans to free-load off it as long as it holds out, and then skip with the silverware. There's one of those hovering around every widow, and no matter if she's a hundred and eight years old and never was much to look at in the first place, he's telling her that she's more beautiful than the Queen of Sheba in all her glory. Those free-loaders are usually kinda easy to recognize; they come into a gal's life saying that they're lifelong buddies of her husband's brother Jeremiah, who lived out West and ain't been heard from in eighteen years. Of course, they get this dope out of the obituary column. She's kinda weak and defenseless about that time, and it feels good to have a strong shoulder to lean on, especially one that was so close to her Hank. Then he starts gently sopping away her tears and making with the compliments, and in her condition she's easy prey.

Another kind of a guy not to be tempted into a second marriage by is the big muscle boy—riding master, sports pro, prize fighter, show-place cowboy on the dude ranch, and so on. They're probably all very good Joes in their place, and their place is right where they ought to stay. For some reason a gal in her middle years, finding herself receptive to the idea of trying married life again, can fall awful hard for this big husky he-man type. She remembers that Hank was getting a little flabby, and how she'd urged him to take exercise for that rubber tire around his waist, and how careful he had to be with his diet or he got heartburn, and here's this gorgeous hunk of man just loaded with health and sun-browned muscles—probably considerably younger than she is, probably without too much on the ball in the culture department, and probably kinda flattered that an older woman with a little cash in hand takes an interest in him. After she's spent a couple of months listening to him grunt, she'll be so bored she'll figure she could have bought herself a dancing bear and got more companionship out of it. This, of course, is a special warning to the gal who's been left a parcel of dough. And here's another warning intended for her ears: don't hook up with one of those real artistic guys who want to paint or write but can't because they have to work at a dull job for a living. Chances are, they'll be real kind and grateful to her, but they ain't looking for a wife: they're looking for a subsidy.

If she wants a new man, she shouldn't let anybody feed her that guff that she's too old to get one. No gal is. But take it a little easy, and bring a little common sense to bear on the choice. If she has any sense at all, it oughta work out real good.

CURIOUS MARRIAGE CUSTOMS

I suppose that the customs and traditions and superstitions that have been connected with weddings at one time or another are about as curious a collection of folklore as you could find anywhere. Of course if you go down to the island of Pago-Pago or explore the habits of little-known tribes in the snowy wastes of the Arctic circle or some of the steamier jungles, you'll learn things that'll bug your eyes out. But that's another subject. I'm talking about the wedding customs of better-known parts of the world, various European countries, for instance, from which most of our ancestors came. It'd take all day to talk about a complete list of wedding customs, but here are just a few which I'll go once over lightly.

Back in the Middle Ages, according to some authorities on this kind of stuff, the Crusaders began the custom of bringing orange blossoms to a wedding and placing a crown of them on the head of the bride. The Crusaders, you might say, were the first real travelers in western Europe, and the boys got around a lot and they brought home sprays and wreaths of the dried flowers, just for this purpose. The fact that the flowers kept their shape and fragrance long after they were picked seemed to have some symbolic significance for a long and happy married life. Also, those Crusaders who actually managed to reach the Holy Land found oranges growing there in abundance, and so the flower conferred a sort of blessing upon a newly wedded pair.

In France, during the sixth century, it was the custom for a bridegroom to give a ring, a pair of shoes, and a kiss to his girl friend. The ring and the shoes were supposed to bind the lady's hands and feet in obedience, and the kiss was to seal secrets between man and wife, so that neither would betray the other to an outsider. In Rome the custom of a bridegroom giving his bride a new pair of shoes was a sign that her father was no longer responsible for the gal's bills, and now she could run up her charge accounts in Hubby's name. In Russia, beginning about the time of Peter the Great, there was a double-ring ceremony. The man's ring was of gold, and the woman's of silver, showing that she was made of an inferior clay to her lord and master. And the boys got away with it, too. I'd like to see a bridegroom try that nowadays. I don't believe he could pull it off, even in Russia.

In Esthonia a little girl was supposed to start working on her trousseau, spinning and weaving and embroidering, when she was four or five years old. And the only lucky time for a proposal was during the new moon. Down in Egypt the Coptic people believed in catching 'em young. The boys and girls were formally engaged when they reached the "age of consent" at six. But that ain't the youngest engagement, not by a long sight. In the year of 1518, in England, Princess Mary, the daughter of Henry VIII, was only two years old when a miniature gold ring containing a valuable diamond was slipped on her finger, and

197

she was actually married to the Dauphin of France, who was about six months old at the time and not even present; the proxy bridegroom was the admiral of the French fleet. Cardinal Wolsey performed the ceremony, and the bride, according to contemporary accounts, was dressed in cloth of gold, with a cap of black velvet embroidered with pearls.

In some country districts in Ireland, where the peasants were too poor to own even enough gold for a wedding ring, some of the bright boys thought up the idea of keeping a few gold rings for hire, and they made out real well, renting the ring, attending the ceremony and eating a good wedding supper, and taking the ring back after the party was over.

Here's kind of a cute one. Gypsy girls claim that they have a sure method of telling just when they will get hitched. All they need to do is to find the longest-eared mule in the camp and whisper the fatal question into its ear. If it nods vigorously, the gal'll get herself a man within the year. If it nods just a little, maybe she will and maybe she won't. And if it don't take no notice whatsoever, she'll have to wait at least a full year before she meets her fate.

PREPARING FOR THE SECOND CHILD

I guess anybody who's ever had a baby knows that getting ready for the arrival of the little darlin' is quite a job. You can spend several hundred, or even several thousand, clams on a handmade layette full of French tucks and fussy lace, and still forget that very essential purchase, a ten-cent paper of safety pins. And if it's your second baby you're having, you can very easily forget that very essential bit of preparation which consists of preparing your first child for the arrival of his little sister or brother, as the case may be. You even have to explain to him, or her, that he, or she, has no choice, no more choice than yourself, in whether a boy or girl is on the way. In fact, this is pretty important, because some kids who have been praying for a baby brother, or sister, have been so disappointed when they got the other variety that they practically tell their mothers to return the kid to the baby factory and get the right kind this time.

About the most important thing about preparing your first child, who is probably little more than a baby himself, for the arrival of the second is to be sure that, during his whole short little life he has learned to be independent and as self-sufficient as his brief years allow. Then he'll be willing to look after himself as much as he can, without pouting and feeling neglected because you have to spend quite a bit of time and trouble on the new baby. Some unfortunate kids are so dependent on their mothers giving them constant and undivided attention that they actually revert to babyhood, even though they're five or six when the new baby arrives. They refuse to feed themselves, for example, and they're not being just mean and stubborn about it either. They actually forget how to eat, and have to be spoon-fed, and they don't do it on purpose at all. It's a reaction against the new baby getting all the attention and they slip right back into babyhood themselves, in order to get attention, too.

For several months before the birth of the new baby, the subject of babies in general ought to be introduced casually into the conversation. You know, yourself, that you're none too crazy about having fast ones put over on you. If you, the object of your three-year-old's deepest affection, disappear for days and nights on end into a mysterious place called "a hospital," and you come back with a yelling, squalling piece of humanity that looks kinda homely and demands all your attention, and, especially, if you spend long hours telling all your friends how you nearly died and what a terrible time you had, naturally your first kid ain't gonna take kindly to your second. Especially, too, if he has to keep quiet and not have any fun, ever, any more, because the new baby has to sleep a lot. Especialy if you're half sick and complaining and he knows that if it weren't for that old baby things would be all the way they were before and he'd still be first in your heart . . . and your lap. Especially if he can't play with or touch or even go near the baby, because he might hurt it in some mysterious way.

One thing that can scare a kid half to death is that babies have a way of coming in the middle of the night. You put Junior to bed at the usual time; he wakes up in the morning to find you gone and the old man is probably gone, too, over at the hospital admiring you and the new arrival, or else he's home acting frantic, and some well-meaning neighbor or aunt or grandmother is telling the poor kid that everything will be all right, and telling it to him in that false cheerful tone that sounds like doom. So don't forget, in preparing Junior for the baby, to tell him that this very thing may, and probably will, happen.

And then, when you get back with your new acquisition, don't clasp

199

Junior fondly in your arms and, with tears streaming down your face, inform him that at times you didn't know if you would ever see him again. That's a dandy way to make him look at his youngest relative with disfavor.

Having a baby in the family is kind of a new experience to your first-born pride and joy, and new and unusual experiences require a little thought and patience, if the wheels are to go round smoothly. Do it right, and you'll have the neatest little built-in baby tender in the world. Do it wrong, and you'll have a sullen, tantrum-y, disobedient kid and an unhappy baby. So it's pretty important, if you're expecting a second, to get the first child ready for the event.

FOUR THINGS REALLY WORTH HAVING THAT MONEY CANNOT BUY

Here's something I've always liked. And, again, I can't credit the author: I have no idea who wrote it.

"1. A baby's smile: You cannot purchase a baby's smile with coin or currency, stocks or bonds. To the soul that has so recently come from paradise, the most coveted things in this world have no appeal. A mother's kiss, a father's caress, a flower, a pretty trinket, may win a baby's smile, but you cannot bargain for it with gold.

"2. Youth, when it is gone: The mill will never grind again with water that has passed. All the wealth in the world cannot buy back the zest and joyousness of youth or the carefree happiness of maidenhood when maturity has blotted them out.

"3. The love of a good woman: Her love, like a baby's smile, cannot be bought with gold. Men may barter silver and gold and precious stones for a base counterfeit, but true love that lasts eternally is the most precious gift a woman can bestow. No man is rich enough to buy it, no man is too poor to possess it.

"4. Entrance into heaven: Money will buy every material thing there is to be found in this world, but not a penny of it can be taken into the next and used to gain admission into a state of immortal happiness. The keeper of the heavenly gate is not susceptible to bribes. There, at least, money has no value."

WHY PEOPLE DOUBT IMMORTALITY
AND FEAR DEATH

It's the most unnatural thing in the world for people to fear death and to doubt immortality. None of the primitive peoples are afraid of death, and all of them have a perfectly simple, natural assurance of some form of immortality. It never occurs to them to doubt that the world existed before them, and probably will for some time after, and, like a stone or a tree, they themselves will go right on existing in wind or cloud or fire even after their mortal bodies have disappeared. Fear of death and doubts of immortality are something that come over us when civilization sets in. Take the ancient Greeks; they had a saying: "If it is, we are not; if we are, it is not." Meaning, simply, that if there is no such thing as immortality, if we do not continue as personalities after death, then all we are, right now, are just animated physical bodies who imagine we have consciousness, and what on earth are we imagining with, anyhow?

Maybe that sounds a little complicated, but there's the general drift of the thing. More speculation has been done by religious teachers and philosophers and wise men and scientists about immortality than about anything else except the existence of matter, I suppose, and now the boys who mess around with psychology have started to take a crack at it. Dr. David Seabury, the practical psychologist who has written more popular books than you can shake a stick at on the subject of what makes mankind tick, has evolved ten reasons why many folks fear death and have doubts of personal immortality. These ten reasons interested me because it seemed to me they help to clarify one's own thoughts on the matter. Here they are: Dr. Seabury's ten reasons, all of which he says you can dispose of by logical constructive thinking; ten reasons why people fear death and doubt immortality.

1. Because many folks are so taken up by mere physical processes of living and put all their emphasis on the pursuit of pleasure. They can't conceive of a bodiless immortality without physical pleasure, so they're scared of death.

2. Because they do not understand the process of death and it seems strange to them. We always fear what is strange.

3. Because most of us are actually unacquainted with our own minds and their capabilities, especially with the subjective aspects of personality. We just don't really understand how our minds and our personalities work.

4. Because of dissent between various religious sects, which disagree with one another as to immortality and the meaning of life itself.

5. Because of misunderstanding the spirit and purpose of science. A little knowledge is a dangerous thing, and a little knowledge of modern science leads the small-minded to doubt all values which cannot be seen, weighed, and counted.

6. Because of emotional maladjustments. Nobody all sick with unhappiness inside has any desire to continue that unhappiness through all eternity. You've got to get yourself straightened out in order even to want immortality, much less to understand and appreciate it.

7. Because of the unmerited feelings of guilt which make man doubt the possibility of happiness and substitute the imagined torments of hell instead.

8. Because of doubt of a Divine Order through the fact that education leaves us so ignorant of it.

9. Because of nervous tension in striving for material advancement, money, position, and power. We become fatigued, and fatigue generates fear.

10. Because we have left undone so much in this life, never having truly learned its meaning. We have no concept of the purpose of a continued existence.

Now, an examination of thousands of people shows very clearly that the guy who finishes his task, adequately putting successive goals behind him, who reads and studies to discover the miracle of personality, who reaches deeply enough into philosophy and science, and religion, to get an inkling that all three are working toward the same thing— well, that guy ceases to doubt the spiritual values. He may or may not be a regular member of any congregation; he may be an astronomer who lives by himself and is awake at night when everybody else is asleep, studying the stars, or he may be a shopkeeper on the busiest crossroads in the world, but if he has the answers to those ten reasons why Dr. Seabury says we fear death and doubt immortality, then he's all right. He'll get along while a lot of the rest of us are floundering around in our own muddle of doubts and despairs. You just turn that over in your mind and see if you don't agree with me.

KING COBRAS

Maybe the biblical story of Adam and Eve and the snake in the Garden of Eden ain't so mysterious and mythical as some of the hard-boiled scientific boys have tried to make it out to be. Only maybe it was Eve who fascinated the snake, instead of the snake fascinating Eve, because that kind of thing is going on right along every day down in Burma and Indo-China. For some reason, and if I wanted to stick my neck out I could dream up a reason or two myself, snakes are extremely susceptible to women, and those Burmese gals are a lot better at snake charming than the men are. At least, that's what Captain Frank Outram says in his account, which he calls *King Cobra Performs.* Captain Outram went deep into Burma, visiting small villages far up the Irrawaddy River, to make a moving picture of the capture of a king cobra and the really amazing performance of the native snake charmers, who work out on only this one kind of snake, the king cobra, or, as it's sometimes known, the hamadryad.

Now a king cobra is nothing to mess with in my book. Even a teeny-weeny little garter snake makes me nervous. Snakes can stay away from my door. And these king cobras are about twelve feet long and as big around as a man's arm. They rear up to a height of four feet off the ground, the rest of them coiled like a pedestal for that four feet of swift and painful death. The natives, especially the women, go out and catch these diabolical things and keep them in baskets, right in the house, and handle them and dance with them wound around their bodies, and at the end of the act they even kiss them. Not for me. When I kiss, it's humans. These snakes act, with their lady snake charmers, as gentle as kittens, but I like my kittens little, and with fur on them.

The queen of the snake charmers was found in the little village of Yenang-Yenang, and her name was Ma Hea. Ma Hea told Captain Outram that her new husband, a big shot in the village, was pretty good with snakes, but she didn't let him handle the cobras too much, because she'd already lost two perfectly good husbands that way. By the way, this little village of Yenang-Yenang is deep in jungles full of beautiful tropic flowers, nestled right at the foot of an imposing volcano, and Captain Outram says that it's just a paradise on earth, except that all the time he was there he was worried about stepping on a snake. The volcano, incidentally, is sacred to the spirit world of the Burmese, particularly the Great Snake Spirit, and on its sunny slopes and in the forest around its foot the king cobras can be found in profusion.

Captain Outram wanted to photograph a real snake capture, follow the cobra through the period of training, and finally snap a full-dress snake-charming show in the village market place. He suspected that this little project of his would take time, and it did. It was a full three months before he packed up his kit and left.

First came the catching. The king cobra is about as vicious a customer as you could wish to avoid meeting up with, and it's the only snake in those parts which will attack man without provocation. Before catching one, the natives ask permission of the Spirit Gods, and if the signs are right and permission seems to be granted, they make a definite contract that the snake will not be harmed, and that it will be released in the forest within a certain period of time. If for any reason the king cobra is kept in the village even a day over this time, the snake charmer believes he will be bitten, with kinda permanent results. And, strange as it sounds, he inevitably is. So the boys are real careful about keeping those contracts.

They catch the king cobras with their bare hands, no net or forked stick, no nothing. Just their hands. As I said, these cobras can raise up to a height of four feet, and a cobra is powerless against anything above its head. So a native walks right close up to a snake, very slowly so as not to excite it, and holds his hand high over the snake's head. The cobra sees the hand but can't do anything about it. Of course the native's bare feet and legs are easy meat, but that hand has the critter worried. And when the guy gets close enough he just swoops down with his hand, catches the snake right at the back of the neck, and stuffs him into a basket tail first, coiling him up like a rope.

When they get a snake home they just set the basket down and forget it for ten days, during which length of time the cobra is supposed to get drowsy and kinda anxious to please its captors, because it ain't getting any groceries during this period of time. After ten days the lady of the household opens the basket, picks up the cobra by the back of the neck, takes it out, strokes it, talks to it, induces it to strike in a series of near misses that would scare anybody except another snake charmer half to death. Then she puts the thing back in the basket . . . and next day she goes through the whole routine again until the snake gets kinda used to her fussing with it.

So now the gal's got herself a trained snake and she's ready to give

a show. Captain Outram says that Ma Hea always started her performance with a slow sinuous dance, during which a squeaky orchestra
played and her baby daughter, about three years old, joined in by
handling a comparatively harmless, sluggish old snake which she held
in her arms like a doll and sang a love song to. Then Ma Hea opened
the basket containing her best and liveliest monster, a giant king cobra
nearly thirteen feet in length. If the snake didn't pop right up, she'd give
the basket a sharp slap and that'd bring him up, and raring to go. Then
the peculiar duel of woman and snake would start. She'd place her face
invitingly near, tap the basket to stir the big boy up, jerk away with
split-second timing. In this job you're allowed just one mistake. After
the cobra struck at her and missed several times she'd take it out of
the basket. It would try to escape, but she'd grab it by the tail, smile,
give the thing a slap like it was one of her own kids that was misbehav-
ing, cradle it in her arms, wind it around her, always keeping one split
second ahead of that striking poisonous fanged mouth, and then came
the big thrill of the show, kissing the cobra. Back in the basket, the
snake coils, rearing up shoulder height. Ma Hea kneels on a small stool,
her face level with the snake's. They stare at each other for a full minute, and the audience is kinda breathless at this point. Slowly, very
slowly Ma Hea's face moves closer to that head, now motionless, until
her lips actually touch the serpent's snout. Her current, and so far
unbitten, husband claps the lid on the basket, crowding the enraged
and yet strangely fascinated reptile inside, and Ma Hea stands up,
takes the bows, and Friend Husband passes the collection box . . .
which after all that nerve-racking performance may contain as much as
a buck and a half for the day's work, if there's a big audience and it's
market day and the crowd is sufficiently thrilled.

So that's a peaceful day in a snake charmer's life, and it's something
I'd rather read about in a book than get too close to at first hand. They
can have it. But I think it's kinda interesting that the gals are the ones
who can tame anything, even a king cobra.

GETTING THE KIDS TO EAT

There probably isn't anything more annoying to a mother—particularly
a young and inexperienced mother—than a kid who fusses about his

meals. And sooner or later most kids develop fussy streaks, and it's kinda up to Mom to get them over it before the habit gets set.

If one of these fussy streaks turns up in an otherwise well-behaved kid, right after he's had a cold or some other minor illness, don't worry. Just feed him a little less and make it look more appetizing, and he'll be right back on schedule, yelling for more, in a day or two. But if he's chronically and habitually fussy, if he's been cold-shouldering the groceries right along, then there's something the matter. If the doctor checks him over and says, outside of his eating habits, he's okay—well, then Mom has to get busy and change some of her own habits, because she's the reason why Junior acts up at mealtime. Maybe she isn't responsible all by herself, but it's her job to find out why the kid has an unpleasant time at meals, and therefore hates to eat.

The first thing to realize is that eating is an established behavior pattern, and it isn't, surprisingly enough, instinctive. Gnawing on a bone is instinctive. The kind of table manners, or the lack of them, that Junior gets his wrist slapped for are instinctive. But civilized eating is not instinctive; it has to be learned, along with wiping your shoes when you come in the house and not banging doors.

Now any kid can be taught what to eat and when and how to eat it without any fuss and botheration at all, provided his mother doesn't work on such a rigid schedule that appetite rebels against it. Grownups have more or less free choice about their food. They forget that, within reason, kids ought to have a little freedom of choice, too. If little Oswald has exactly three tablespoonfuls of creamed spinach put in front of him at exactly five-thirty, and he knows he has to eat it within the space of exactly six minutes or he won't get his tapioca pudding that he likes, and if every look and word and gesture of the grownups reminds him of this, and reminds him, too, that he has to eat every scrap, and not spill any on the tablecloth, then creamed spinach is the last thing on earth that little Oswald wants to eat. He'll go to any lengths to get out of it. He'll sulk, he'll scream, he'll dawdle and daydream, he'll throw the spinach on the floor in a tantrum, and he'll actually get sick at his stomach, but he won't eat that spinach. He won't eat it because there's been so much bruhaha about supper at exactly five-thirty, and eating it all up on time, exactly three tablespoonfuls, and Mom has told him a million times that spinach is good for him and it's full of vitamins and see, how nice it is this time, creamed and everything! So he gets set against spinach, and he don't eat it, no matter what. Mom can dissolve in tears, and Pop can spank him, but he don't

206

eat spinach. It had too big a build-up. He was bored with the idea of spinach before he sat down to the table.

Now, if Mom gives him a build-up and insists on an exact schedule for everything, spinach and meat and prunes and potatoes and orange juice and milk and all the rest of it, pretty soon the kid is set against food in general. He just won't eat nuthin'. He'll start to scream the minute she mentions that this or that is good for him. He disappears at mealtimes. He shudders when he sees food. And, of course, he frightens his mother out of her wits; he seems to be living on air. But it's very surprising how little kids can eat and get along, after a fashion.

The only thing you can do if you have a situation like that around the house is to throw the schedule out of the window, and feed the kid any time he seems hungry. Don't feed him much at a time; let it be a treat, and don't say one word about how nice and rich the milk is, or how many vitamins there are in the bread. Once you shut up, Junior will, too. And he'll start eating regular meals when he sees they aren't quiz sessions on food values.

Another thing—a kid is likely to eat what's good for him, in the correct amounts, if you don't supervise him too closely and nag too much about his table manners. Those he'll learn as he goes along. But eating is a comparatively new adventure to a young child; every few days some new food that he's never tasted before is added to his diet, and he has to get used to food before he knows how to be polite about it. So go a little easy on the directions. If he's obviously nuts about carrots, don't take the spoon out of his hand and make him eat them with a fork. He won't like you or the carrots. He'll eat them with a fork, as a matter of course, just as soon as he's ready to, and not one day sooner. How can a kid have an appetite when, every other minute, he's reminded that his manners don't measure up to standards that are so far beyond him that he doesn't even know what they're for?

Don't coax him to eat. And don't load his plate so full that eating it all seems an insurmountable task; he'll get discouraged before he starts. And don't make him "eat it all." Nobody makes you. Give him a little less than you're pretty sure he wants, and let him ask for seconds.

Don't make him eat, or expect him to, if there's been an emotional upset around the house just a few minutes before, even an emotional upset that has nothing to do with him. Emotional upsets are awful catching. And they have a physical effect on the digestive processes which either keep you from eating by taking away your appetite, or give your indigestion if you do eat.

Most of all, make eating fun. It ought to be. Most people get a great deal of pleasure out of eating, even if they don't like to admit it. So why shouldn't a kid get pleasure, too, out of his meals? Just try to think of what you enjoy most about your meals, and give him the same breaks too. You'll find yourself with a happy, eager youngster who eats everything set before him—well, almost everything. You have a few very strong food dislikes, haven't you? Maybe you don't like beets, or liver, or salt codfish. And you don't eat 'em. Well, just take into account that there could be a couple of things that don't taste so good to Junior, either. Don't insist on his eating them. Nobody does that to you.

THAT BOY

A boy is a bank where you may deposit your most precious treasures—the hard-won wisdom, the dreams of a better world. A boy can guard and protect these, and perhaps invest them wisely and win a profit—a profit larger than you ever dreamed! A boy will inherit your world. All your work will be judged by him. Tomorrow he will take your seat in Congress, own your company, run your town. The future is his, and through him, the future is yours. Perhaps he deserves a little more of your attention now.

Anonymous

JUNIOR'S CHANGING VOICE

Maybe you've been going through kind of a trying period at your house, all on account of Junior's voice. In addition to other rude virtues, like daydreaming and door slamming and excessive blushing and growing so fast that he always looks as if he had his little brother's clothes squeezed on him, your thirteen- or fourteen-year-old pride and joy has developed a trick voice that varies from the piping whistles of an asthmatic canary to the boom of a basso working on the lower notes of "Asleep in the Deep."

Now, you know that eventually Junior is going to get over this thing he's got in his throat, but it seems to be taking a long time and it's mighty embarrassing, especially to him, and that boy soprano who used to lead the choir is lost forever, and sometimes, when company comes,

208

you sort of wish he wouldn't open his mouth at all, because heaven only knows what's going to come out. And there's nothing you, or Junior, can do about this situation, because only time can cure it. Junior's voice is changing, and that's that.

But what makes those strange squeaks and booms?

Well, of course, we know that the sound of our voices is produced by air being forced through our vocal cords and vibrating them to produce sound. The vocal cords of children are short, so their voices are high and piping, like the notes struck in the higher octaves of the piano, where the wires are very short and thin compared with the wires down in the bass. Women's voices are a little deeper than children's, because their voice boxes grow in proportion to their bodies.

But early in adolescence a boy's voice box starts growing with astonishing rapidity and the vocal cords just can't seem to keep up. Some of them get stretched tighter than others, and the result is an instrument that's badly out of tune, and that's going to stay out of tune until the vocal cords can catch up with the voice box that holds them. The deeper the adult voice of Junior is going to be, the more trouble he has with its changing, while the changing process is going on. If Junior is intended to wind up as a tenor, he may get through his voice changing with just a few minor squeaks, but if he's been designed to sing fourth in the barbershop quartette, he's going to run the whole gamut of every sound you'd think possible to human speech, and quite a few that sound anything but human. He's really in for it, and it's going to take a while.

So, if Junior has been a-squeaking and a-scraping as long as you can stand it, and maybe a little longer, don't give up hope. He'll probably end up as a second Bing Crosby, and very plushy in the lower notes, at that.

THE CLOSED DOOR

Here's a weird little yarn that's calculated to send the creeps up and down your spine. It's had folks down in the island of Haiti kinda worried for pretty near a hundred years now.

Seems there was a French nobleman by the name of the Vicomte de Troismoulins de Saint-Saturnin—jumpin' Jehosophat, what a mouthful!—who escaped from France during the French Revolution and fled to Haiti, where he did all right for himself and raised a large-sized family, whose descendants are today tops in the aristocracy of Haiti.

Now this nobleman was an ardent supporter of the Royalists back in France, and in memory of the beheading of Louis XVI on January 21, 1793, every January 21 for the rest of his long life he tied a red ribbon around his neck as a symbol of mourning for the beheaded monarch.

Well, at the ripe old age of ninety-four, this old aristocrat, still hale and hearty, went to bed with the frayed and frazzled old red ribbon tied around his throat, and in the morning when his servants went to wake him, they found him stone dead, with his throat cut from ear to ear. And the mystery of his murder was never solved. It remains a puzzle to this day. The only possible explanation was that it was a political murder, because the old boy had great power in those days, but, on the other hand, it just don't seem reasonable that a man ninety-four years old could be any real political threat, one way or another.

Now here's where the creepy part of this yarn comes in. The frail old body of the nobleman was laid out in the great paneled library of his house, which was practically a castle, and it stayed in state there until sundown, and then was carried out through the french doors of the room and buried in the garden. The grave is still there, plainly marked. As the coffin was carried out, the doors closed of themselves behind the funeral procession, and *nobody* has ever been able to open them since!

Now, no bolts or bars or trick hinges are holding that door shut. It's still there, worm-eaten and battered by tropical storms, and experts have examined it on both sides and even taken it down off its hinges, and it's a perfectly normal door, or rather a pair of doors; it fits snug, it don't sag, and nary a thing is blocking it. But it won't open, not by brute force or by gentle jiggling or by anything. Ali Baba could holler "Open Sesame!" till he was blue in the face for all this door would budge!

Now there are a lot of unexplained things going on down in Haiti. It's a fertile place for superstition and voodoo and zombies and all manner of outlandish hobgoblins and spine-chilling spooks that the mind of man can dream up. But even with a dozen assorted zombies, you just can't explain that door that banged shut the day the old nobleman was being carried out, and that has never opened since. It's one of those things the smart fellers can't figure out.

WHAT CHILDREN FEAR

Fear has always been an important consideration with the psychologists. The boys have studied every aspect of it, as it appears in a day-old baby, in a child, or an adult, and they've come up with some conclusions which I think are pretty interesting. Maybe you'll get an idea or two out of this, to put to good use in your own life, or with the kids. It might help, next time little Suzybelle cries, because she's afraid of the dark.

The instinctive fear reaction of a very young baby is called the "Moro reflex." Babies are afraid of very few things; a loud noise, falling, or a sudden blow are about the only things that scare them. In the "Moro reflex" they stiffen, throw themselves about, and scream. The purpose of this seems to be mostly to warn the mother that Baby is in danger. Well, this kind of action wears off very shortly, in maybe two months or so, and then the baby acts startled if he's afraid. He cries out, tucks himself up in a scared little ball, clamps his hands together, shudders, and sometimes breaks out in a cold sweat. He crawls inside himself. The kid is in full retreat from some terrible danger, and by weak, shrill cries, curled-up body position, and so on, he's acknowledging that whatever scares him has him totally licked; he isn't even going to try to fight. Various methods of coping with fear take up from there; as a child learns more and more about the world he finds out how to run away, how to retreat gracefully, how to size up a dangerous situation, and how to fight back.

Now, it's not only scared babies that curl up weakly when they're afraid. Some grown folks act the same way when confronted with danger. You've read about tough criminals whose knees turn to water when they're face to face with personal danger. That knees-turning-to-water stuff is the sort of fear we call cowardice; it's an admission of complete failure and inadequacy to cope with the situation, and, generally speaking, it's frowned on and it gets knocked out of kids pretty early in life. If they haven't gotten over it by the time they go to school, the other kids will see that they do, in short order.

Of course, it's a good thing to get rid of this curl-up-and-die attitude as soon as possible, because it renders a person incapable of action and

211

decision at a time when he needs both. But it ain't smart to educate all fear out of a kid. We don't want little Oswald to be afraid of bugaboos, but neither do we want him so utterly fearless and foolhardy that he tries to beat the streetcar across the tracks, or climbs into the lion's cage at the zoo.

The things most kids are afraid of are: the dark, imaginary monsters, being abandoned by their parents, kidnapers, weird things they see in nightmares, and ridicule. The very real fears of dangerous things, such as falling and loud noises, are all gone by the time a kid is about four or five. What he has now is a set of imaginary fears, and except for the fear of ridicule, which most people keep to some degree all their lives, and which may serve some purpose in keeping us from giving in to crazy impulses, these fears are all ones he can be educated out of, and it's just as well to get rid of them as soon as possible. Fear feelings can get mixed with guilt feelings, as the kid grows older and begins to realize all the do's and don'ts of life. When that happens, the kid can show such anxieties as nail biting, queer grimaces, jerky movements, stuttering, and the like, and those things get to be habits that are pretty hard to lose.

Most fears are learned. You can actually teach a small baby to be deathly scared of a rabbit, a rabbit he's previously enjoyed petting and stroking. Every time he pets the rabbit you bang hard on a loud gong, making an unholy noise that always makes him shudder and cry. After ten or twelve times the very sight of the rabbit he used to love will send him into a fit of terror. It's a mean trick, but you can do it.

Since fears, especially these foolish fears, are learned, the main thing to do is not to teach them to the child in the first place, or, if he learns them outside the home, explain them away as soon as possible, before they get set in his mind. Don't threaten Junior with a bogeyman when he's bad. If you do, you ought to have a bogeyman chase you; that's all I can say about it. Don't shiver and shake when you go to the dentist or the doctor. Don't hide in the closet during a thunderstorm. Don't act as if every harmless little poodle is a vicious mad dog. Don't encourage the kid to run up to every strange dog and pet him, either, because the best dog in the world might misunderstand attentions from people it doesn't know. But don't act scared yourself, and dollars to doughnuts you won't have a scared, whiny kid on your hands.

One of the hardest childhood fears to get rid of is the fear of the dark. Pretty near every child between three and five years old gets a spell of being scared of the dark. And if you aren't wise, this fear will persist, and when the kid gets old enough to read spooky stories he can work himself into such a nervous, fearful state that it amounts to a breakdown.

You can ease him over this fear of the dark by making kind of a game out of it, getting him to go in a dark room and turn on a light ahead of you, putting a fluorescent button on the end of the light cord so he won't have any trouble finding it, getting him to name over all the familiar objects in the room with his eyes shut, and so on. And don't let some addlepated friend or relative tell him that there's a bear under the bed. It just makes trouble for you, getting rid of the bear. I heard a story a while ago about a kid who got the notion that there were owls in his room every night, and night after night his distracted parents had to go through the motions of catching imaginary owls and putting them out the window. That kind of thing can be pretty annoying, if it keeps up. So don't let it get started in the first place. If you keep the kids from having fears, you'll have a lot more sleep.

SHEPHERDS ON STILTS

When I was a kid, I thought it was a lot of fun to walk around on stilts. I could look into people's windows, and scare the wits out of some fat old boy doing his setting-up exercises, or some gal prettying herself up. If I was lucky, I could snake a warm fresh apple pie off my mother's kitchen window and never leave a trace. Of course, I walked around on stilts for fun. And fun is about all stilts are good for in this country. Clowns use them in the circus, and not so long ago men used to dress up in stilts and funny suits and walk around the streets of the town to advertise something. That's about as useful as stilts ever got.

But I was reading the other day about a place where stilts are just as important as shoes or pants or anything else. In fact, without stilts, the people who live there just couldn't make a living.

This place is the Landes district near the Bay of Biscay, in France. The principal industry around those parts is sheep raising, and you wouldn't think there'd be any connection between sheep and stilts. As it happens, this part of France is very boggy, with shallow waterways completely surrounding fields of rich pasturage. Sheep, who are constantly on the move, don't get bogged down, but a shepherd would

213

not only get wet and muddy scrambling after his flock, but if he stopped to rest for a minute, he'd be in over his boot tops.

So the shepherds of the Landes district do their sheep tending on stilts, very strong, secure stilts securely strapped to their legs, leaving their hands free. To keep his balance, the shepherd carries a long pole with a crotch at the upper end. When his flock gets to a good grazing spot and he wants to stop and rest, he puts this stick behind him and sits on it, so in combination with the stilts it forms a tripod and holds him up. And there he can stay for hours, busily knitting. Knitting is the way he whiles away his time.

It sounds like a nice, peaceful life, healthy outdoor exercise—all that fun of cruising around on stilts, and at the end of the day you've got a sock or a stocking cap or a scarf to show for it.

But it must be a very odd sight to see half a dozen men, each up on the top of his tripod, knitting away and watching over his flock. The nearest we can come to it, around our neck of the woods, is a pair of elevator shoes.

TYPES OF MOTHERS

There's a book by two psychologists named Ferdinand Lundberg and Marynia F. Farnham that's caused quite a little talk. It's called *Modern Woman: The Lost Sex*, which certainly is a title to make you stop, look, and whistle, although as far as I know, women as a sex aren't any more "lost" than men are.

The theory these psychologists advance—and by the way, one of them is a woman—is that the modern gals, generally speaking, are restless, unhappy, and dissatisfied, and that this dissatisfaction is having a pretty disastrous effect on the whole social and moral structure of our civilization.

In the course of their analysis of modern woman, they devote quite some space to modern mothers. Now some of these books on psychology and behaviorism kinda give out the impression that a mother is just one degree removed from a first-rate monster. The boys blame everything that's wrong with everybody on mothers and how they bring their kids up, but Dr. Lundberg and Dr. Farnham take the view that on the whole Mom isn't such a bad old girl after all. In fact, they say that at least fifty per cent of the mothers couldn't be improved on, which is quite an admission for a psychologist, because a psychologist is usually a guy who wants to make improvements in everybody.

But what they say about the other fifty per cent of the mothers of the world is mighty interesting. They divide them into four types: the rejecting mother, the oversolicitous or overprotective mother, the dominating mother, and the overaffectionate mother.

Now these four types of mother don't do their kids any harm if they're just a little too dominating or a little too overprotective, or the rest of it, but they don't do them much good, either, and the extreme cases of these four various kinds of mothers probably are responsible for most of our juvenile delinquents, our neurotics, and our alcoholics. They're neurotic themselves and they make the kids that way. As I read this list over, I recognized several women I know among the lot, and I'll bet you will, too. There probably are mothers who live right across from you, or down the street, or who belong to the same club you do, and they're working Junior over with one of these deals right this minute.

Take the rejecting mother, to start with. She's the one who wasn't overly eager to have the kid in the first place, and now she's got him, her opinion hasn't changed any. She misses the freedom she had before he came along, and she's firmly convinced she might have had a great career if she'd gotten the breaks, instead of tying herself down with a husband and a child and a house to look after. And she don't do much looking after, either. If she can't afford a maid she lets things slide, because she's too busy with her own interests to tend to her home. In extreme cases the rejecting mother abandons the kid outright on some doorstep. She's the type who lets a baby cry for hours without attention, who locks the door and goes off gallivanting for hours at a time, who is never home when little Oswald comes home from school, who puts him to bed "to get rid of him" when company comes in the evening. Naturally, she makes him feel unwanted and nothing he can do pleases her. She shouldn't have had a kid in the first place. Fortunately, very, very few mothers are like this, but the ones who are account for the abandoned babies and neglected waifs you read about in the papers. Of course, the rejecting mothers who belong to the idle rich can hire nursemaids, who usually are kinder than their unnatural employers.

The overprotective mother may seem to be the model mother in the community: she constantly sacrifices herself for the kids. She's in a tizzy all the time about their health and she supervises every detail of their lives. It just don't seem possible to her that her kids are normal and well and happy. She thinks there's something wrong all the time. Of course, she gives them a whole assortment of fears and worries, with her constant fussing, and as they grow up they remain babyish and emotionally immature and they have a terrible time adjusting themselves to life and its responsibilities.

The dominating mother is beset by a constant need to crack the whip over everything and everybody. She can be very fond of her kids, but they have to toe the mark right up to a hundredth of an inch and she frets and fumes if they don't carry out her orders to the last word. She nags and scolds when they're little, and when they grow up she keeps right on running their lives as if they were still three years old and not quite bright. The dominating mother is responsible for in-law troubles and broken marriages, among other things.

The overaffectionate mother is unhappy in her own life and she turns all her love, without restraint, on the kids, but she does it in such a way that it's sticky and clinging rather than loving and helpful. She turns away from her husband and actually falls in love with her own babies. She is so afraid of displeasing Junior, for fear he won't love her any more, that she gives in to his slightest whim and overwhelms him with hugs and kisses and cake and candy and expensive presents. This type of mother is especially rough on sons, because they grow up to be sissies, and it ain't exactly their fault, either; they can't help it.

Against these four wrong types of mothers there's the truly loving mother, who accepts her children and never resents the fact that she has them, who really likes kids in general and hers in particular, who finds them fascinating and companionable but not all-absorbing, who can teach them discipline without harsh punishment, and who can tell if a baby is hungry or wet or cold or lonesome without having to read a book on the subject. She just sorta knows how to be a mother by instinct, and she likes the job. It's a full-time job, but she gets in a little relaxation, so she don't go stale. She's in balance herself, and she has balanced kids who don't have to live in an alien world when they grow up, because the world is a friendly place to them, a place they've enjoyed living in from the first moment they were born.

SOME RULES FOR A HAPPY, SUCCESSFUL LIFE

1. Keep skid chains on your tongue. Always say less than you think. And remember to cultivate a low persuasive voice. How you say it very often counts for more than what you say.

2. Make promises sparingly and keep them faithfully, no matter what it costs you.

3. Never let an opportunity pass to say a kind, encouraging thing to or about somebody, and praise good work, regardless of who does it. If criticism is merited, and you feel you must criticize, criticize helpfully, but never spitefully.

4. Be interested in others—interested in their pursuits, their welfare, their homes, and their families. Make merry with those who rejoice, and mourn with those who mourn, and let everyone you meet, however humble they might be, feel that you regard him, or her, as a person of importance.

5. Be cheerful. Keep the corners of your mouth turned up. If you've got pains, worries, and disappointments, hide them, don't show them to anybody else. Laugh at good stories, and learn to tell them.

6. Preserve an open mind on all debatable questions. Discuss, but don't argue; there's a difference. It's the mark of superior minds to disagree and yet remain friendly.

7. Let your virtues, if you have any, speak for themselves. And refuse to talk about somebody else's vices. Discourage gossip. Make it a point to say nothing to somebody else unless it's something good, that is, about somebody else.

8. Be careful of other people's feelings. Wit at the other fellow's expense is very rarely worth the effort, and it may hurt when you least expect it. Just pay no attention to ill-natured remarks about you; simply live so that nobody will believe them.

Anonymous

POKER NELL'S DIAMOND TEETH

Out West, in the early days, some of the small mining or cattle towns played pretty rough, what with shooting and cattle rustling and claim jumping and dance halls and Indian raids. A peaceable man like a doctor or a dentist could run into some pretty unusual experiences in a town like that without even half trying.

For instance, take Dr. Will Frackelton: he has been a sagebrush dentist out in Wyoming for going on sixty years now, and he's got some tales about those early days that'll really curl your hair.

One of the funniest ones has to do with a gal named Poker Nell, in the little town of Casper, Wyoming, about 1894. Casper was a cattle town, and still is. The population in Casper now is close to twenty thousand, but in 1896, if you added up everybody, man and boy, you'd find maybe six hundred people in the whole county.

Well, Poker Nell was a big handsome black-haired doll, and she was owner—and manager—of the biggest dance hall in Casper. She could ride like a man, and shoot straighter than most of the buckaroos in those parts, and when she played poker the sky was the limit; hence her nickname, Poker Nell. Poker Nell was a tough dame, and a flashy dame, and when she wasn't on hossback she was dolled up in silks and satins and low-cut gowns with plenty of cleavage showing, and she went in for sparklers. She had enough diamonds hung on her to set a good-sized jewelry store up in business.

So one day Poker Nell wanders into Dr. Frackelton's office, and he can't imagine why, because Poker Nell's teeth aren't the type you have trouble with. They're big and strong and white and she can bite through a bullet with 'em without even crunching down hard.

"Doc," she says, "see these here sparklers?" And she flashes a couple of hunks of ice of fair size, maybe two carats apiece. "I want to know if you can set these in my front teeth," she says.

Well, Doc Frackelton didn't think much of the idea, because it didn't seem like a job quite up to his ethical and professional standards as a reputable dentist, but after all, they were Poker Nell's teeth. He was a young fellow trying to get along in the world in as peaceable a way as possible, and Poker Nell was fingering a six-shooter very lovingly as she made her inquiry. So Doc Frackelton allowed as how he could set the diamonds in her teeth, but it was going to be a long, painful job and might not turn out too well after all, so Poker Nell would have to go into the thing at her own risk.

She agreed to those terms and the work began. Now, in those days, dentists' offices in the Wild West didn't carry much supplies in the way of bridgework and crowns and porcelain facings; it was mostly yank 'em out and slap in a store set of teeth you got by mail order from

218

Chicago or somewhere. Doc Frackelton was a capable man, but he had to invent methods as he went along, because he'd never done a thing like this before, and he even had to make some of the instruments specially for the job. But finally everything was done up down to the last polish, and Poker Nell sat up in the chair and grinned her diamond grin into the mirror.

"That'll rock the dames around here back on their heels," she approved. "And it's gonna help out with the poker playin', too. If the boys get to watchin' the sparklers in my teeth, they won't watch the deal too close!"

She paid her bill and sashayed out with the rustle of satin and the click of six-shooters, and Doc Frackelton mopped his brow and wondered what would come into his office next.

EARLY MORNING MANNERS

What kind of a mental attitude do you have when you first get up in the morning? Somebody once said that the first hour of the day is the rudder that points out how all the other hours are going to go. And the things that happen during that first hour can pretty much set your whole state of mind for the whole day.

Suppose you and the old man open your eyes at the same time, and leap out of bed and practically have a fight to see who's going to get into the bathroom first. You both want the shower, and Father has to shave and pretty himself up, and either words are passed right off, or there's one of those silent arguments when one of you dives for that important door, races in and locks it, and the other one paces up and down while the one that's inside makes with all the preparations.

Well, it's a lead-pipe cinch that if Father makes it in there first, and stays in about twice as long as he ought to, there's a good way to start a divorce, right off. And of course he will stay in twice as long, because he's shaving, and if you've ever watched a guy shave, and go through all that routine of the soap and the water that has to be just the right temperature, and the funny faces and the close inspection from every angle, and the bending down to see how the bald spot's getting on, and the lotion and powder, you can say that you've been watching a very vain guy. That's the way every man is when he's shaving; the mere flash of a razor does it to them. Of course, he leaves his shaving things out, and the shaving brush full of messy lather, and the cap off the toothpaste, and if he takes a shower he throws the wet towel on the floor, and when Mother gets to go in, the place looks as if a pack of monkeys had romped through it.

Then, the minute he's out, while she's still in there trying to pin up her hair, he wants to start right in operating on breakfast, and he puts up a howl if things ain't exactly to his taste and within his reach so he don't hardly have to glance up from the newspaper more than once to feed himself.

Well, Mother is about ready to take him over by then, and he don't help matters a bit by starting a long conversation, the minute he sits down to his bacon and eggs, about how he don't know what's the matter with him, but he didn't sleep a wink all night; he never closed his eyes, and he thinks he'd better have a good thorough examination and find out if he's mortally ill or something.

Of course, Mother didn't get her eyes closed for the simple reason that Father was sawing logs over there so loud that nobody could sleep, and when he hit a knot it sounded like a bear caught in a trap, and the neighbors three houses down the street looked out of the windows to see where the fire engine was coming from. She might mention these things, but if she's smart she's careful not to. She just smiles and says, "Yes, dear, what do you think caused your sleeplessness?"

So the old man says it might have been those crackers and milk and pie before he went to bed, and she better ask his mother how to make that good tender piecrust they always had back home. By this time she's fit to be tied, but she still keeps quiet.

Then, while he's got his paper up in front of him, she starts in with "Now, look, I want you to be sure to bring me home a spool of white thread, number sixty, when you come tonight, now don't forget it, like you forgot it the last three days, and I want you to clean out the cellar tonight, so come home good and early, and call up the meter man and tell him that meter don't work right and there's too much on the gas bill this month, I know I used only about half that gas, and you should order the coal early this year, earlier than you did last year, anyhow, and bring home a new garden rake and two packages of pink sweet pea seeds, I said pink, don't get red ones just because you like them better."

So Father just grunts and keeps on reading the paper, and after a while he says, "What's the matter with you, why don't you look at me when I'm speaking to you?" and he says, "Why should I?"

That's the sort of stuff that starts the day off in great shape. And, seriously, a little consideration could have prevented the whole thing. If two folks can't spend a pleasant morning hour together they don't have much hope of having evenings that are much better. It makes sense to try to work on these troublesome morning hours, in the interest of creating a happier and brighter day for all concerned.

KNOW YOUR RIGHTS

The business expert, Richard P. Calhoon, has made a list of things that you have a reasonable right to expect from your employer. Here goes:

"1. The right to a reasonable explanation. Everyone has a right to a reasonable explanation of an assignment. You have a right to ask questions at the beginning in order to be sure you understand the assignment. You also have the right to check back with the boss as the work progresses. If you know the object of the work, you will do it far more intelligently.

"2. The right to reasonable completion dates. Some bosses expect everything to be done at once. If you insist on a reasonable time to do the job, you won't be in the position of having to explain why you can't get it done according to the whims of the boss.

"3. The right to service. A man in a high position in business has a right to better service, simply because his time is worth more to the company and his requirements are more urgent. But the little fellow in a minor capacity has a right to service too. He can't work efficiently without it. So insist on your right to expect statistical data, stenographic help, information, etc. Service within an organization isn't a matter of doing favors; it's working together.

"4. The right to know where one stands. If a person is perpetually in fear of losing his job, or disturbed as a result of not knowing how he's doing, he has the right to check with the boss . . . to ask if his work is satisfactory, and, if not, what's wrong with it.

"5. The right to recognition. Outstanding work of any kind deserves recognition . . . even if you have to blow your own horn to get attention. Try not to blow it too loud—a gentle toot usually gets attention.

"6. The right to consideration for promotion. If a man feels confident that he can successfully perform the duties of a better job, he has every right to ask for it, and to have his request considered with fairness.

"7. The right to be heard. Today, good businessmen believe that every member of an organization has a voice. If yours goes unheard, it's usually because you are letting the rest of the boys drown you out.

"8. The right to consideration. In a business, it is frequently necessary to make changes, often very drastic. But you have the right to know about these changes, and to what extent they will affect you personally. Don't be the one whose desk is always shoved into a dark corner, who must always take the most inconvenient lunch hour.

"9. The right to one's convictions. It is a mistake to yield one's personal convictions or to grovel, mentally, before the boss. There are matters upon which you should agree if only for the sake of peace . . . matters concerning the integrity of the business. On the other hand, don't swallow everything he says whole. Don't feel that you have to ape him, especially outside the office. Don't surrender your convictions about your church, or your country, or how to bring up your kids, or what color necktie to wear . . . just to obey the whims of the boss or to set yourself up good in his eyes."

WHEN THE KIDS ASK QUESTIONS

I remember, when I was a kid, somebody was always telling me, "Don't ask so many questions!" I don't think I was any more curious than other boys, but I was a question-asking kid, the same way all average, normal kids are question-asking. And I asked 'em so fast and so indiscriminately that my folks stood it as long as they could and then told me to shut up and be quick about it, before their ears dropped off.

But my folks did one thing that a lot of people forget to do, along about the time they get the screaming meemies from question-asking kids and make them shut up. They introduced me to the encyclopedia and the dictionary, and told me to look things up, and showed me how. And that took care of my question-asking, and if I really got stuck I came around to them and asked, but not so often that I was a headache to them.

222

You've probably noticed that most of the questions kids ask can't possibly be answered, at least not in the form they ask 'em. Questions like "Where is up?" and "Did God make the pussycat?" and "How far is high?" and "Who is 'they'?" and "Where does the sun sleep?"—you just can't answer things like that right off. And that's the main reason why you get so discouraged; a barrage of unanswerable questions can get anybody down. But the kid isn't trying to annoy you; he really wants to learn. And if you give him a swift brush-off on these vague impossible questions, he'll come back with a thousand more, and consider you pretty dumb because you don't know the score.

If you can possibly get him to stop asking vague general questions and ask specific ones, you're well on the way to teaching him to think for himself. If he asks, "Where does electricity come from?" you're stuck, but if you can steer him into asking, "How does electricity get into the light bulb and make the light go on and off?" you can answer after a fashion, even if you have to sneak out and look it up so's you don't fall flat on your face in front of your own kid.

And just as soon as you can get him to put questions in a concrete form, he can learn how and where to look up the answers. And then he can learn to put these isolated scraps of information together and get himself a real background of knowledge.

A lot of parents think that this sort of teaching is what schools are for, and they don't take the time and trouble to do it at home. So the burden falls on some poor overworked teacher who has a roomful of fifty kids all squirming with questions, and she's got her hands full already without doing the job which should have been done at home, the job of showing Junior how to ask the right questions and get the right answers.

FATHER DOES THE WORK

Among civilized peoples, all the fussing and care and excitement during childbirth go to the mother, and Pop's left out in the cold. All he gets a chance to do is to pace up and down, and have jokes made about him, and pass out the cigars.

But among the Indians of British Guiana, it's just the reverse. Pop does all the suffering—or is supposed to—and he gets all the glory.

Here's how they work the deal in those parts:

Mama works up to within a few hours of the blessed event, but about a week before the expected birth, Pop takes to his hammock. He is prohibited certain foods for fear they will make the child thin, or cause its teeth to be crooked. For instance, there's the flesh of the water cavy, which is a delicacy in those regions, but which has big buck teeth. Pop can't eat any of that, no matter how much he wants it.

Then, when the time comes, Mama goes silently into the woods, while Pop moans and groans in his hammock of pain, and the witch doctors and medicine men make a hullabaloo around him. As soon as everything is over, Mama returns, as quietly as she went, and for the next ten days she takes care of herself and the baby, and of her husband, who mustn't set foot to the ground, or lift a hand to feed himself, for this length of time.

This whole screwy business is really a very naïve attempt at deception, to fool the evil spirits and trick them away from the birth scene, in order to give Mama and the baby a better break. And, from the fuss some civilized fathers make, you'd think they were trying to do the same thing.

TEN COMMANDMENTS FOR HUSBANDS AND WIVES

Here's a list of ten commandments for husbands and wives that might come in handy when the family temper is straining at the leash:

For Husbands:

1. Thou shall not think that thyself are "It."
2. Thou shalt not praise thy neighbor's wife; praise thine own.
3. Thou shalt not share the love of thy wife with the booze shop. She deserveth it all.
4. Thou shalt not be stingy with thy wife.
5. Thou shalt not keep any secrets from thy wife. Secrets breed suspicion and wreck confidence.
6. Thou shalt not refuse to talk with thy wife after the day's work is done.
7. Thou shalt not fail to provide life insurance for thy family.

8. Thou shalt not scold thy wife when the meat burns. Blow up a powder mill instead!

9. Thou shalt not fail to kiss thy wife good-by every morning.

10. Thou shalt not forget through all the years of thy life that thy wife, whom God hath given thee as thy companion, is thy superior.

Now, any guy who's only half bright knows those things by instinct, but sometimes he forgets and has to be forcibly reminded. Let him hereby paste the list in his hat and read it over every morning while he's on his way to work. Now let's turn to the other ten commandments:

For Wives:

1. Thou shalt not be a spendthrift. Do not squander thy husband's money.

2. Thou shalt not talk shop when thy husband returns at night.

3. Thou shalt not fail to have his meals on time.

4. Thou shalt not quiz thy wedded husband. Hit him with an ax. It is more kind.

5. Thou shalt not nag thy husband. Shoot him with a revolver. It is more kind.

6. Thou shalt not fail to dress up for thy husband as thou didst before marriage.

7. Thou shalt not try to fight thy husband. Crying will fetch him sooner!

8. Thou shalt not expect thy husband to apologize—even when he is wrong. Let it pass.

9. Thou shalt not hesitate to assure thy husband that he is one great guy.

10. Thou shalt not remind thy husband what a big sacrifice thou didst make to marry him.

WHEN WOMEN GOT THE VOTE

Did you know that the amendment to the Constitution that gave women a vote was passed in the House of Representatives because a man made a mistake?

Here's what happened. The gals had worked and struggled and pushed and shoved for years to get the right to vote, but the men didn't want to give it to 'em. They'd been ridiculed and thrown in jail and beaten up, but they wanted that vote and they fought until they pretty near got it—but some of the men were still holding out.

At last the vote to ratify the amendment was taken in the House of Representatives on May 21, 1919. The session was punctuated by cheers and wild shouting as one congressman and then another cast his vote, and when it was all over the women had won, 49 to 47.

And then there was a dead silence, while everybody suddenly realized that the vote was meaningless. The House, that term, consisted of ninety-nine members. Two were ill at home and one had resigned before the vote was taken. So, while 49 to 47 was a majority of those present, it wasn't a constitutional majority of the whole House. It lacked just one vote of being that. And on that technicality, the anti-suffragists could throw up legal barriers and hold up ratification past the next November election, in which the gals had their heart set on voting. They were gonna vote in the 1920 general elections, or bust trying.

And then Representative Seth Walker, Speaker of the House and leader of the anti-suffragists, made his immortal boner. He was thinking fast—but not fast enough. According to parliamentary rule, he could change his vote and then call for a reconsideration, since the vote was not a constitutional majority. So he jumped up and did just that, and the shrieks of the crowd told him, just a little too late, what he'd done. He'd changed that vote into a constitutional majority, 50 to 46, and the suffrage amendment was ratified. Of course, he never lived it down. He was a marked man after that. People used to go around talking about "doing a Seth Walker" whenever a horrible boner was mentioned. But that's the real inside story of how the ladies got the vote, and it's a good thing they did. They've proved themselves capable of taking on their share of the obligations of citizenship, and the women's vote is pretty important in the country nowadays. But as far as Seth Walker was concerned, it was all a terrible mistake.

WHAT MAKES MOTHERS-IN-LAW MEDDLE?

I dunno just why it is that we assume, generally speaking, that mothers-in-law are meddlesome busybodies. Maybe I've been kinda lucky in my acquaintances, but practically all the mothers-in-law I've ever known have been real nice people, and they haven't meddled to speak of, and even if they did, nobody minded much. But you and I both know that the stock character of a meddlesome mother-in-law does exist in people's minds; otherwise there wouldn't be so many mother-in-law jokes. Incidentally, why not father-in-law jokes? But we'll get around to that in a minute. We also know that in some cases a mother-in-law, sometimes with the best intentions in the world and sometimes with positive malice, can make an awful lot of unhappiness. Now why is that?

Well, to start with, let's leave the malicious type of woman, the kind who deliberately wants to break up a marriage because she can't stand having her darling boy or girl out of her clutches—let's leave her out of it entirely. What she needs is expert treatment by a psychiatrist, because she's a sick woman with a sick mind. Let's take up the perfectly nice, well-intentioned mother-in-law who just wants to be kind and helpful and who gets her feelings and everybody else's hurt in the process.

For twenty years and upwards that mother-in-law hasn't been a mother-in-law. She's been a mother. And she's worked hard at that job of being a mother. Now she's been notified that her job is finished and her services are no longer required, just as if she'd held down a desk job in an office for twenty years and suddenly she got the pink slip saying that she was out at pasture, as of the 15th inst., etc. Of course, she figured on retiring sometime, but she was doing her work well and there'd been no complaints, and now, all of a sudden—that pink slip. That's exactly what it amounts to when her children marry and she turns them over to a new and sometimes to her eyes not too attractive management. So she kinda hangs on and keeps on managing anyhow, and she's just about in the position of a retired bookkeeper who trots down to the old place every other day and starts telling the new incumbent how to keep his precious books.

Now don't get me wrong. I don't mean that mothers-in-law shouldn't take a very active and happy and generous part in their married children's lives. And they'll find that they're taking that part, if they'll only be patient. But they can only take it on the invitation of the young folks. There's no other possible way. As much as they ache to help out, with advice or money or anything at all, they must keep hands off until asked. Raising the kids was a big job, a job they're proud of, and now it's done, mothers-in-law can't help feeling kinda sorrowful that it's over. But if they take it easy, if, say, they find some real interesting temporary work to fill in time for a little, they'll find their job back and better then ever. Seems like there's an old Chinese proverb to the effect that you never really know love until you have grandchildren.

That temporary work I mentioned: well, maybe there's a course or two they've always wanted to take, or some clubwork they never had time for, or hobbies, or some young people, other than their own, who need a spot of mothering. Anything at all that will keep out the emptiness and loneliness until the new mother-in-law has had a chance to adjust herself to the fact that there are lots of jobs in the world to be done, and raising Junior was only one of them.

Of course, the best thing is if they figured out, when they were young mothers, that the kids were going to grow up someday and have to stand on their own feet, and if they can kinda prepare for that time and make plans, just as Father makes plans for what he's going to do when he retires. Both men and women can and often do have a far richer and fuller life after retirement—on the one hand, freedom from an office job, and on the other, freedom from the care of young children—than they ever dreamed of in their younger years.

And, by the way, why no father-in-law jokes? Because Father, of course, has his work to interest him, as well as his home and family. Mother, all too often, and all too tragically, has only the home, and it sees mighty lonesome when the birds have flown. So she keeps on doing the only job she's fitted herself for, the job of raising kids that have already been raised for several years now. You can't exactly blame her, but you can feel sorry for her and wish she could take a deep, healthy interest in something else, at least, till the grandchildren come along.

FISHERMAN'S PRAYER

Dear Lord . . .

When Gabriel blows his blast
And I come home to rest at last,
Don't measure me for harp and wings,
Let me instead have these few things—

Some tackle and a rod and reel,
A pair of waders and a creel,

A gushing, frothy, laughing stream,
A placid lake by which to dream,

An angel pal with whom to angle,
Magic lines that will not tangle.

And permission, Lord, with fingers crossed,
To lie about the fish I lost.

Anonymous

SOUTH SEA ISLAND BEAUTY

Anybody around your house complained lately that you take too long to get prettied up when you go out? Do your menfolks growl and grumble, all slicked up, including their eyebrows, while you're standing around in your petticoat still wondering which dress to wear to the dance? If they do, you better see that they hear about this one:

When a gal down in the South Sea Islands wants to look beautiful, she don't dress, she undresses, and it takes her so much longer than it does for you to get your clothes and face on that it ain't even funny. That guy who's been naggin' you to hurry up ought to wait for one of those doll babies.

In the first place, it takes a number of years for a South Sea gal to get ready to start the beautifying process, because she has to be tattooed from head to foot, and a complete tattoo job like that can't be done all at once, especially with the crude and painful instruments the natives use.

Well, now, suppose she's all through her tattooing ordeal, and the natural light brown of her skin is completely covered with a tracery of pale blue tattoo like lacework. She's, say, sixteen and real pretty and she hears that her best beau is coming over to call that evening. She's gotta start early in the morning if she wants to get prettied up real nice for her date.

She's in a Mother Hubbard when she hears the big news, and her hair is in a sort of loose string nightcap to preserve the elaborate coiffure, as big as a bushel basket, that she's been nursing along for years. First thing is to get out of that Mother Hubbard. No self-respecting South Sea girl can receive callers with a thing like that on. While she's climbing out of her clothes, Momma is grating a coconut, shell and all,

229

and she proceeds to pound and pummel and massage the gal with this grated coconut until both of them are out of breath, but the gal's skin is a shiny rich brown and the blue tattooing stands out twice as bright as before. This coconut rubdown may take three or four hours, with time out to rest, if the kid wants to look real pretty and the boy who's calling is a good catch.

Then she gets her hair out of that string nightcap and Momma gives it a workout with what's left of the shredded coconut to make it glisten, and then combs it out with a long-pronged wooden comb. This combing is quite a process, because that head of hair ain't been combed since the last time a boy came to see her, and if by any chance this is her first beau, it just ain't been combed at all. Not since she was born. By the time it's done, the rest of the afternoon is shot.

Then she puts on a couple of grass petticoats, or maybe three, if she has 'em. Each one is a different color, maybe a deep henna-brown one, a yellow one, and a blue one to match the tattooing, and over that an apron of white leaves. All these skirts have to be adjusted so that the layers will fall just right, sorta concealing and revealing at the same time, so to speak. And with no full-length mirrors to practice by, it's pretty tricky.

Then, through each pierced ear lobe she puts a sprig of a certain purple flowering herb that, the authorities say, acts on her future boy friend like cheese acts on a mouse. The flowers in her hair take another half an hour or so, and then come her necklaces, made out of glass beads and shells and seeds and dog's teeth, and, finally, the big shiny crescent of mother-of-pearl which every girl, however poor, must own if any boy is ever going to give her a second look.

Then she has to get her feathered arm bands and anklets on. These have to be wound carefully so they're not too tight and not too loose. And she chews up a fresh mouthful of betel nut, to make her teeth the nice bright cherry-red approved in those parts.

Maybe you noticed at the beginning I said a South Seas gal takes more time to get undressed than you do to get dressed. Well, when she's all finished, she's reasonably modest. All the strategic spots are covered up, you might say, but what she's actually got on in the way of clothes is a couple of grass skirts. The tracery of tattooing all over her and the heavy necklaces that cover her body like armor plate make her a whole lot more modest than these gals waltzing around in midriff evening gowns.

Well, now she'll all fixed up beautiful, it's dark as pitch, and when her boy friend arrives he can't see a thing. She might as well have stayed in her old Mother Hubbard. But apparently the thing works, sight unseen, because nobody ever heard of one of those babies not catching a husband at a real early age.

INFIDELITY

One of the most abused words in the English language is "unfaithful," when it's applied to a wandering (or supposedly wandering) husband or wife. I guess we abuse the word "unfaithful" so much because by the time we've gotten into a state of mind to apply it to somebody, we're so stirred up emotionally that we hardly know what we're talking about.

Of course, it isn't exactly a pleasant moment for anybody when the realization comes that a husband, or wife, as the case may be, has been out tomcatting around with somebody else. It's no fun. Your pride is hurt, and all you want is to get away from the person who's done this thing to you. Maybe you even want revenge. But it's a sure thing that you're blowing fuses, emotionally speaking, and right then you aren't fit to make decisions. You have to try to put aside your emotional reaction before you can know the truth of the matter, or take steps to counteract it.

For one thing, the psychologists and marriage experts say that nine tenths of the accusations of infidelity made by angry wives, or angry husbands, are based on the shifting sands of suspicion and there's absolutely nothing to them. The fact that your Joe can't make his eyes behave in public, and that at a party he always has to be the one to sit out on the porch swing with the visiting siren don't mean a thing. He's just built that way, and he'll run for cover like a scared rabbit if things start getting serious. But just let him play patty-cake often enough, and you're bound to get suspicious of him, and then, the next time he stays out late—brother, look out! As far as you're concerned, where there's smoke, there's fire . . . and after all, he brought it on himself. He's a deep-dyed villain for sure. He's unfaithful. Now maybe, technically speaking, he ain't done a thing he shouldn't, but the evidence sure is agin him. If you've got somebody around the house who's unfaithful in that sense, some lad with wandering eyes but a home-loving disposition, you'll probably just have to put up with it. There's no known cure. You can take comfort in the fact that dynamite couldn't blast him out of his comfortable little niche, the pleasant, cozy home you make for him. But you'll get pretty disgusted now and then, even though he always comes trotting back safe and sound . . . and usually scared.

But suppose that you find out for sure, in the real sense of the word, that your mate has been unfaithful to you. This isn't a matter of suspicion, or a case of his just fooling around some; this is it. The real thing. Well, what are you going to do about it?

If it only happened once, try to remember that accidents can happen in the best-regulated families. After you get over being mad about it, and you will, eventually, because after all you love the guy, and he really loves you, you'll probably decide that both you and he have been punished enough by what's happened. The accidental type of unfaithfulness that happens only once, under great temptation, is the commonest kind. There's a lot to gain by a mite of forgiveness, and an awful lot to lose without it. Even such an august church dignitary as the Most Rev. Cyril Forster Garbett, Archbishop of York, has pointed out that momentary temptation can make both men and women do things entirely contrary to their real nature and inclination. Modern life, particularly the war and its aftermath, have thrown people together under unusual circumstances and have created tempting situations which would never be encountered in normal times. On the whole, our young people took the long separation of the war years pretty well, but there were some slips, and most of them come under this heading of temporary infidelity. Things can be patched up, even though you don't think so at the time.

On the other hand, chronic infidelity is pretty hard to take. Even that isn't always fatal to a marriage, but it's a severe strain. If your Joe has strayed from the fold not once, but frequently, or if he's been conducting a long-standing affair that he shows no signs of giving up, then you're in a spot. But remember one thing. No matter what your wandering boy does outside the home, you're still ruling the roost. Morally and legally you're in command of the situation. What you do about it is up to you and your conscience, always keeping in view the attitude of your particular faith toward a broken home and divorce. Whatever you do, don't break with your church just because your husband can't behave. If you do that you'll have neither home nor the comfort of your beliefs. Naturally, if there are children, every possible effort must be made to keep the home fires burning, on a basis of understanding and tolerance, even if love has flown out the window. It may not be an ideal sort of home life, but if bitterness and recriminations can be kept out of it, it's better than none at all. A lot of reasonably pleasant homes are run on that basis, and eventually a very satisfactory adjustment can be, and often is, made. It's a well-recognized fact that a great many men pass through a phase, usually when they're somewhere in their middle age, when they get mighty restless and they're open to temptation and easily become involved in affairs which really don't mean much of anything. They're just trying to prove to themselves that they're as young as they think they are, and after a while they wake up and realize that home and Momma are what they want after all. So if you have the patience to stick it out, he'll be back. It'll take awhile, but he will.

So you have to take all these things into consideration in a case of infidelity. In the first place, nine times out of ten, there's nothing to it but your own suspicions; in the second, temporary infidelity is better forgiven and forgotten; and in the third, chronic infidelity will probably cure itself someday—if you stick around long enough.

On the other hand, it don't do to be too broad-minded. Foolish broad-mindedness isn't found as often as foolish suspicion, but in some high-flying social circles it's actually considered smart and sophisticated to get away with as much as possible. The results, needless to say, are disastrous.

If nothing else should deter mankind from promiscuous infidelity, the threat of disease should keep our feet on the ground. And in addition there are the heartaches, the sense of betrayal, the general laxity of standards that accompany every indiscretion. It's nothing to get mixed up with. But if you find yourself gazing into the eight-ball, while Sonny Boy is out sowing a couple of wild oats, think it over and give yourself time to cool off before you do anything drastic. No situation requires calmer thinking, and there's no time that it's harder to be calm than in that first minute after you hear of unfaithfulness, either apparent or actual.

THE POTTO

They've got a very curious animal out in the jungles of West Africa, a little animal which goes under several names, the commonest of which is the potto. They're also called bush bears and bush babies and any number of long scientific jawbreakers which we'll just leave out of this little discussion entirely, for the very good reason that nobody but a scientist can pronounce them.

These pottos are really small tailless lemurs, and lemurs are second cousins to monkeys, but except for the fact that pottos live in trees, they're as unmonkeylike as possible. They're plump little brown woolly critters, and they hang upside down, of all things, on the branches of the trees, so low down that you'd think all you had to do is reach up and pick one off, like a bunch of grapes. However, if you tried it, you'd get a couple of surprises.

In the first place, this potto wouldn't stick around for you to pick him off. He'd be off like greased lightning, fifty feet up the tree, and still upside down, before you could get your hand up to touch him. And even if he did stay, and you got hold of him, you couldn't get him off the branch. His feet are so constructed and his muscles are so strong that you can't make him let go. A potto can be torn apart by a wild animal, but his hands and feet will go right on clinging. There are records of hunters shooting at pottos, mistaking them for the head of some larger animal, and then coming up and finding just half a potto, latched securely onto the tree and clinging in death as firmly as it did in life. What's more, the potto, if he's going along a branch and suddenly decides to go in the other direction, can turn and walk back on himself, with his head and front feet coming out between his back legs. Then he swivels around by means of a special joint in his hips which turns the hip completely over, and he can walk that way just as well as the other. In fact, he doesn't care which way his hips are swiveled. That's being double-jointed for you! The beauty of it is that in turning around he actually doesn't let go of the tree at all; he just sort of turns himself inside out inside his own skin. The boys who have seen this done, and not many have, because the potto is extremely rare, say that it is decidedly uncanny and not a thing to watch if you're the worrying type, because you'll spend the rest of your life trying to figure out how he does this thing, and nobody knows that except another potto. But it's just one of the reasons why you can't reach up and pick one off a branch.

And a third reason why you can't is that a potto has a row of very sharp spines around its neck, and if you did get your hands on one, it would let go with its front feet, double up on itself so its head completely slips back into the loose skin surrounding this collar of spines,

234

and quick as lightning it would swing like a pendulum and about that point you'd be letting out yells loud enough to wake the whole jungle, because your hand would be neatly pinned against the tree with those spines, which are tough enough to pierce the bark of the tree. So there are three reasons why you don't go around in West Africa picking pottos off the trees like ripe fruit, even though they look like little plush toys strung up there by nature in a jovial mood. They ain't. They can take care of themselves.

But once you catch one, and it can be done, by throwing a net around it and then sawing off the branch and taking branch, net, potto and all, he'll settle down and live just as happily in captivity as he ever did in the jungle. Pottos have been exhibited in zoos, both here and abroad, but they're pretty scarce, because of their rarity and the difficulty of capturing them alive. I believe there are a couple of them, right now, at the Bronx Zoo in New York, hanging upside down as happily as ever they did in Africa. One of these days I'm going to take time to go up there and find out.

SCARS

Life wounds all of us. At best there is sorrow enough to go around. Yet because the deepest wounds are those of the soul and hidden to mortal sight, we keep hurting each other day by day, inflicting wounds that time mercifully scars over. But the scars remain, ready at a touch to throb angrily and ache again with the old gnawing wild pain.

You remember that day in school when the teacher laughed? You were only a little fellow, shy and silent, sitting in the shadow of the big boys, wistfully looking toward the day when you would shine as they did.

That day you were sure your chance had come. You were sure that you had just what the teacher wanted on the tip of your tongue, and you jumped up and shouted it loudly and eagerly, triumphantly—and you were very, very wrong.

There followed a flash of astonishment, an instant of dreadful silence and then the room rang with mirth. You heard only the teacher's laughter and it drowned your heart.

Many years have gone over your head since that day, but the sight of a little lad trudging along to school brings it back and the old pain stirs and beats against the scar. You cover it over, hush it to quiet once more with a smile. "I must have been funny. She couldn't help it." But you wish she had.

And there was that time when your best friend failed you. When the loose-tongued gossips started the damaging story and he was pressed for a single word in your defense, he said, "Oh, he's all right. Of course, he's all right but I don't want to get mixed up in this thing. Can't afford it. Have to think of my own name and my own family, you understand. Good fellow, but I have to keep out of this."

You felt forsaken; for weeks and weeks you carried the pain in your heart. The story was bad enough but that would right itself. The idea that he should fail you, that he had not rushed to your side at the first hint of trouble, was bad enough, was unbearable. He came back again after it was all over but the sight of him renewed the ache in your breast and the throb of pain in your throat. The scar was thin and the hurt soul beneath it quivered.

We all bear scars. Life is a struggle and hurts must come. But why the unnecessary ones? Why hurt the souls of little children? Why say things to them that they must remember with pain all their lives? Why say the smart, tart thing that goes straight to the heart of someone we love because we would relieve ourselves of the day's tension and throw off a grain of the soul's bitterness?

Who are we to inflict wounds and suffering and scars on those about us? Staggering, blind mortals, groping our way from somewhere "here" to somewhere "there," conscious of little but the effort to stay "here" a little longer.

It behooves us to travel softly, regardful of one another's happiness, particularly where our path crosses that of those dependent upon us for comfort, or enters into the heart of little children.

Anonymous

THE GIRL WHO READ IN HER SLEEP

You can find some mighty interesting material by skimming through old medical journals. Maybe, a hundred years or so back, the boys didn't have all the fancy frills in the psychological department worked out the way they do now, but they got all the facts down on paper just the same.

One of the oddest cases I ever came across in these old accounts is the one about a seventeen-year-old servant girl named Jane Rider, who lived up Massachusetts way something over a century ago.

Up until her seventeenth year, Jane acted like any other normal young girl. She did her work, and got a little dreamy-eyed over the delivery boys, and was known for her pleasant, cheerful disposition.

236

But in June 1833 her employer, Festus Stebbins, a prosperous Massachusetts farmer with eleven children, called in a doctor to look over the little housemaid. She'd been acting strangely lately, and both Mr. and Mrs. Stebbins feared that she had acquired some rare and unidentified illness that had made her insane to the point where she might injure herself or some member of the family.

After the family physician had examined her, it seemed necessary to apply to a mental specialist, Dr. Lemuel Belden, of Springfield, Massachusetts. Dr. Belden reassured the Stebbins family that the girl was far from insane, but that she certainly was suffering from some kind of physical disturbance, possibly due to "undigested food"! Otherwise, why would she rise from her bed, sound asleep, and go through complicated household chores, including *reading* and *writing* in her sleep? After these somnambulistic wanderings, she returned to her cot and rested quietly until morning. She had no memory of anything unusual going on during the night.

Dr. Belden questioned the girl closely about her personal life. She came from Brattleboro, Vermont, where her father was a blacksmith. Her mother died of a brain tumor when she was a baby. Her first job was with the Stebbins family, where she was treated as a member of the household and was completely happy. In fact, there were plans afoot that someday she might marry the elder Stebbins boy, and her prospective mother-in-law had already endowed her with generous gifts of heirloom silver and linen. The original verdict of "undigested food" stood.

About a month after his first visit, Dr. Belden was again called to the Stebbins home. Jane was walking in her sleep again. Arrangements were made so that he could observe the girl, and during the first night he spent in the household he watched her rise about midnight, with her eyes closed, dress completely, and go downstairs to the kitchen. There, she began to get breakfast for the family. Moving swiftly, she set the table, went to the closet and took down the coffee cups and other china, and placed them on a tray. Although she lit the lamp in the kitchen, the pantry, closet, and dining room where she meticulously arranged the dishes were completely dark. When passing through a narrow door with the tray, she turned sideways in the darkness, so as not to knock and jar the china.

Dr. Belden, along with the now awakened Mr. and Mrs. Stebbins, watched in amazement. Jane went out to the milk room and proceeded to skim and separate the milk, pouring cream into one pitcher and skim

237

milk into another without spilling a drop. Her eyes remained closed, and the only light was in the kitchen, where her fascinated audience stood aghast. At times, one of the spectators would place a chair where it would obstruct her movements. She avoided it deftly, but her lips tightened with impatience. Finally, she went to bed of her own accord, got up in the morning, and, finding the breakfast table ready, inquired, "Why did you let me oversleep while someone else did my work?"

Then Jane began having attacks two or three times a week. Sometimes she never rose from her bed, but sat up, talking, singing, and reciting poetry. Often she asked for food; sometimes she rose and cooked an entire dinner, seasoned correctly, and she became extremely annoyed that the family was not present to eat it. Although her eyes were closed, when she came into a room where a lamp was burning, she turned it off petulantly, muttering that she never could understand why people would keep lights burning in the daytime!

Very soon Jane began having somnambulistic attacks in the broad daylight. She would sit in a chair, gently swaying to and fro, complaining of pains in her head, a ringing in her ears, and extreme drowsiness. Suddenly her face would become flushed, her eyebrows drawn as if in severe discomfort, and she would begin to moan. Her hands and feet grew cold as ice, and every attempt to wake her by normal methods was useless. Once Dr. Belden poured a bucket of cold water over her; she murmured that he was trying to drown her, and went quietly upstairs to change her clothing, returning to her chair in the sitting room apparently sound asleep.

During these somnambulistic periods, which lasted as long as two to three hours, Jane answered questions which were put to her. Her loquaciousness led to a fantastic happening on a Sunday evening in November of that year. "It was proposed," Dr. Belden said later, "to discover if the girl could read and write with her eyes shut. As she sat in a trancelike dream in the parlor, the lamp was removed and she was screened so as to be in almost complete darkness. A stranger, called in for the purpose, wrote some words on a card, which she read correctly after some urging. Another visitor wrote so dimly that none of the observers in the room could read it, but Jane, in the dark and with her eyelids covering the pupils of her eyes, made the letters out easily."

Within the space of a week, her strange powers developed amazingly. On November 12 she fell asleep while pumping water, outdoors on a bright sunny day, and for forty-eight hours she remained in a sleepwalking state. During this time more than a hundred people came to visit her; she obligingly read cards and other written messages for them, told time by watches that were shown her, and recited poetry. When her eyes were tightly blindfolded by two handkerchiefs, she continued to make these amazing demonstrations. Dr. Belden, and several other scientific wiseacres who observed her, could find no signs of any trickery.

Jane was exhausted by the forty-eight-hour trance. Dr. Belden, believing that the crowds who flocked to see her were bad for her, arranged for her to come to live at his house, where she could be closely guarded. Unfortunately, she got to be too difficult to care for, and Dr. Belden, after calling in other specialists, turned the girl over to the Massachusetts Hospital for the Indigent Insane in Worcester. Even as she was carted off, on a freezing cold December day, she suffered one of her trance attacks.

At the hospital Jane lost her odd sleepwalking tactics, possibly because of the unpleasant and uncomfortable remedies forced upon her. After a week or two she was pronounced cured, and her official record ends with the certificate issued by the asylum doctors to the effect that she was having no more attacks.

I've read about a lot of fakes who tried to get attention by pretending to have some unusual quirk, and perhaps Jane Rider was one of those. On the other hand, her story reads straight as a string. Perhaps today the boys who mess around with psychology could figure it out—but I'm just telling it according to those old medical journals written more than a hundred years ago.

THE GHOST HORSE OF THE PLAINS

The records of every race abound in tales of strange monsters and fantastic creatures on land and sea, and most of them stay fantastic creatures. But every once in a while one of these yarns comes true, and then you rub your eyes and gasp. One of these legendary critters was the Ghost Horse of the Plains, the Pacing White Stallion that the plainsmen used to talk about, back in the early days of the Southwest. What probably happened was that there were several fleet white stallions running wild at the time, descendants of the horses the Spaniards brought into Mexico more than four hundred years ago, and every once in a while one of the boys would see one of these white horses and he'd come back to camp with kind of an exaggerated story about how big and how wild and how fast it was, until the Ghost Horse of the Plains was built up into a supernatural critter a million times more beautiful and more fiery and faster and stronger than any horse in the world, and any plainsman would gladly have laid down his life for the chance to ride him.

Around the 1840s, the boys started seeing the Ghost Horse of the Plains pretty frequently, in the vicinity of what is now known as Mc-Kinney Falls, on Onion Creek in Travis County down Texas way. The horse they saw looked like a pure-bred Arabian. He was snow-white, with a mane down to his knees and a tail that almost swept the ground, and his only gait, outside a walk, was a pace, so they called him the Pacing White Stallion. He was wild as the wind, and nobody got more than a fleeting glimpse of this paragon of horses, but plenty of the boys were out chasing him. His range covered several hundred square miles, but he always seemed to come back to Onion Creek, which was his favorite watering place. Finally his fame spread so far that a doctor in San Antonio, who was something of a horse fancier, put up a reward of five hundred dollars for the horse, delivered to him alive and in a "sound condition."

Santa Ana Cruz, a Spanish-born rancher living in those parts, decided that five hundred dollars was more hay than he could grow just by ranching, so he took out after the Ghost Horse, and chased him four days and four nights, running hard with no rest, but he lost the horse somewhere along the Rio Grande and had to give up the search.

And then, maybe a month later, a cowboy out riding herd spotted a gaunt, weary animal in a box canyon, a white stallion that had evidently been without water for a long, long time, because watering places are few and far between out in that country. He recognized this unhappy animal as what was left of the Ghost Horse of the Plains, and, without too much trouble, he roped him and brought him in, two hundred miles through the desert from his usual stamping ground.

Well, they staked the King of the Mustangs out to pasture in green fresh grass, and put a trough of water beside him so he could drink his fill, but not a mouthful of water or of grass did that stallion take. For ten days and ten nights he stood quiet as a statue. He didn't kick or pull or make any effort to break away; he just stood there, and on the morning of the eleventh day he lay down and died without having touched the grass or the water. Seems he just couldn't stand having a rope around him, and after his first efforts to choke himself to death, as wild stallions sometimes try to do if tied up, he calmly and quietly starved himself to death in the midst of plenty. I don't know how many humans would do a thing like that. It was sorta like Patrick Henry saying "Give me liberty or give me death," but then, Patrick Henry was just taking his chances with the rest of the boys in his fight for liberty, and with the Ghost Horse of the Plains it was the real thing, face to face, and he never flinched a moment.

JUST A FRIENDLY WORD WITH YOU

A veteran of the Civil War, who had served his country in its army for twenty-one years, was talking with his boy, who was pretty much the apple of his eye, on the front porch of a modest cottage far away from here. The man was more than seventy. The boy was just forty. . . . And the father said among other things:

"Stand upon your own feet. Make your own way. Pay your own way. Ask no man, woman, or child to do you a service but you pay what the service is worth, otherwise you are a parasite, seeking to get labor of value for nothing.

"Owe no man what you cannot repay. If you are called to pay what you owe, make all your borrowings with care and deliberation, remembering that to evade a debt honestly contracted is to steal money.

"Own your own soul if you have to give up every possession you have. For it is the only thing that can ever be really yours. Misfortune or disaster may sweep away your properties, if you gain them, but rightly considered, misfortune and disaster will make your soul bigger, brighter, and better. If you lose your own soul you have nothing left, and you have justly gained the contempt of honest men.

"Do not pledge that soul for anything of place, power, office, or money. For once pledged you cannot fail to redeem it without breaking your pledge. And that is dishonest. And if you keep a bad pledge you dishonor your soul. In either way you are beaten.

"Take no gifts of value, beyond the worth that may be attached intrinsically to some slight token of friendliness or sentiment. For every gift beyond that you take, you may sometime be called upon for payment. And beware even of those gifts. I am speaking to you as a man that should know human nature is weak and the gift giver sometimes thinks the gift taker ungenerous if he does not make some repayment if called upon, and it may be that repayment is something that should not be made.

241

"And lastly, I have no money to leave you. This may be the last time I shall see you. If you will remember what I say and put it into practice you will need no money beyond what you can earn. And what you cannot earn you do not deserve to have."

Anonymous

THE WAY MEN SHAVE

The boys who mess around with psychology say that a guy is at his worst in the morning before breakfast when he's shaving. Of course, wives know that without being told.

A while back, Judith Chase Churchill, who writes a lot for the women's magazines, got together some material on the male animal during this daily shaving period. I know I'm sticking my neck out when I bring this subject up, because I have to go through the process every morning myself, but here's the gist of what Miss Churchill has to say:

A man takes his shave very seriously. Men come in two types: the kind who like to be watched and admired during the business of shaving, and the kind who don't. One guy has to have an audience or he'll practically cut his throat, and the other goes through the entire repertoire of facial expressions, scraping away methodically, behind barred doors. Neither type is much of a bargain during that ten minutes or so that he's working over his jawbones.

Mankind, collectively, spends about eighty million dollars a year on shaving, and individually, approximately three months of his life span. No matter how unimpressive it may be to his wife, that stubble on Buster's chin is the badge of masculinity to him. Ever since, in his early teens, he sheepishly fingered the first signs of fuzz on his upper lip, he's had mingled feelings of pride and touchiness about the whole affair.

The average husband has to make a whole great big ceremony over scraping off his whiskers. Half asleep, he staggers into the bathroom, gets out his brush, razor, soap or cream, and balances the implements precariously on the edge of the washbasin. He starts the water running, and if it's cold he yowls for hot, but if it's hot he lets it run anyhow, while he stares long and hard in the mirror to see (1) if he looks his age, and (2) if he really needs to shave, after all.

After a good three minutes of dawdling and reflection, he slaps the lather on his face at record-breaking speed. He wants not too much

242

and not too little, and only the individual knows the answer. If he's right-handed, he starts on the left side of his face, and vice versa. He goes through several dozen changes of expression, glowering head on, or with sidewise scowls, with head upraised or glaring down his nose. Why he don't scare himself silly we'll never know. He eases up a bit when he's tackling his jawbone just under the ear and when he's working over his upper lip, because those are the spots where he's most likely to cut himself. If he does carve himself, he blames everything from his wife's hurrying him to the guy who sold him the razor.

And, when he's finished, he leaves his brush, razor, soap or cream balanced on the edge of the basin and wonders where breakfast is.

Man, who hates change in everything from easy chairs to the weather, is a pushover for all kinds of shaving gadgets. He'll fall for before-shaving lotions, during-shaving lotions, and after-shaving lotions, to say nothing of talcum powders, quick shaves, brushless shaves, lathers, astringents, stroppers, holders, and blades. His wife's hopeful contribution is a box to keep the stuff in.

A man usually has three or four razors, but, like hats, he uses only one and never throws the rest away. It's a funny thing about a man; he'll spend fifty cents on a cigar, or fifty dollars on a night-club blowout, but he'll go all out to promote the life of a two-cent razor blade. He'll experiment with everything from rubbing it on the inside of the tooth glass to buying a three-dollar sharpener, just to drag it out for one more shave and then boast about it. Back around fifteen years ago, when the electric shaver came in, man cultivated a new early morning wanderlust, for now he could shave almost anywhere. He didn't have to hide in the bathroom any more. Guys took to shaving in bed, in the dining room, and down cellar—wherever there was an electric outlet.

Beards aren't the height of fashion right now, but there's never been a guy on earth who hasn't kinda hankered after having one and wondered how he'd look in a full set of chin spinach. There have been times in history when men have worn 'em, pampered 'em, dyed 'em, hennaed 'em, and woven gold thread, spangles, and pretty ribbons into 'em. Beards have been braided, curled, waxed, oiled, dusted with powder, starched, and kept in elaborate gold and jeweled beard cases. Just where man got the idea of shaving is a doubtful point, but back in the Stone Age he was hacking away at his whiskers with a piece of flint and looking into a brook for a mirror. Around the time of Alexander the Great he started shaving conscientiously, because some of the boys found out that a big, jutting, ornamental beard made a good handle to

243

catch an enemy by, and the Persians, who went in for those fancy tonsorial deals, were kinda out of luck on the battlefield.

A mustache is a lot easier and pleasanter to grow than a beard. It takes only about eight weeks to raise one to full flower, while a good husky full beard needs from four to six months. When a guy's growing a mustache, everybody knows what he's up to, and he can talk about it to his friends and get quite a lot of interesting conversation about how it's coming, and so forth, but when he's raising a beard people just think he's careless and forgot to shave. When he's mustache growing, he can roam at large, but when he's beard growing, he usually hibernates like a bear or goes on a camping trip. And there's one mystery that's never been solved, and that's why man spends half his life trying to scrape the hair off his face, and the other half trying to put it back on his head.

Just the same, if you gals think we and our shaving troubles are funny, we'd like to ask just one thing. If *you* had it to do, how would *you* make out?

DON'T BE A DICTATOR

Generally speaking, American women tend to deprecate the poor male animal until he don't know if he's coming or going. Shortly after the war a whole slew of books and magazine articles were written in an attempt to explain why the overseas soldier so often came home with a cute little package of foreign manufacture tucked under his arm. If you read some of these books and articles you probably noticed that they all boiled down to one central basic idea: the European gal is brought up to think that even though a man ain't exactly a superior being, if she can keep him thinking he is, a marriage runs like clockwork. And the funny part of it is that it works, not only in theory but in practice.

Now I'm the last person on earth to criticize American womanhood. I think that our American women are just about the smartest and trimmest and prettiest, not to mention the most intelligent and the healthiest Bedelias that there have been on earth ever since Eve bit into that fatal apple. But on this one little point I've got a bone to pick with them. They push their men around too much.

244

From the time a guy gets that first pair of three-cornered pants pinned on him, they have him boxed in. They pin things on him from there on in. They operate on their husbands and their sons and their brothers and their family friends; they even work on male business competitors and the butcher, the baker, and the candlestick maker.

It's not exactly that woman really wants to compete with man. But, finding out that she can meet him on equal grounds in the fields of business and the professions, she proceeds to swing her equality like a club. And this growing "masculine streak" in women loses them more husbands than the proverbial "other woman" ever kidnaped off their doorsteps.

By nature, men like women; they like to please them and take good care of them and if they get a word of thanks into the bargain, that's so much gravy. But how can a man exert his perfectly natural function of sheltering and coddling a woman who's determined to prove that she's more self-sufficient than he is?

No, he's the one who is "taken care of," from the cradle to the grave, by assorted relatives, mother, grandmothers, aunts, and older sisters, and finally by a wife, and later on by daughters who demonstrate clearly that Daddy is a sweet old fuddy-duddy who don't know enough to come in out of the rain, but who ain't bad at writing checks if the checkbook is shoved under his nose. These dominant females may not go out in the world and fight for their men in open battle, but in private life they wear the pants, whether pants are becoming to them or not, and the old man is reduced to a "yes, dear" and "no, dear" status. He's trained that way. The feminine dictatorship to which he's been exposed all his life makes him expect love and affection from women, and also punishment and correction. When he was a kid his mother spanked him and his Sunday school teacher told him all about what a hot place he might go if he was a bad boy, and during the week his teacher kept him in after school. And then he grows up and falls in love, and the whole business starts over again.

The poor guy is a pushover for any gal with a streak of aggressiveness in her. And nowadays the gals are aggressive. They work him over in no time flat, and it's a very unusual guy who ever gets to call his soul his own, except maybe while he's asleep and dreaming.

Of course, I don't mean all American women are like that, but enough of them are to make it pretty noticeable, especially when you compare them with women of other countries, as the G.I.s found out in short order. It's the difference between making a guy feel like a great big he-man who's wiser and smarter and handsomer than anybody else in the world, and making him feel like an underprivileged worm whose only function in life is to bring home the pay check, and why ain't he got a raise yet, anyhow? There's an old saying about catching more flies with honey than with vinegar.

There's a sixty-four-dollar word, "symbiosis," which means the process of living together to the greatest advantage of both. Nobody wants you gals to be doormats. A doormat is about the least interesting and attractive part of the household furniture. Rather, be like a hearthfire—warming, comforting, and cheery to come home to. Be a true and harmonious mate, physically as well as spiritually. The good marriage is always a symbiotic partnership, with both man and wife contributing their unique qualities to make a united whole.

It seems to be absolutely necessary to male happiness for the guy to do some strutting and crowing and peacocking around the joint. So let him, and don't laugh at him, except maybe up your sleeve, and don't belittle him, even though you think you could do his job a dozen times better . . . and maybe you could. It's smart to stay as feminine as possible. If you do, you'll find that nine times out of ten you'll have your own way without a breath of argument. Whatever you do, don't run the poor jerk down. Build him up. It can't do any harm, and you may find that what was originally very mediocre husband material may turn out to be one of the greatest guys on earth, after all.

Only God can make a man, but a wife can make—or break him.

THE GUY WITH A WHINE

I don't mind the man with a red-blooded kick at a real or fancied wrong; I can stand for the chap with the grouch if he's quick to drop it when joy comes along; I have praise for the fellow who says what he thinks, though his thoughts may not fit with mine. But spare me from having to mix with the ginks who go through the world with a whine!

I am willing to listen to a sinner or saint who is willing to fight for his rights, and there's something sometimes in an honest complaint that the soul of me really delights. For kickers are useful and grouches are wise, for their purpose is frequently fine. But spare me from having to mix with the guys who go through the world with a whine!

Anonymous

FLOWERS ON CALAMITY'S GRAVE

I don't know who wrote the following little fable. Maybe it's like the famous "Doc Brackett: Office Upstairs" story, which maybe Damon Runyon wrote, and maybe his father did, and maybe there were six other guys who worked it over before and after. But here it is, and I think you'll like it. There's a little moral tucked away in it which you may want to pass on to somebody you know who needs it.

It's a little fable about a guy named Calamity Crab Howl, believe it or not. Calamity Crab Howl was an important guy in his home town, and he admitted it. According to the census taker, he was only one man, fifty-seven years old, but Calamity classified himself as a group.

His age was really much greater than fifty-seven, because he lived everybody's life, including his own. He knew everything, especially everything that was depressing or scandalous—that is, he and his father did. His father was dead.

He could see a wolf at every door. In fact, he could see the wolves coming before they got to the door at all. He was the original loud-speaker for Old Hard Luck himself.

He never agreed with anything or anybody. One of the unsolved mysteries of the community was how he agreed with his wife long enough to marry her. He always affirmed that matrimonial alliances were failures, and he did his best to present a concrete example of that theory to his wife.

His business was insurance. How he happened to get into that line nobody knew. The town wisecracker claimed that insurance was the only thing in this world, or elsewhere, that Calamity really knew nothing whatsoever about. So, true to form, he claimed to be an insurance man.

Thereafter he was in it, but not at it. He was too busy anyway minding other people's business to pay any attention to his own, which is a common failing, of course.

He was the champion dissenter. When the sun shone, he said it was going to rain, and sooner or later it did, which made him a first-class prophet. He never said when.

When anybody started in business in the home town Calamity gave him six months, and then did his best to make his prediction become a fact.

He made a special effort to be present at the demise of as many lines of business as possible each year. He was the permanent pallbearer for retired business firms. He never minded having helped them to early oblivion.

He was such a cheerful oaf that a robust citizen in perfect health on meeting him would, in ten minutes, go home and take to his bed. That's the effect Calamity had. A fellow with a thousand dollars at eight per cent on first mortgages, farms, and other gilt-edged securities, after taking a look at Calamity and hearing him howl, would immediately snatch back his thousand and hide it in an old shoe. And that's the way it went in Howl's town.

Things were going great in other nearby districts. People were busy, money was working, and everybody was prosperous.

But one bright sunshiny day Calamity died, and the doctor that examined him said it looked to him like an extreme case of pessimism. He said Calamity's eyes were worn out looking for trouble. His feet were all shot from running down bad news. His heart was wrecked from excitement incurred in learning of impending trouble.

Calamity had been such an expert howler, and was so letter-perfect in the part, that no ordinary pessimist had the temerity to attempt to take his place. So, on his death, the town just had to get along without another gloom dispenser.

Five years after that, every street in town was paved, the bank had a surplus, and everybody carried a lot of insurance, but there were no flowers on Calamity's grave.

And that's the story. Did you ever know anybody like that? There are people who delight in bad news, and people who enjoy poor health. No matter when you ask them how they feel, they've always got something. They're ready for you. And they know when their story is wearing a little thin. After they've talked about their rheumatism for so long that you get a kind of dim look on your face when you see them coming, they develop something else, so they won't bore you with the same thing all the time.

I think we could do very well without these professional pessimists, these people who've always got something the matter with them and who can see absolutely no future in anything; who are sure that a new war is going to start up at least by tomorrow night and that the younger generation is going to the dogs. There's only one cure: refuse to listen.

They'll go away, because they're mighty bored themselves unless they have an appreciative audience.

HOW TO CLEAN YOUR MENTAL HOUSE

Long about April or May, a lot of folks are doing their spring house-cleaning jobs. But there's one big job, maybe the biggest one of all, that a lot of us neglect. That's the job of cleaning our mental houses, getting rid of all the old junk and shining the joint up to make room for a new idea or two.

I found a little piece in Margery Wilson's book, *Make Up Your Mind,* that I think maybe you'll like. It's called "How to Clean Your Mental House":

"First, brush off the dust of laziness and inaction. Be sure to dig in the corners for the cobwebs of self-justification. Use plenty of the soap of self-confidence. It shines things up right away. For stubborn spots, use the abrasive of honesty.

"Use a powerful disinfectant, like forgiveness. Then open the windows and let the breeze of joy blow it sweet and dry. Now spray everything in sight with a liquid called faith which prevents the hatching of the little moths of envy and other destructive insects that eat holes in your nicest attributes when you hardly know it. Faith also kills the eggs of that dreadful microbe, 'fear of the future.'

"Now your house will have a clean, wholesome smell, but if you want to create a more alluring atmosphere, then spray it with the perfume of content. Content is that beauty shining in the faces of lovers. It is a sense of rightness, of fulfillment. It does not say, 'I shall never want more or other than this' . . . it says, 'All's well,' instead.

"As in most housekeeping, a place is easily kept clean if a little brushing up is done every day. Try to arrange your mental house into an orderly and peaceful place every night before you go to sleep . . . you will find it an invulnerable fortress into which you can retire, and you will rise refreshed as though by magic."

I kinda like that.

WOLVES IN THE FOLD

Of course there isn't anything funny about murder. Murder is always serious and vicious. But every once in a while you read about a case that has some angles to it that are kind of ridiculous, in a grim sort of way.

The case of Laura Fair, who shot her lover on the Oakland ferry while they were crossing San Francisco Bay, back in 1870, has some queer twists that make it a gruesome little comedy, if there ever was one.

Laura was an extremely pretty blond girl from Holly Springs, Mississippi. When she was sixteen, she ran away to New Orleans and married a questionable character named William Stone, who died of cholera and too many trips through those swinging doors about a year later. Laura was brokenhearted, but she forgot her grief after two months and married Thomas J. Grayson, who made frequent trips through those swinging doors, too, and whose chief delight was banging away at Laura's bedroom wall with a six-shooter to show her what a good shot he was. One night he dragged her out of bed and made her march out to the hen coop, where he dispatched fifty chickens, one after another, trying to prove he was a great hand with a revolver.

Well, Laura found all this a little too noisy and disturbing, so she left Mr. Grayson and ran away to San Francisco, where, after getting a kind of shaky divorce from the sharpshooter, she married a Colonel William D. Fair. Colonel Fair didn't pan out too well either. After two years of married life he blew his brains out.

So there was Laura, a beautiful young blond widow with a year-old baby girl and no money whatsoever. She went to Sacramento and tried to run a boardinghouse, but it failed. She got a couple of minor jobs in the theater on the strength of her looks, but she couldn't act for sour apples.

Well, about that time the great Comstock Lode was discovered in Virginia City, and Laura headed there, and opened a hotel which, for once, was successful. But very soon something happened to take Laura's mind off her business. She met a handsome, dignified family man named Alexander Parker Crittenden, a regular Kentucky colonel type, the father of seven children and grandfather of two or three more. Crittenden was devoted to his wife. The only trouble was that he forgot to mention to Laura that he had a wife at all.

When Laura found out about Mrs. Crittenden, she started asking some very pointed questions. Mr. Crittenden said everything was going to be all right, because he was going to get his Clara to give him a divorce. And for seven solid years he strung Laura along, with bland promises that he was getting the divorce, that Clara was getting it, and that it wouldn't be long now before he was free to marry her.

Laura had a very pretty face and a cute figure and a blond "follow-me-lad" curl draped over her shoulder and he couldn't give all those things up, nohow. And he couldn't give up his plump, comfortable little Clara, the ever-loving wife of some twenty-odd years, who ran his house and mothered him, along with the seven kids. So he tried working both ends against the middle, and the affair came out about the way those things always do; it came out bad.

Sometimes he took both gals out to dinner, at one of the fashionable San Francisco restaurants. They'd all moved to San Francisco by that time. It didn't look good, or make anybody very happy, but he did it. That guy must have thought he could get away with anything. Laura would come over and visit the Crittendens during the evening, and then she'd go home, and Crittenden would get his Clara all tucked in bed and asleep, and he'd sneak out and go over to Laura's place, returning at dawn and crawling in beside the slumbering Clara, who never dreamed that her husband had been out tomcatting around all night.

Laura got pretty sore a few times, because she couldn't see that she was getting any closer to marrying Crittenden. She packed up and went to Havana for a trip, and then she actually accompanied Crittenden on a trip to Virginia, where he was supposed to get a divorce put through in a hurry, but his plans fell through. Laura didn't scold; she just went out and bought herself a gun, a small, ladylike little gun she could carry in her handbag.

About 1867, Laura noticed the trousseau she'd bought to marry Crittenden in was getting out of style, so as not to waste nothing, she up and married Jesse W. Snyder, who seems to have been a very patient guy, because he never complained about her going right on spending her time and attentions on Mr. Crittenden.

Well, things stayed pretty much on an even keel for three years. And then, in 1870, Mrs. Crittenden went East to visit her family, and Crittenden came around and told Laura that now Clara was gone for good, and she was to get a divorce from Snyder right away, and they'd be married immediately.

So Laura got her divorce from Snyder, who took the whole thing lying down. And she got a new trousseau ready, and Crittenden was more attentive and loving than ever, but Laura just happened to hear that he was furnishing a beautiful new house for Clara as a homecoming present. In fact, Clara and the kids were already on the way home.

So Laura put her little gun in her pocketbook and went down to meet the ferry which would bring Clara over from Oakland. When she saw the touching reconciliation of husband and wife, she drilled Mr. Crittenden as neatly as her second husband, Mr. Grayson, used to drill chickens.

Laura was tried and convicted, but she demanded a retrial and got it, and this time the verdict came in "Not guilty" by reason of emotional insanity. And it wasn't long before Laura hit on a way to turn her disastrous adventure to a profitable business. She traveled around giving a lecture, the title of which was "Wolves in the Fold," concerning her own case and the perils of an innocent young girl alone in the wicked world, generally speaking. After she worked that one to the bone, she had various jobs, as a practical nurse and a housekeeper and one thing and another, and she died at the age of eighty-two, still cheerful and active to the end of her days, and still landing on the front page of the newspaper every once in a while, when she did something like suing somebody for a huge amount because of supposed libel, or making a spectacular attempt to kill herself, or some little thing like that. Laura, whatever else you may think of her, was a colorful character.

YOU TELL ON YOURSELF

You tell on yourself by the friends you seek,
By the very manner in which you speak,
By the way you employ your leisure time,
And by the way you use a dollar, or dime.

You tell what you are by the things you wear,
By the spirit in which your burdens you bear,
By the kind of things at which you laugh,
By the records you play on the phonograph.

You tell what you are by the way you walk,
By the things of which you delight to talk,
By the manner in which you bear defeat,
By so simple a thing as how you eat.

By the books you choose from a well-filled shelf,
In these ways, and more, you tell on yourself.
So, there's really no particle of sense,
In an effort to keep up false pretense.

Anonymous

WATCHING A HABIT GROW

You know, one of the silliest statements anybody can make, and one
which is made fairly often by reasonably bright people, is that crack
about "I never allow myself to form habits. The moment I find I have
the beginnings of a habit I break it at once."

Well, of course that's even more ridiculous than it sounds right off.
Because if we didn't have any habits at all, we'd be as helpless as newborn babies—even more helpless, because babies start acquiring useful
habits from the first moment of birth. Some authorities in this field claim
that some habits are acquired even before birth. If we had no habits, we
couldn't walk or talk or feed ourselves; we probably couldn't swallow
our food, and if we could, our stomach wouldn't have the habit of di-
gesting it. What those dopey people who say they refuse to have habits
really mean is that they feel kinda superior to other folks because they
consciously avoid forming some little obvious habit that's no trick to
make or to break, and they get all set up about this and have to keep
yakking it up until everybody wishes this person would run afoul of a
great big bogeyman habit that would swallow him, feathers and all.
He's got only a few million habits he don't know about. If he didn't
have, he wouldn't be living, because breathing is kind of a habit, too.

Not long ago I learned kind of a cute way to teach yourself a simple habit in short order, and then find out how it feels to break it. You may not have time to do this now, but remember the simple rules and try it out sometime. I think you'll get a little surprise. All you need is a pad of scratch paper and a pencil and a mirror.

First draw a good-sized five-pointed star on a piece of paper. Draw it as neatly and evenly as you can. Then tear off that sheet of paper and draw another, and keep going till you've done this maybe fifteen or twenty times. You'll find that you draw faster and faster as your muscles acquire the habit of drawing five-pointed stars. Make each star on a separate piece of paper. You don't need to waste the paper, you can use the other side for grocery lists or figuring out your taxes or something.

Now take a mirror and prop it up in front of you and take a piece of paper and the pencil, and hold up a piece of cardboard so you can't see what you're doing directly, but you have a clear view of your hand and the pencil and paper in the mirror. Now try to draw a star. You can't do it. You absolutely can't. So take one of the stars you drew and try to trace around it. There's the star. All you have to do is follow the lines you drew in a couple of seconds, only now you're looking in the mirror. I'll give you about five minutes of concentrated effort to get around the outline of that star, and the muscles of your arm will knot up till they hurt. You'll pretty near go nuts, because the pencil is glued to the paper; you can't push and you can't pull. But keep it up, and try another and another. Each one will get easier. By the time you've traced around the twentieth one, you can probably do it in ten or fifteen seconds; not as fast as you could draw if you were looking directly at it, but pretty fast.

And now that you've learned the habit of drawing a star, and unlearned it by drawing mirror-fashion, take a piece of paper and draw a star the regular way. You may draw something—but it won't be star-shaped. About this time you'll be sorry you ever paid attention to me in the first place, but you'll have learned something real interesting about yourself. In the space of less than an hour you've learned a habit, unlearned it by learning an opposite one, and now, whichever way you try to draw the star, it's a mess. By tomorrow your muscles will stop being confused and you can draw a nice neat star again, but right now you're in a complete state of being all snarled up. I think it's kind of an interesting little experiment, and if you ever had any cockiness about breaking habits, it'll take it out of you.

NAPOLEON AS A HUSBAND

It's a well-known fact that a great many famous men who've spent their lives in the limelight have had very unhappy private lives. Of course, I don't mean that just because a guy is famous his home life is bound to go on the rocks, but somehow it works out that way often enough to be real noticeable. Maybe we just pay more attention to the details, especially the gruesome details, when a guy's name is in the news. Maybe that's a way of working out our own envious desire for fame and fortune. I dunno. But the records show that a lot of very important Joes have been mighty poor husband material, and nothing to take home to Momma to show her what a good picker you are. And yet the gals are wild to marry these guys. After they get 'em, they're just wild, and with good reason.

Take Napoleon, for instance. He had two wives, and any number of more or less hectic romances, and there never was a woman who got real well acquainted with him who wasn't crazy in love with him to start with, and equally frantic to call the deal off and get shut of him real soon afterward. Apparently Bonaparte didn't wear well, and we know the reasons why. Marie Louise, his second wife, set 'em all down in her diary.

In addition to being an absolute dictator in his home as well as in his country, Napoleon had any number of irritating little habits. He prowled around the palace most of the night; he had keys to every door, and if he felt like talking to somebody he just opened their bedroom door, walked in, woke them up, and started talking, usually telling them off in a tone of voice that could be heard ten blocks down the street. If he wasn't dressing somebody down, he spent the wee small hours pacing the corridors and singing at the top of his voice, and he couldn't carry a tune in a basket. He cracked his knuckles loudly and constantly, and he loved to pick up a poker and bang it on the fire irons until you'd think the whole chimney would fall in. Those were just some of his peculiarities. If he was fond of a person, man, woman, or child, he took delight in pinching them, pulling their hair and nose and ears, and since he wouldn't have anybody around that he didn't like well enough to pinch, his entire court was always covered with black-and-blue marks.

Somebody said once that all the crowns of Europe couldn't make Napoleon into a gentleman. Although he was extremely fussy about his clothes, his personal habits were slovenly, and wherever he went he left a trail of mess and disorder. No matter how many servants there were to pick up after him, the place was always untidy. Napoleon hung his clothes on the floor, ate his meals standing up, threw the bones to the dogs, and all I can say is that it's a good thing he didn't chew tobacco. He wouldn't have found the right place to put that, either.

Life with his first wife, Josephine, was a continual Donnybrook. Napoleon did have a kind of casual good nature which made him shower his wives and sweethearts with extravagant presents, but he wanted to do the showering. He didn't want them running up bills on him, and Josephine was a gal who knew how to run up bills. Contemporary records say that the screaming and hollering that went on was something scandalous. Divorce was inevitable.

Marie Louise, the timid Austrian princess who became the Emperor's second wife, ran away from him after a few years of married life, and afterwards described her life with him as "a bad dream." She said it was "slavery" and that she "was afraid of him." He used to make her go without food until she was ill with a headache, and then tell her that "women should never want to eat." Actually, he wasn't being cruel, just thoughtless. He himself ate very sparingly and often went a whole day without so much as a swallow of water, and he thought it proper for his wife to eat when, as, and if he did, and at no other time. He insisted on long walks, sometimes at night or in the rain; Marie Louise was always subject to rheumatism, but if she stopped to get a cloak to keep the rain off he went into a fury. As like as not, he'd keep her up until three in the morning reading to him, and then wake her up at four saying to get ready in ten minutes, they were going out hunting. And when Napoleon said "hunting" he meant just that. He didn't come home till he'd gotten the game he'd gone after, and if Marie Louise had to spend a couple of days and nights in the saddle that was okay with him. He was a soldier, and used to it.

One time that he was put out with Marie Louise, he took her for an all-night drive in a carriage with every window open and the rain pouring in, just because she suggested that it was a bad night and she felt a cold coming on. Next morning she wrote in her diary that all men were insufferable and if she should ever be born on earth a second time she certainly wouldn't marry again. On another occasion when they were walking along a beach in Belgium and the waves gave her a good soaking unexpected-like, he refused to let her change her wet clothes and as a result she got a fever. That time she wrote mildly in her diary, "I really do not know what has become of my iron constitution; it seems to have disappeared entirely."

And here's another revealing sentence: "I dread nothing more than to see the Emperor angry with me, but would sooner die than give him the pleasure of seeing my pain by crying on account of his reproaches, so I restrain my grief until he is out of the room."

In between these violent scenes there was love-making just as violent. Marie wrote that when the Emperor came into a room where she was she never knew if he would pinch her and pull her hair because he was full of exuberant affection or because he was punishing her—and it hurt just as much either way.

So if your old man has been kinda getting out of hand lately, and you're beginning to think that some drastic changes have gotta be made or you can't stand it any longer, take comfort in the thought that he's probably about a thousand per cent better than any number of guys who've made their mark in the world, but around the house they've been just one big mistake. And that goes for kings and emperors, great scientists, great musicians, and almost any great you can think of. Probably the best thing for a gal to do is to settle for that Joe down the block—the one with the freckles and the good disposition. He may be no ball of fire, but at least he's housebroken, and guys like Napoleon weren't.

SOME REASONS WHY I GO TO CHURCH

You ask me why I go to church?
I give my mind a careful search.
Because I need to breathe the air
Where there's an atmosphere of prayer;
I need the hymns the churches sing—
They set my faith and hope a-wing;
They keep old truths in memory green,
Reveal the worth of things unseen.

Because my neighbor needs to go—
His faith in right is rather low.
He needs the church to hold him fast

To those great truths that always last;
And when he sees me on my way,
It draws him to the church to pray,
And both our hearts are lifted up
To heavenly places where we sup.

Because my boy is watching me
To note whatever he can see
That tells him what his father thinks,
And with his eager soul he drinks
The things I do in daily walk,
The things I say in daily talk;
If I with him the church will share,
My son will make his friendships there.

Because the church builds up the state,
Breaks down the barriers of hate,
And helps to spread unselfish life,
Allay all bickering and strife;
Sustains a wholesome public health,
And builds a righteous commonweath—
A joyous place in which to live
With all the blessings God can give.

Anonymous

BASTA, THE CAT

If you ever happened to see a statue of one of those ancient Egyptian
cats, the kind the boys thought were sacred, back in the days of the
Pharaohs, you've probably noticed that they don't look like ordinary
cats. You've doubtless seen 'em; there isn't an art museum in the country that hasn't got at least one, or, if you didn't happen to meet one of
these critters, you've seen a picture of such a statue somewhere, and
sorta wondered if they were the same kind of cat that we have around
nowadays. Well, as a matter of fact, they are and they aren't. They
don't look the same; they're sort of longer and slinkier, and their necks
are longer and their heads smaller in proportion, and their yellow fur
is much shorter and stiffer than most kitties', and somehow or other,
even though all cats are kinda uncanny, the Egyptian cats are even
more so.

Oh yes, they have plenty of them today, alive in Egypt. The original Egyptian cat was the first cat; in fact, the historians say, the very first animal to get friendly with man and become domesticated. In the days of the Pharaohs these early ancestors of cats were actually worshiped, as incarnations of the goddess Bubastis, and if a cat died she was mummified and buried with solemn rites, and all the men of the household shaved off their eyebrows and sat around wailing and beating their breasts in anguish. Today, in modern Egypt, it's considered very unlucky to hurt a cat; and in Cairo and other cities hundreds and hundreds of cats are fed every day at public expense. They say they feed poor pussy because she's so useful in killing off rats and mice, but superstition hangs on a long time. These same early Egyptian cats were imported into Greece and Italy by the Phoenician traders, and there they mixed with the smaller native wild cats, and after hundreds of years passed, traders from China brought oriental cats into the breed . . . and that's how our domestic tabbies and toms developed.

The English naturalist and novelist, Arthur Weigall, had a pureblooded Egyptian cat for a pet during the time he lived in Egypt, and this cat, which he called Basta, had some weird little habits that could be counted uncanny even among Egyptian cats. If you lifted her off a chair, she'd jump right back on and then very deliberately get down of her own accord, just to let you know she couldn't be bossed around. There was a square slab of stone out on the lawn which had once been part of an altar to the ancient sun god, and Arthur Weigall used to have a good deal of trouble keeping servants when Basta was with him, because they were scared green by her daily habit of depositing a mouse on this slab and then sitting and gazing raptly straight into the sun, like an old-time priestess at an altar.

This habit of Basta's led to more than one unfortunate episode. Not only did she terrify the more superstitious natives within an inch of their lives, but, one day when a dignified and famous archaeologist came to call, and Weigall was using this square stone slab as a sort of outdoor table for refreshments, Basta deposited a small mouse on the archaeologist's plate alongside some fresh dates. As it happens, nobody noticed her, and this archaeologist was extremely nearsighted, so the mouse was almost into his mouth before he saw what it was, and flung it into the air with a bloodcurdling yelp that echoed up and down the Nile.

Well, Weigall tried to explain that the cat put it there, but the archaeologist gent thought some sort of schoolboy trick was being

259

played on him, and he angrily snatched up his hat, which lay beside him in the grass, unaware that the mouse had landed in it. As he clapped it on his head, the mouse tumbled out into the front of his loose silk shirt and slipped down inside.

At this point the poor man more or less went mad, dancing up and down and howling and, in the process, stepping on Basta, who promptly dug her claws into his leg. The pain of this final indignity did the trick; the mouse shook loose, and Basta calmly let go her hold on the archaeologist's leg, picked up her unwanted offering, and departed with the same dignity with which she had come on the scene in the first place—a dignity which was entirely lacking, at that moment, in either man who had taken part in the scene.

Weigall reported that not long after this incident Basta fell in love with one of the wild cats who lived in the trees beyond his garden wall, and, sorry as he was to see her leave, at least he didn't have mouse trouble any more.

LOVE AT FIRST SIGHT

An awful lot of poems and stories have been written about love at first sight. To listen to the poets, you'd think that love at first sight is the greatest thing going, but the boys who mess around with psychology and behaviorism don't agree with that at all. They're of the opinion that love at first sight isn't real love at all.

For instance, they say that if some older couple, who have been happily married a long time, talk about having fallen in love at first sight—well, that couple just don't know what they're talking about. If it makes them happy to think so, that's all right, but it just ain't true. What really happened is that they liked each other at first sight, and every time they met they liked each other better, until the thing blossomed into true love and they lived happy ever after. Their liking turned into love after it stood the tests of time, of occasional situations that maybe weren't quite so agreeable as they might be, of all the big and little humps and bumps that life deals out. But as far as that love-at-first-sight and floating-on-Cloud-Seven stuff goes, it very, very rarely pans out. But it's a phase most people go through.

For instance, if you happen to be the mother of a twenty-year-old boy, old enough to be through with puppy love but not yet quite settled down in life, and he busts into the house after his first date with a new girl and gasps out: "Mom . . . she's gorgeous . . . she's got everything . . . she's dreamy stuff for sure, and it's love at first sight!" —if he does that, you don't have anything to worry about. Chances are, after the second or third date he'll suddenly notice that she's kind of a funny-lookin' Bedelia and there are some things she just ain't quite bright about. Or if your grown-up but not yet married daughter goes all moony over some guy she's only seen once, stick around and she'll get over it.

There's a very simple reason for this, and that is that nobody is perfect. But everybody has a kind of dream image of his or her ideal, and that dream image is the sum total of everybody you've ever admired from afar, plus all the books you've read and the movies you've seen and the daydreams you've cooked up for yourself. So a young person who hasn't knocked around enough to know the dream from the reality meets someone new who has one or two qualities just like the dream image he's built up, and right away he takes a nose dive in her direction, and doesn't even notice the things about her that aren't the least bit like his ideal. In fact, in the state he's in, he'd get very sore if anybody tried to point out that the gal isn't exactly perfect. And if it just happens that he's a little bit unhappy, and doesn't feel sufficiently appreciated at home, or in his job, or at school, he may drift along in his blissful self-delusion until it's too late. If he wakes up and finds out he's married to a complete stranger and then he tries forcing the gal to live up to the image he has created as the girl of his dreams, it's no good. That way, everybody's unhappy. And it isn't the gal's fault; she didn't even know what was going on. Maybe she's got the same problem in her attitude toward him.

"Love at first sight" is just an intense and impulsive emotional reaction to very fragmentary impressions. It has to be tested by many and frequent meetings, and it has to come down out of the clouds and take root in reality before it's worth much; certainly before it's worth marrying. If we stopped believing in love at first sight, except as it crops up in romantic literature, we might be able to do something about that shocking divorce rate—one out of every three marriages headed for a smashup.

THE TRUE MEASURE OF A MAN

The place to take the true measure of a man is not in the darkest place, or in the amen corner, nor the cornfield, but his own fireside. There he lays aside his mask and you may learn whether he is an imp or an angel, cur or King, hero or humbug. I care not what the world says of him; whether it crowns him boss or pelts him with bad eggs. I care not a copper what his reputation or religion may be if his babies dread his homecoming and his better half swallows her heart every time she has to ask him for a five-dollar bill, he is a fraud of the first water even though he prays night and morning until he is black in the face and howls hallelujah until he shakes the eternal hills. But if his children rush to the front door to meet him and love's sunshine illuminates the face of his wife every time she hears his footfall, you can take it for granted that he is pure, for his home is a heaven—and the humbug never gets that near the throne of God. He may be a rank atheist and a red flag anarchist, or a mugwump, he may buy votes in blocks of five and bet on the elections; he may deal them from the bottom of the deck and drink beer until he can't tell a silver dollar from a circular saw and still be an infinitely better man than the cowardly humbug who is all suavity in society but who makes home a hell, who vents upon the helpless heads of his wife and children an ill nature he would inflict upon his fellowmen but dares not. We can forgive much in that fellow mortal who would rather make men swear than women weep; who would rather have the hate of the whole world than the contempt of his wife; who would rather call anger to the eyes of a King than fear to the face of a child.

W. C. Brann

THE WOMAN WHO TRIED TO BE PRESIDENT

There was a pretty interesting woman who popped into the limelight in this country right after the Civil War, and she held the limelight for over five years, and to this day, long after she is dead and gone, nobody knows whether she was an extremely clever Bedelia or a prime screwball. Sometimes she acted like a mixture of both.

This gal's name was Mrs. Victoria Woodhull, and she blew into New

York in the fall of 1869, without Mr. Woodhull, who don't seem to have figured in the picture at all, but with her sister, Mrs. Tennessee Claflin, who was just as smart, or as screwy, as she was.

Mrs. Woodhull has been described as a picturesque but bedraggled bird of paradise. She was exquisitely beautiful, with a slightly faded opulent beauty that made her even more attractive than if she had been in the full flush of youth; at least, that's how some of the tycoons of the time, like Commodore Vanderbilt and Gould and Astor, felt about her. And, before her extraordinary career was done, she'd managed to drag everybody she knew into that limelight we mentioned, with her, and sometimes the limelight wasn't such a pretty color.

Victoria and her sister, Tennessee, were astonishingly clever at making money. They operated a broker's office, and once they made half a million bucks in a single transaction, on a tip from Commodore Vanderbilt. However, quite a few shady deals passed through that office, too, and there were shady deals aplenty in the years right after the Civil War. The girls were joint editors of *Woodhull and Claflin's Weekly,* a magazine crammed with brilliant writing which just skirted the edges of respectability. They were both avowedly in favor of free love, and they were both mystics. Victoria had a "spirit control" named Demosthenes, who was supposed to dictate the clever editorials in her magazine, but it's more likely they were written by General Benjamin Butler, who had more than a passing fancy for the pretty lady.

And, to top everything off, Victoria scouted around and dug herself up a political party—it was called the National Radical Reformers' Party—and managed to nominate herself for President of the United States, on a platform of everything free: free love, free trade, free suffrage, government-guaranteed employment for all, and a new federal Constitution, which Victoria was going to write when she got elected.

Either the general public is awful credulous, or it gets fascinated easy by pure crazyness, but Victoria managed to keep the pot boiling briskly. She seems to have been half squirrel and the other half wildcat. In a day when Susan B. Anthony and the other women's rights leaders had their hands full, she was a horrible example, according to the men, of what could happen if women got any political power. But, at the same time they were accusing her of dreadful deeds, they fell in love with her by the carload. And she had an uncomfortable little habit of boasting about her love affairs with prominent citizens, so after a while it got so that if Victoria didn't have a scandal to tell on a man, it was sort of an indication that he wasn't very important in those parts.

It would take a whole book to tell some of the messes she got herself and her friends into, so I'll just give one of them the once over lightly. Henry Ward Beecher, who was famous for his eloquence in the pulpit, got himself pretty badly involved with a gal named Elizabeth Tilton, the wife of a close friend of his. Her husband, Theodore Tilton, was willing to forgive but not forget, and he took his wife back, but he kept reminding her every so often of her indiscretion with Henry Ward Beecher. As it happened, both Mrs. Tilton and Beecher were friends of Victoria's, and they sobbed out the story of their star-crossed love on her sympathetic shoulder. Victoria thought it was just too, too sad and beautiful: this great man and this courageous little woman trapped by convention when they ought to be enjoying the privilege of free love, unencumbered by the shadow of Mr. Tilton. So she asked Demosthenes, her spirit control, what he thought about it, and Demosthenes agreed with her. And so she published the whole thing, naming names, and adding all sorts of lurid little details of her own, in her weekly magazine.

Copies of *Woodhull and Claflin's Weekly* were selling for forty dollars apiece before the day was out, and an outraged member of Beecher's congregation, who happened also to be a United States district attorney, clapped Victoria and her sister into jail, and the Beecher-Tilton affair roared into an unsavory trial in the New York courts. So poor old Henry Ward Beecher, who'd been eminently respectable all his life, except for just this one slip, got his reputation all gummed up, and Victoria ogled the judge until he let her and her sister off, and everybody was unhappy, especially the Tiltons, who had no use for one another whatsoever by this time.

When you read about things like that, it makes our doings seem pretty tame nowadays.

After about 1874, Victoria sorta calmed down a little, because she was losing her looks, if not her ability to make mischief. Years passed, while she amused herself by usurping the floor at political rallies and talking a mile a minute about nothing until she either succeeded in breaking up the gathering or the police were summoned to put her out. She became a drab, shrill-voiced, rather pathetic old body . . . pathetic, that is, if you didn't know who she was. If you did, you lit out for the high hills until she moved on, because even when she got real old Victoria was still half squirrel and half wildcat, and nobody ever knew what impossible thing she'd do next.

LEARN TO LOOK FOR SURPRISES

That book, *Don't Be Afraid,* by Dr. Edward Spencer Cowles, has a real good section on surprises which is worth a bit of your attention. I dunno if you've ever thought much about how the element of surprise can practically make over your life, but the Doc has gone into this subject real thoroughly, and I think what he has to say makes sense.

He says that the reason why so many young folks, and older ones, too, act kinda torpid and fed up with life, why they feel that life is dull and there's nothing to look forward to, why they contemplate and sometimes commit suicide, is just this: they never learned to look for surprises. Dr. Cowles says there's something actually called "the law of surprises," and by the operation of this law, surprises happen. And they happen to everybody. "No today is so fixed that tomorrow cannot be quite different and next week as different from that which now surrounds you as the landscape of Peru from that of Pennsylvania."

This surprise-creating element makes life continuously worth living. At the very moment that you're trapped and helpless in some intolerable situation, *something* happens, and you're immediately set free. Now, it's possible that the something which happens may make things even worse, but at least you've got a fighting chance that it'll make them better. Suppose you miss the train that you absolutely had to catch, or else. While you wait for the next one, it's conceivable that you'll get into a conversation with a total stranger and as a result the whole course of your life will change for the better. Such surprises, or opportunities for surprises, come to us every day by a hundred different routes. Occasionally one of them latches on and then things are all changed for us. It's kinda like the maple tree that showers down thousands upon countless seeds every year, out of which three or four take root and maybe one gets to be a tree.

Now, unless you have a philosophy of life, and, in fact, a philosophy of fixed optimistic opinions, these surprises pass by like wind and water. You're ready to give up living. You're a dead duck from there on in, because you're blind to the possibility of life being full of pleasant surprises. All you can see is the effort and the unpleasantness, and just being alive ain't worth it.

265

But if you've been taught from childhood to look for good surprises—the unexpected piece of candy, the picnic that was scrabbled up in a hurry and was more fun than if it had been planned long ahead, the new dress or the new bicycle—all these happy surprises and only one little measly disappointment! What a difference it makes when you look at it that way!

If you know in your heart that it is possible for gloomy forebodings to turn into happy events, if you have seen dull days become bright ones, if you have that conviction rooted in you, you won't have much trouble. If you don't have it, and you want to achieve mental freedom from fear and worry, learn to look for surprises. Remember that Friday is a bad-luck day because men started taking notice of certain dark events that happened on that day. The thirteenth of the month is supposed to be hard luck for the same reason. The boys looked for something kinda horrible in the way of luck on the thirteenth of every month, and if you look hard enough for a thing, especially a thing like hard luck, you'll be pretty sure to find it. They could just as well have looked for and kept track of the good things that happened on the thirteenth, and the record would probably have been ten to one on the bright side. An awful lot more good things happen to people than bad things, only the bad ones stand out more.

You can count on your surprises to come and perch on your doorstep, but when they do the next move is up to you. All you have to do is open the door and let them in, and the old, bad conditions will break down pronto. Don't let your surprises languish outside the door. Make the most of them. Almost every one of them is all to the good.

I KNOW SOMETHING GOOD ABOUT YOU

Wouldn't this old world be better
If the folks we meet would say,
"I know something good about you,"
And then treat us just that way?

Wouldn't it be fine and dandy,
If each handclasp warm and true
Carried with it this assurance—
I know something good about you?

Wouldn't life be lots more happy
If the good that's in us all
Was the only thing about us
That folks bothered to recall?

Wouldn't life be lots more happy
If we praised the good we see,
For there's such a lot of goodness
In the worst of you and me.

Wouldn't it be nice to practice
That fine way of thinking, too,
You know something good about me,
And I know something good about you.

Anonymous

HOW TO CATCH ONE

I suppose people, especially young people, spend more time and trouble figuring out ways for boy to meet girl, and boy to hang onto girl, or vice versa, than on any other one thing. That problem of how to catch the eye of the nice boy down the street, or how to get the girl you've danced with a few times into the mood to go dancing through life with you is mighty important, not to mention that it supports more dress shops and beauty parlors and candy factories than you could shake a stick at.

Dr. Clifford R. Adams, that up-and-coming psychologist and marriage counselor, has figured out a set of rules for the girls to use when they want to make it known that they have marriage on the mind, and for the boys to paste in their hats when they go a-courting. Dr. Adams doesn't say these rules will guarantee results, but he says they sure make prospects sit up and take notice.

First, let's name over a few things a girl can do to set the wedding bells a-ringing:

1. She can talk about the man's basic needs, such as good food, comfortable furniture, fireplaces glowing with friendly light, slippers laid out to get warm, a nice home to bring his friends to. She has to talk about these things in an optimistic way, and never, never mention

drawbacks like bills and cleaning the furnace. They say returned veterans go for this line because their disrupted life has given them a profound desire to settle down with creature comforts.

2. She can appeal to the guy's yearning for mastery. She can let him do most of the talking, approve all his ideas, and fall in with his plans. She must skip over any mistakes he makes, keep her complaints to herself, and show that she's having a wonderful time on dates, even if she doesn't think much of his choice of places to go and things to do.

3. She must make herself extremely attractive in appearance.

4. She must never discuss illness or hard luck or her possible knack of blundering into awkward situations or troubles.

5. She must let the boy get the impression that plenty of other guys are interested in her, but they don't interest her nearly as much as he does.

6. She must not run down other girls.

7. She must make it clear that she is sure he is popular, and very successful in his work.

8. She ought to talk casually about her married friends, and get over the idea that these friends have been terribly happy ever since they got hitched.

9. She should make every date real fun—keep it light and gay.

10. And, finally, she shouldn't be afraid to show the guy that she likes and trusts him, and cares how he feels about her.

Well, that's the findings for the gals with a matrimonial gleam in their eye. That routine is supposed to hog-tie the victim and get him before the altar in no time flat.

And here's what Dr. Adams says the boys can do to fascinate a girl right into holding a lily-of-the-valley bouquet and soulfully breathing the fatal words:

1. Find out what she's feeling inferior about. Everybody feels inferior about something. And then angle his compliments accordingly. Maybe she's self-conscious about thick ankles or mousy hair. Word the compliment so that the girl gets so grateful she'll want you around just so she can sit and listen to the nice things you say.

2. The guy should be romantic . . . if it kills him. Things like Valentine's Day were practically invented by wimmenfolks. So he has to remember anniversaries and make much out of sentimental tokens and such, even if they don't mean a thing to him.

3. He can play on her longing for security, show her pictures of houses in the magazines, tell her about the great future he has in his

job, and, if she happens to be employed, talk about her job, too—not exactly running it down, but emphasizing how hard she has to work and how pleasant life in a vine-covered cottage or a three-room flat could be. He mustn't mention dishwashing or any other housekeeping tasks. This is a dream house where nothing ever gets dirty or out of place . . . as if she'd believe it. But, if she likes him, she will!

4. He should be self-assured and just a bit masterful. Women like to be swooped up and whisked away and relieved of all their problems.

5. He must be considerate and gentle and be very careful about all the little politeness deals that he usually doesn't fuss with. Women are impressed by etiquette.

6. He must never mention any worries he has about his job.

7. He should let the idea sorta leak out that he's in a marrying state of mind and there are quite a few cuties who are more than a little interested in him.

Now, I don't know if I'm doing right in broadcasting this here set of rules. I don't know if the world is ready for this stuff. Maybe Dr. Adams is causing a matrimonial rush that's only equaled by the California miners back in '49. Back where I was raised, a gal who was weak and wistful and a boy whom nobody understood could be figured to get closer together than ham 'n' eggs. But maybe times have changed. You have to do all your courtin' by a set of psychological rules. All I thought it took was a few evenings, a-settin' on the porch swing and holdin' hands. We weren't so scientific back when I went a-courtin', but we sure got results.

BE POLITE TO THE KIDS

Did you ever notice how often older people are rude to kids? They don't mean anything by it, and they probably don't even realize that they are, but they'll say things to small fry that they'd get—and expect— a poke in the kisser for if they tried it on anybody their size. I don't mean the things parents have to say in bringing up the kids, or the rules and regulations teachers have to keep in school. I mean downright disrespect for the rights and privileges of one human being to another, as frequently exhibited toward children by grownups who should know better.

It's like the old yarn about the professor who was accosted by a little bootblack who wanted to shine his shoes. The professor was a little disgusted by the fact that the boy's face was kinda dirty.

"I don't want a shine, my lad," he said, "but if you'll go and wash your face I'll give you a dime."

So the kid said okay, and he went over to a drinking fountain and washed his face, and came back looking cleaner, and the professor said: "Here, boy. You've earned your dime."

"I don't want your dime," said the kid. "Hang onto it and get yourself a haircut sometime."

And yet we expect kids to be very smart and very kind and considerate and pleasant and courteous to everybody. There's something wrong someplace.

THE PEEPHOLE LIFE

I guess every one of us knows some busybody who spends all his or her time taking a disapproving interest in other people's business, especially if that business can have a whiff of scandal read into it. Usually this busybody is an older person who doesn't have normal outlets for the very normal impulses that everybody has, so he or she takes it out in spying on others, in gossip and talebearing, and all too often in writing poison-pen letters or making anonymous telephone calls that cause plenty of unhappiness all around.

Dr. George Lawton, in his book, *Aging Successfully*, makes a pretty thorough analysis of these "unofficial and self-appointed old women of both sexes" who spend their time witch hunting and are only happy if they can sniff out a bit of scandal. He says that this sort of thing happens when normal human impulses are denied satisfaction and the person who is so denied is either too stubborn or too stupid to find indirect satisfactions which are, so to speak, harmless and socially acceptable.

Now, we have many major physical and mental needs, and anybody who's emotionally mature knows that one of these needs is sex. But, whether through circumstances or choice, a lot of people never find the right life partner. Hence, they never marry, or if they do, they're not very happy in their marriage.

270

Taking it for granted that the ideal state is a happy marriage, it does not follow that the unmarried or unhappily married person will become maladjusted or even insane, as some of the early psychologists believed. Nor does it follow that sex is a cure for psychological disorders of any sort.

The person who doesn't find direct satisfaction for normal, healthy impulses will doubtless find indirect satisfactions which serve just about as well. The unmarried teacher who finds great satisfaction in her class work and who takes a personal interest in the pupils and rejoices in their successes and sorrows in their failures is just exactly as happy and useful and well adjusted a person as she would be if she married and had children of her own to take an interest in. Nursing and medicine and social work, indeed, any absorbing job that deals with human relations, will serve just as well. Friendships and close family ties and a healthy interest in romantic movies and novels and radio programs are perfectly harmless substitutes for idyllic happiness, and to some degree, they work out all right.

But when a man or woman is deprived of normal satisfactions and he or she starts taking an abnormal interest in the affairs, particularly the love affairs, of other people, they better start taking stock of themselves. They're well on the way to turning into busybodies and peephole watchers who devote long, loving, and venomous hours to observing and recounting the escapades of the young and the not so young. Dr. Lawton says that the life of such a searcher for juicy scandal would be empty indeed if everybody around him was absolutely pure and antiseptic.

He tells about one woman who came to his psychological clinic to complain about a gal who lived in the same apartment house where she and her husband resided. "The most awful things go on in that apartment!" she wailed to Dr. Lawton. "Why, I just bought a pair of binoculars, and I can see through a window a hundred feet away, as close as though it were right in the next room! And, speaking of what goes on in the next room, why last night I heard——"

"Wait a minute," said Dr. Lawton. "You mustn't judge people by a chance word . . ."

"Chance word!" she snorted. "Those walls are as thin as tissue paper; all I have to do is keep my ear tight against one of them and I can hear everything!"

Well, the young girl she was spying on with the binoculars and the couple next door were equally innocent of any wrongdoing whatsoever, but her unhealthy curiosity and imagination had put a highly colored interpretation upon nothing at all.

Dr. Lawton records another case—this one is really astonishing—of a single man who was prominent in the public life of his city and who lived in an eminently respectable residential hotel, most of whose residents were wealthy enough to have considerable spare time on their hands. A good many of them were elderly widows and retired business couples.

Well, they had a normal, healthy curiosity about this prominent single gent until, one afternoon, someone saw an attractive woman enter his apartment. She was recognized as a prominent woman in town; she was known to be single, and she was engaged in the same sort of public work as the hero in the case.

By the time this woman had made her second or third visit, even though she came with a brief case of papers and sometimes brought a secretary with her, the entire hotel was agog. The idle snoopers and gossips set up an elaborate espionage system, with a member of the "secret service corps" constantly at a vantage point to keep the man's door "covered." They operated in relays, each "agent" giving so many hours to the watching job, and then turning it over to the next one.

Dr. Lawton says that what is most surprising about these otherwise well-behaved snoopers is that they brushed aside the moral aspects of the affair they suspected was going on. None of them ever indicated either approval or disapproval. Their attitude was one of sheer curiosity, impure and non-objective. Without even being aware of it, they wanted to capture every single salty detail, so that they could participate in what they hoped would prove to be a shocking adventure. And the fact that there was a perfectly sound and reasonable and innocent explanation for the woman's visits didn't hold them back one bit. In fact, they refused to recognize the reasonable and innocent explanation that these two were engaged upon some project requiring a typist and brief cases of papers. That sort of thing didn't interest them. Nothing less than a clandestine love affair could keep them happy.

The vast "peephole" and underground life of gossips and snoopers, both male and female, would be hilariously funny if it were not so cruel and destructive. It has probably accounted for more broken hearts and broken marriages and broken careers than poverty or illness ever did. And there's a lot more of it going on than we think, and, as a rule, it's almost always directed at innocent victims. The people who are actually doing something wrong are pretty smart about covering up their activities. A snooper doesn't stand a chance with them. But the rest of the world, the folks who have nothing to conceal, aren't afraid to leave their window shades up and to speak above a whisper, so of course they're the ones the snoopers go to work on. But if these snoopers were told to their faces that what they're actually doing is getting a sort of perverted thrill out of other people's business, I guess they wouldn't be so anxious to snoop.

A CREED FOR THE DISCOURAGED

I believe that God created me to enjoy the blessings of life, to be useful to my fellow beings, and an honor to my country.

I believe that the trials which beset me today are but the fiery tests by which my character is strengthened, ennobled, and made worthy to enjoy the higher things of life, which are in store for me.

I believe that my soul is too grand to be crushed by defeat; I will rise above it.

I believe that I am the architect of my own fate; therefore, I will be master of circumstances and surroundings, not their slave.

I will not yield to discouragements. I will trample them underfoot and make them serve as steppingstones to success. I will conquer my obstacles and turn them into opportunities.

My failures of today will help to guide me on to victory on the morrow. The morrow will bring new strength, new hopes, new opportunities, and new beginnings. I will be ready to meet it with a brave heart, a calm mind, and an undaunted spirit.

In all things I will do my best, and leave the rest to the Infinite. I will not waste my time in idle waiting; I will not waste my mental energies in useless worry. I will learn to dominate my restless thoughts and look on the bright side of things.

Anonymous

WISDOM FROM SOUTH OF THE BORDER

This is the instruction that the ancient Aztec fathers gave their sons who were about to enter adult life and take on adult responsibilities:

"Honor all who are older than you are. Never blame a man for making a mistake; you may be the next one to commit an error. If someone talks to you, listen to him attentively. Never walk directly in front of an older person if you can help it. At table, wait for your elders to begin. If you receive an expensive gift, don't brag about it, and if you receive a cheap gift, don't disregard the fact that, however humble it is, still someone wishes you well. Do not let wealth make you arrogant. Never tell lies. Do not indulge in slanderous gossip. Sow no enmities. If you are entrusted with an office, think it over first. Perhaps someone is trying to tempt you by it. Do not accept it too readily, even if you know you are the best-qualified candidate. Accept it only if they urge you—this gains you their esteem. By this advice, I try to fortify your heart. Your life's happiness depends upon it."

And here's what the Aztec mother said to her growing daughter:

"Never neglect your spinning and weaving, your sewing and your embroideries. Don't sleep too much and don't lie about on the shady grass. Don't be shy and sensitive; don't be idle. Never show that you dislike your tasks. If you cannot always fulfill your parents' wishes, explain why, and excuse yourself politely. Do not be proud of your face and figure, for the gods distribute their gifts according to their wisdom. Have no dealings with disorderly, untruthful, or idle women. Do not walk alone too much in the streets or the marketplaces. Such places cause your ruin. When you have finished your errands, return home at once. If you visit your relatives, show that you are useful, and pick up a bit of weaving or sewing as soon as you enter the house. That is enough to learn for one day, my daughter, but be sure you learn it well."

TONY'S TRAFFIC TIMER

I heard of a little yarn that struck me as kinda unusual. Seems that a guy named T. F. Roselle got caught in a traffic jam on one of the main streets in Atlanta, Georgia, a while back. I think this occurred around 1942. What happened was that Roselle started crossing the street on the green light, the light turned red while he was out there in the middle, and there he was with about as much chance for his life as a goldfish with Pussy prowling the room. As it happened, he didn't get hit, but it was kind of a near thing. I've been in the same spot myself, and I know how the guy felt.

That night at dinner he was telling the family what a close call he'd had, with the angels breathing on his neck, so to speak, and his son, T. F. Roselle, Jr., generally known as Tony, said that there sure ought to be some way a traffic signal could be rigged to give some indication of how much of the green light there was left for folks to get across the street.

Tony had always liked fooling around with tools, inventing things, so he tinkered for three months in his workshop and came out with a thing he called a "traffic clock." The idea was to have a half-moon dial, and a big hand climbing up it, showing motorists and pedestrians how long the light has been on and how long it has to go. When the light changes, the hand falls back to the bottom of the dial and starts climbing again.

Well, four of these traffic clocks were installed, right off, on one of the busiest corners in Atlanta and the traffic policemen said that conditions were much improved, which was putting it mildly. Now that everybody knew how much time there was left to cross the street, there weren't any more of those wild and scary and dangerous dashes to beat the light. And city-wide installation was being considered. Frankly, I dunno if this city-wide installation was ever carried out. I haven't been down in Atlanta for quite some time. All I can say is that Tony had quite an idea, and if it would work on a large scale a lot of lives would be saved and a lot of folks wouldn't turn gray so young.

But one of the most interesting things about the yarn is that when Tony invented the traffic clock he was just ten years old.

A DEFINITION OF A WELL-ADJUSTED PERSON

Here is a list of items which, taken on the whole, paints an ideal picture of a well-adjusted, emotionally grown-up individual with a mature outlook on life. I think you may get an idea out of this, although that noted psychologist, Dr. Lawton, says that most of us should feel real set up if we can pass muster on half of the items:

1. The well-adjusted person is able and willing to assume the responsibility appropriate to each age or period of life as he reaches it.

2. He participates with pleasure in the experiences that belong to each successive age level, neither anticipating those of a later period nor holding onto those of an earlier age.

3. Though he may object to a certain role or position in life, as long as he must fill it he willingly accepts the responsibilities and the experiences that pertain to this role or position.

4. He attacks problems that require solution instead of finding means to evade them.

5. He enjoys attacking and destroying obstacles to his development and happiness, once he has decided that they are real and not imaginary obstacles.

6. He can make important decisions with a minimum of worry, conflict, advice seeking, and other types of running-away behavior.

7. After making a choice, he abides by it, until new and important factors enter the picture.

8. He accepts the authority of reality; he finds the major satisfactions of life in accomplishments and experiences that take place in the real world and not in the realm of daydreams and make-believe.

9. His thinking is a blueprint for action, not a device for delaying or escaping it.

10. He draws lessons from his defeats instead of finding excuses for them.

11. He does not magnify his successes or extend their application from the field in which they originally occurred.

12. He knows how to work when working, and play when playing.

13. He is able to say no to situations that may provide temporary satisfaction but that, over a longer period, run counter to his best interests.

14. He is able to say yes to situations that are momentarily unpleasant but that will ultimately aid him.

15. He is able to show his anger directly when injured, not to brood and sulk, but to act in defense of his rights, with both indignation and action appropriate in kind and amount to the injury.

16. He is able to show his affection directly and to give evidence of it in acts that are fitting in amount and kind to its extent.

17. He can endure pain, especially emotional pain or frustration, whenever it is not in his power to alter the cause.

18. He has his habits and mental attitudes so well organized that he can quickly make essential compromises if necessary.

19. He is able to bring his energies together and concentrate them

effectively upon a single goal, once he has determined to achieve that goal.

20. He would not change, even if he could, the fact that life is an endless struggle. He knows, and makes use of the knowledge, that in this struggle the person who fights himself least will have the most strength and the best judgment left for the outside battle.

THE LEGENDS OF GLAMIS CASTLE

You know how people go week-ending with friends in the country, and when they get back Sunday night they're so worn out they gotta take two days off to get over the week end? I don't go much for that week-end stuff, but even if I did, there's one place I sure wouldn't accept an invitation to. And that's the historic old heap of stone in Scotland known as Glamis Castle.

Glamis Castle is considered the most haunted spot on earth by the authorities on ghost hunting. There's more funny stuff going on there than any other place they've looked into, and personally I wouldn't care to hang around the joint, even in the daytime. As far as I'm concerned, ghosts are in the same class as poison ivy. I happen to be one of those fortunate people who don't seem to get poisoned by poison ivy, but I don't go out and pick an armful and bring it into the parlor, either. I'm kinda careful about things like that. So I don't believe in ghosts but I ain't going out looking for any on a dark night, either. But, like everybody else, I'm a real sucker for a good spook yarn.

I was looking up some stuff on haunted castles the other day, and this Glamis Castle kinda stuck out as having more and better hants than any other place going. Glamis is the family castle and traditional home of the earls of Strathmore and the Lyon family, to which the present Queen of England is related. But how they stand it I dunno.

Let's start easy with some of the run-of-the-mill ghosts which have been reported, not once or twice but literally hundreds of times by people who live there—in an almost continuous state of nervous fright, I should imagine, although they seem to take the spooks more or less as a matter of course. I dunno what goes, in a deal like this; I'm just telling you what the books say.

Guests sleeping overnight at Glamis, especially if they are quartered in the older part of the castle, which dates back to the days of Julius

Caesar, say that they are awakened about four o'clock in the morning by a loud pounding and hammering just outside their window. They come to the conclusion that the Scots, being a thrifty and industrious people, have got the carpenters out at the crack of dawn putting up a scaffolding or something, and they roll over and put the pillow over their heads and try to sleep. At breakfast time, they comment on how early the carpenters start to work, and the owners of the castle just smile and say, oh, that's nothing. There was a Lady Glamis back in 1537 who was hanged for witchcraft and poisoning a couple of husbands, and what you heard is ghosts; every once in a while they build the scaffold and hang her all over again.

Then it seems that a very tall figure of a man clad in a coat of armor is often seen striding about the halls, and the family think that he's either the ghost of Malcolm II, an early Scottish king who was murdered in Glamis, or else he's Sir John Lyon, who died in a duel back in 1383. They ain't exactly sure which, and this tall gent in the tin suit ain't never told them. But it seems he don't do much harm; he's only good for leaning over folks in their sleep and waking them up and practically making them take leave of their senses, at that point. But he don't harm 'em none.

A while back there was an Earl of Glamis who was popularly known as "Beardie." Seems that Beardie had a very unattractive habit of lopping off people's heads if they disagreed with him in the slightest, and on account of this very few folks cared to associate with him. He was nuts about gambling, but he had a lot of trouble getting guys to play poker with him, because word got around that unless Beardie won the hand, you lost your head. So one night he's sitting there jiggling the cards and nobody will play, so he says something to the effect that, since nobody else will play with him, he wishes the Devil would. A stranger appears and the room gets full of fire and brimstone and to all intents and purposes Beardie has a terrible hand-to-hand fight with this stranger who, on getting the worst of it, vanishes into thin air. That's too much for even Beardie, and he has that room in the castle sealed off forever. But legend has it that every year, on that particular night, horrible noises of combat and the rough voice of old Beardie swearing blue murder can be heard coming out of the stone walls in that part of the castle where the sealed room is supposed to be. Incidentally, nobody has ever found this room, and all the space in the castle seems to be present and accounted for, but the legend and the noises and shouts keep right on going.

Then, to make things real cozy, you'll remember that Shakespeare's Macbeth was Thane of Glamis, Thane of Cawdor, and finally King of Scotland, and he had to ease Duncan off the Scottish throne before he could climb on it. What isn't too well known is that all that is historically correct, and Macbeth and his lady actually did murder King Duncan, right in Glamis Castle, and the deed is supposed to have been done in still another mystery room that can't be located, though why anybody should want to locate it I wouldn't know. But every generation of the Lyon family takes its turn tapping walls and taking up boards looking for it.

They've got a lot more ghosts wandering around, including the figure of an attractive young Bedelia who is supposed to lie on a sofa in a dead faint while her gentleman friend comes in, selects a dagger from the collection on the wall, and stabs her, whereupon they both vanish into thin air, and the dagger is left quivering in the sofa as evidence. They've got the figure of a man who walks barefoot, surrounded by a ghastly blue light; that's supposed to be a farmer that that unpleasant Beardie character hanged back in the fifteenth century. Beardie, of course, does his bit in the general haunting, and there was another Lord Glamis who locked up a whole family named Ogilvie in the attic, if you can say a castle has an attic, and left them to starve to death. He and his victims just rattle chains and howl, though; nobody sees them. And to top it off, some of the boys who mess around with this ghost-hunting stuff have unearthed a legend to the effect that because of an ancient curse, every once in a while a vampire is born into the Lyon family, and a vampire is a very uncomfortable sort of critter to have for a cousin.

No, that's one place I ain't going for any week ends. Not now and not never. Maybe there's nothing to it, and maybe there is. But as far as I'm concerned there's no future in hanging around to find out. The reputation of a place like that could get a nice quiet guy's imagination so riled up that he'd be seeing things before he got inside the door.

GETTING ALONG WITH THE REST OF US

It's just human nature to want to feel important. Maybe you know some old buzzard who acts like he was weaned on a pickle, and you say to

279

yourself, Well, he sure don't care what other people think of him, or he wouldn't act the way he does! But the funny part of it is, he does care. And that's why he acts that way. Somewhere back along the line, maybe when he was just a baby, he was made to feel that nobody liked him or wanted him, and that he didn't count for much. So he built up this reputation of being a sourpuss, a real important sourpuss, one that you remember. It's his way of making himself important. He actually wants to be liked and thought well of, just as much as anybody, only he goes at it inside out.

Dr. Karl S. Bernhardt, who's a professor of psychology up at the University of Toronto, worked out a pretty good set of rules for getting along well with other people, and it's practically guaranteed to make you a well-liked person, even if folks take one look and run when they see you coming as of now. Of course, they don't, but let's see how this works out in your case anyhow.

First; one over-all rule: remember that you're most successful in your social contacts when you make the other fellow feel that he's the important one, and you're least successful when you blow your own horn and elbow everybody else out of the spotlight. Now for Dr. Bernhardt's eleven rules:

1. Be genuinely interested in other people. Without a sincere interest in others, it is impossible to get along very effectively with them. Effective social relationships are based on mutual liking and respect, and liking and respect are only possible between those who have an interest in one another.

2. Avoid creating a feeling of inferiority. Try to put the other person on an equal level with yourself, or on a higher level. If, even temporarily, we can forget our desire for importance, and if we can allow the other party the lion's share, we succeed in getting along with him.

3. Make use of sincere appreciation. We're usually too stingy with our words of praise, mostly because we're too busy listening for somebody to say something nice about us. Let's never resort to hollow flattery, but if the next guy does something as good or better than we can, let's be sincere in telling him so.

4. Eliminate criticism and disapproval. Criticism is usually not only unnecessary but totally unwanted. And it's wasted effort, because even if it's justified, it's invariably resented, and nobody can profit by what he resents.

5. Let the other fellow correct his own errors. Don't be one of those eager beavers who has to show him how to hold his tools or his

280

golf clubs; don't suggest that this or that cake recipe is better, or that Suzybelle is going to the wrong dancing teacher. It's none of your business, and it always sets up a faintly unpleasant feeling toward you and your great wisdom, even if you're right, which like as not you aren't. Don't be a chronic mistake correcter.

6. Never try openly to make other people over. Nobody likes to feel that he needs to be reformed. And don't ever marry anybody to "reform" them. A little undercover urging in the right direction won't hurt, though it probably won't do much good, either. But don't ever come right out and start a remodeling job. You'll get nothing but heartaches.

7. Cultivate the habit of sympathy. By "sympathy" we mean "feeling with the other person." Imagine how the other fellow feels, and try to feel the same way. That way you'll never make anyone resentful or hurt.

8. Cultivate the habit of tolerance, and appreciate the other person, whether or not his religious and political views are the same as your own, and whether or not he happens to be of the same race, nationality, or economic status. Tolerance does not mean adopting the beliefs and opinions of others; it means accepting them at their face value, just as we accept the fact that some people live in brick houses and some like stucco or frame better.

9. Remember that all people are different. What works with one won't work with another. We must respect each other's interests and not think there is something peculiar about other people because they happen to like something different from what we like.

10. Check first impressions. It's possible to take a violent dislike to some perfectly grand person just because the color of his hair or the way he wears his necktie reminds us of someone whom we had cause to dislike, long ago. Try to reserve judgment until we really know a new acquaintance. Look for and find some good point in every new person you meet, but, on the other hand, don't go overboard in one of those temporary enthusiasms that are painful memories later on.

11. Think of giving more than of getting. It's all too easy to slip into the habit of looking for personal advantage in our relationships with others. If we keep our minds on what we can contribute, rather than what we'll get out of a friendship, our rewards will be more than we could ever hope for! Just from a selfish point of view, we'll reap a far greater harvest in the long run if we give richly to start with.

WHY DON'T YOU TRY . . .

To live—be loved and to love mankind—
To smile when things may hurt you most—
To speak no word of scorn of men—
To praise all good but never boast.
To listen another's story through—
To measure faults with liberal rule—
To never say, "I told you so,"
Or judge the other man a fool—
To say the things you'd like to hear—
Remembering that praise is sweet to measure,
That deeds, like doves, return to roost,
That a friend is life's most hallowed treasure.

Anonymous

WHAT IS REAL YOUTH?

Here's a little thing I clipped out of a paper so many years ago that I can't even remember what it was published in, except that I know it was written by that famous author, Mr. Anonymous. I think you'll kinda like this. It's called: "What Is Real Youth?"

"Youth is not a time of life—it is a state of mind. It is not a matter of ripe cheeks, red lips and supple knees; it is a temper of the will, a quality of the imagination, a vigor of the emotions; it is a freshness of the deep springs of life.

"Youth means a temperamental predominance of courage over timidity, of the appetite of adventure over the love of ease. This often exists in a man of fifty, more than in a boy of twenty. Nobody grows old by merely living a number of years; people grow old only by deserting the ideals.

"Years wrinkle the skin, but to give up enthusiasm wrinkles the soul.

"Worry, doubt, self-distrust, fear and despair—these are the long, long years that bow the head and turn the growing spirit back to dust.

"Whether seventy or sixteen, there is in every being's heart the awe of wonder, the sweet amazement at the stars and the starlike things and thoughts, the undaunted challenge of events, the unfailing childlike appetite for what-next, and the joy in the game of life.

"You are as young as your faith, as old as your doubts; as young as your self-confidence, as old as your fear; as young as your hope, as old as your despair.

"In the central place of your heart there is a wireless station; so long as it receives messages of beauty, hope, cheer, grandeur, courage and power from the earth, from men and the Infinite, so long are you young. When the wires are all down and all the central place of your heart is covered with the snows of pessimism, the ice of cynicism, then are you grown old indeed and may God have mercy on your soul."

ISRAEL

Out of the roaring fray
A nation was born today
Nurtured on blood and tears
Oppressed for so many years.

Never again to know
The homeless wanderer's woe,
Israel . . . reign supreme!
You are a people's dream!

Thus ends the endless quest,
The harrying east and west.
No more does he have to roam.
The wandering Jew is home!

Nick Kenny

THE PERFECT HOME

There was a man who was rich, and he married a wife who was rich. And they builded them a Beautiful House. And they invited me and Keturah to come and dine with them and see the new home. Now this was in the days when our children were small, and we had a houseful of them. And Keturah got the baby to bed, and told the older children to take care of the younger ones, and be good to each other, and be sure and wash their hands and faces before they went to bed.

And we sat at meat at the rich man's table. And it was Some Dinner.

And we saw the New House, and it was beautiful. And they took us to the Nursery, where an Hired Nurse kept the children while the rich man's wife wrote addresses on Child Study. And it was all very fine.

And when we got home, before we sat down, we took a Ball and Mitt out of one chair and a Doll out of another, and there were skates hanging to the back of another chair and School Books in another.

For we had no Hired Nurse, neither did Keturah write addresses on Child Study.

And I said unto Keturah, "We have seen a Perfect Home."

And she said, "I do not think so."

And I said, "I did not refer to the home of our friends, but to this one."

And she said, "O my Lord, I know not a thing about Child Study. I know only that I love my children. And I cannot keep my house looking like a Palace, for I will not make it a Penal Institution for mine offspring. I just do the best I can."

And I went into my Study, and behold, the white wall bore the marks of little hands where the children climbed to where their father wrought. And in various other parts of the house there was evidence of children.

And they were the happiest, noisiest, hungriest children in town. And we looked at them as they lay asleep, and thanked God for them.

And I said, "O Keturah, God might have kept this world free from all scratches and finger marks and have lived in isolation and written books about Child Study without my children, or with children trained by angels in a kindergarten in the Moon. But He hath permitted this system of Rough House which prevaileth on this distracted Planet because it is better to have chairs with skates and balls and mitts, and walls with scratches and finger marks, in order to have a perfect world. For in the sight of God a world unmarred doth not appear so perfect as one in which God's children scratch the furniture, but learn to glorify God and enjoy Him forever."

HOW NOT TO BE POPULAR

The other day I was going through a file of real old magazines, and I ran across a little item called *The Dining Room Magazine*, date, September 1877; seventy-two years ago. And, like in the magazines you find now on the newsstands, back then they had all kinds of little hints about keeping a nice home, and making yourself popular, and how to be charming, and even how to catch a man. Some of them were real frank on the subject. In those days they wouldn't publish a picture of a lady's stocking or any part of what were considered "unmentionable" garments, but they sure were outspoken on dropping hints as to how to charm the male critter into submission.

However, the piece that kinda intrigued me in this old magazine wasn't about that at all. It was a set of things to do if you want your friends to need ya like they need a hole in the head. And I think it's kinda cute. Here goes: as of seventy-two years ago:

"Always come whenever possible on washing day, even though an ironing day will suit your purpose just as well.

"Endeavor to drop in just before mealtime, and stay on any pretext until the bell rings, when it is very probable you will be asked to sit down at table, no matter how inconvenient it is to the family.

"Be sure and report all the unpleasant things that the neighbors have said, of course in the smoothest and most disinterested manner, which will not lessen the effect of the scandal in the least.

"Do not fail to notice any defects in the house, the furniture, or surroundings, and draw unfavorable comparisons between them and the neighbors' home arrangements.

"Give a detailed description of Mrs. Smith's or Miss Brown's parlor ornaments, especially if new, and remark how much finer they are than those around you.

"If your child has the whooping cough, of course don't mention the fact until the child has played with your host's children for half an hour, and then insist on their kissing each other at parting.

"Act with charity toward none and malice toward all, then go and wonder why people don't seem cordial or ask you to call again."

MONGOOSES

When I was a kid I used to get a lot of joy and satisfaction out of reading about Jack the Giant Killer, maybe because I was such a little shaver and I got my share of being kicked around, from the big fellows in our block. Little Jack polishing off that great big old giant boosted up my ego no end, just as it has the egos of thousands and thousands of kids.

And then, when I was a little older, I read Kipling's *Jungle Books,* and there I found the Jack the Giant Killer of the animal kingdom, the mischievous little mongoose who took care of the villain of the piece, Nag the King Cobra, in no time flat. The name of that mongoose was Rikki-Tikki-Tavi, and when I thought what it would be like to have Rikki-Tikki-Tavi for a pet—well, Old Dog Tray and the pussycat just had to take a back seat, that's all. They couldn't do nuthin', compared to him.

I also used to wonder whether the plural of "mongoose" wouldn't be "mongeese," and where the "mongander" was—nobody ever talked about *him.* And I remember an old movie of a fight between a mongoose and a cobra that was one of the most fascinating and terrifying things I've ever seen. Both the cobra and I had cold chills up the spine before it was over, only the cobra's chills were permanent. He didn't have no future, no more.

Well, that movie about the mongoose and the cobra wasn't so special after all. That sort of thing goes on every day, in India and Burma and southern China. Mongooses just naturally don't like snakes, except to make a meal out of, and they go for them every time. A mongoose a foot long can kill, and eat, a seven-foot snake, and not even feel a little tired afterwards.

The mongoose doesn't seem to have any close cousins in the animal world; the naturalists seem to think he's an offshoot of some special animal family, all the other members of which are extinct. He's kind of a cute-looking little guy; he can sit up pretty as a squirrel and he can flatten out and go faster than a streak of greased lightning. He can dig like a badger and he can wiggle his toes like a monkey, which is more than humans can do. Toe wiggling among humans is no great shakes, maybe because we've had our feet in shoes for so many generations.

There are a lot of different kinds of mongooses. There's the crab-eating mongoose; he's the biggest one, as he gets to be maybe two feet long, and he goes in for crab salad, with or without mayonnaise, I wouldn't know. There's the stripe-necked mongoose and the water mongoose, who works on frogs, and the Javan mongoose, and a few others. There's even one small variety who lives in Spain, and how he got there nobody knows, because outside of the Far East he's the only one, and it's a long hike from Spain to India.

Now, you'd think that since snakes, especially poisonous snakes like cobras, are the favorite diet of mongooses, some bright boy would think of importing a few of the little critters to clean up the copperheads and moccasins and rattlesnakes and other undesirable customers we've got in this country. But that don't work. That's been tried out, and it's strictly a no-good idea.

The reason is that a mongoose would a lot rather suck eggs than fight snakes, if he has any choice in the matter, and once he's gotten loose in a henyard and found out how to get a living the easy way, he isn't inclined to go back to killing snakes very soon. And you can't keep a mongoose out of anything. He burrows under fences, gnaws through things you'd think were ungnawable . . . and he himself is practically indestructible. Let a flock of mongooses loose on the countryside, and the poultry farmers would go out of business, but quick.

Just the same, I've got kind of a sneaking affection for the little fellow, the ferocious little giant killer who can take on a seven-foot snake and think nothing of it. It boosts my ego up.

HOW TO TEST YOUR OWN PREJUDICES

Any of you who have been in on these little chizzy-chats from time to time know that I can get just a little roiled up on the subject of race and religious prejudice. That's a subject I've got very definite ideas on —in fact, just one idea—I'm agin it. And when a new books comes out dealing with the subject of prejudice, I'll take off a couple of hours to find out what the boys are saying now.

Well, the other day I found a book called *Glass House of Prejudice*, by Dr. Dorothy W. Baruch, who is a consulting psychologist and specialist in intercultural relations, and has lectured all over this country and most of Europe on her pet subject, how to dispose of race hatreds. She's real well known for another book, *You, Your Children and War* which received the *Parents' Magazine* Gold Medal back in 1942. Personally, I like this new volume, *Glass House of Prejudice*. It's a hard-hitting book, and not recommended for light and amusing reading, because she names facts and figures, and some of the incidents of prejudice she tells about, right here in this country, maybe in your town and in the school your kid goes to, would kinda make the hackles rise on the back of your neck.

Dr. Baruch says that, no matter how tolerant and broad-minded we may think we are about our relations with peoples of other races and religions, we still have to do some powerful soul-searching and ask ourselves some pretty sharp questions before we can be absolutely sure that we have clean hands when it comes to the prejudice business. Here are some of the questions she suggests that we ask ourselves:

1. Am I conscious of being prejudiced against any particular group of people? Do I avoid sitting next to them on public conveyances? Do I have them come to my home, and do I go to their homes? Do I count any of them among my friends, and, if so, do I act patronizing toward them?

2. Do I dislike any particular persons individually among the minority groups, or, if I belong to a minority group myself, do I dislike particular persons among the majority groups? If so, why do I dislike this individual? Is it because of unpleasant qualities loosely associated with the group to which he belongs?

3. Do I realize that troubles in my own life, past or present, can set up a chain of resentments which eventually crop out as prejudice?

4. Do I realize that facing such feelings and conquering them can help me, as an individual, to become not only a more effective person but also a less prejudiced one?

5. Do I still tighten up inside over things that bothered me as a child, made me feel misunderstood, unloved, unworthy, or inferior?

6. What is my first and most ready reaction today when I am bothered and in trouble? Do I feel hostile, and, if so, do I feel hostile toward some specific racial group or toward an individual in that group?

7. What am I doing, right now, to handle my present troubles? What am I doing to handle the resentments and hostilities which remain after the troubles have been taken care of?

8. Am I doing anything at all, any specific thing, to add to decent and cohesive relations between racial and religious groups? Do I study the available and well-founded scientific information which proves that catch-phrase name-calling of various races is baseless? Do I do anything in my own community to improve minority problems?

9. Am I honestly trying to make new friends among various groups, and to *feel with* them instead of merely observing their (to me) curious customs?

10. What am I doing to see that my own need for love and affection is met? Am I openhearted to others? Do I show others that I appreciate them? Have I found some degree of pleasure and beauty and warmth in my own life? Am I square with my own conscience?

288

Dr. Baruch says we have to ask ourselves these questions because a happy person, a person without resentment, a person who feels that life has dealt him a pretty good hand after all, is invariably a person free from prejudice. And the guy with the chip on his shoulder, the guy who gets up in the morning looking as if he'd been weaned on a pickle, and goes through the day grumpy and barking at everybody, and then comes home and kicks the cat and takes a whap at Junior—well, he's the boy with the prejudices. Maybe he don't even know what's the matter with him. But until he finds out why he's got this sour attitude toward the rest of the world, and why he thinks everybody is agin him and he always gets the dirty end of the stick and so forth, he continues to be a very dangerous guy as far as the people he associates with are concerned, because he for no reason at all will take a violent dislike to somebody and if that somebody happens to be a member of some racial or religious group different from his own, or if the somebody's ancestors belonged to such a group, why then this guy with a chip on his shoulder promptly transfers his whole unreasonable dislike to that whole group, and starts up his own little campaign to discredit that group in his community. And right there, in a nutshell, is the way prejudice gets started in the first place, because some guy has a mad on with the world and not enough self-control or knowledge of his own emotions to work it out chopping wood or hitting a golf ball or working crossword puzzles. He takes it out on some perfectly innocent character that he's always been kinda leery about anyhow because this character has an accent or celebrates his Sunday on Saturday or has a different color to his skin.

The minority problems in your own community are the problems of the majority in your community, just as the minority problems of a nation have to be solved by the majority of the nation. You know that old saw about how one bad apple spoils the whole barrel? Well, the bad apple in your neck of the woods ain't that foreign family living down at the end of the road; it's the guy in your community who starts saying, "What are they doing here? How dare they move in and live with us and take the bread out of our mouths and send their kids to our school and snag off that job my shiftless cousin Hank fell down on?" That's the kind of bad apple that spoils the barrel—and no mistake. And there's an awful lot of that stuff going on, right here today; more than you'd ever guess unless you start studying the subject. Nevertheless, there are folks in there pitching to scrub away the ugly stains of prejudice, and maybe someday we'll make it, if we keep trying.

TWO BITS

I was kinda surprised to learn the origin of our expression "two bits," "four bits," "six bits," and so forth. I guess it stops there; can't say as how I ever heard of anybody saying "eight bits." And for some reason we never say "one bit" or three or five or seven bits, but we could, and make sense, supposing we wanted to. Here's how the thing works:

Back when pieces of eight, those old Spanish coins so dear to the hearts of pirates, was in wide circulation—and, as a matter of fact, it was perfectly good legal tender right here in our own country—a piece of eight was a coin equal in value to our dollar. Contrary to the general idea nowadays, a piece of eight was not made of solid gold. It was an alloy with a yellow sheen like gold, and it was called in Spanish *peso duro*, which means hard dollar, to distinguish it from a true gold coin, because gold is a soft metal and this alloy was hard. And it was called a piece of eight because it was grooved in eight sections, like a pie is sometimes marked off in eight pieces before cutting, and when you wanted to make change with the thing you broke off one or more of these sections and they worked just like small change. The sections were called "bits": the whole coin was "eight bits" and a quarter of it, two sections, which was twenty-five cents in our money, was called two bits. Half, or fifty cents, was four bits; three quarters, or seventy-five cents, was six bits. And though we haven't had pieces of eight floating around for maybe a hundred and fifty years or more, the terms still stick.

It's kinda interesting, how we'll go along for dog's years using a term like "two bits" without ever knowing where it came from. The study of words is more than fascinating. At least, it fascinates me, and I kinda thought this would interest you too.

HOW TO WARM UP TO YOUR WORK

It's a good idea to make haste slowly, when pitching into a hard job. Maybe it's okay for kids to go zooming out of bed like Superman in a high breeze, and snap into it with every bone and muscle and nerve fiber, but if you're anywhere upwards of the age of sweet sixteen, it won't hurt a mite to sit down and consider the situation before you start hitting on all eight cylinders.

About ten years ago Dr. David Seabury, whose books on popular psychology you've probably read, put out a little volume called *How to Get Things Done*, along with another psychology expert, Dr. Alfred Uhler. I've picked a few sentences out of this book, thinking that you might get some use out of them. The general theme is: Warm Up to Your Work.

"After you've been idle, it takes time to warm up. That's true of your car and your radio. (Why not you?) After a vacation, start on routine tasks. Attend to details. Sort things out. Then you will find yourself in full swing again.

"First, select what you will do. Cease looking for the perfect opening . . . start on the first part of it that you touch. Promptness is a habit, built on the art of beginning where you are, and with what you know.

"Few people know what to do first; fewer still do it. If you give yourself to your task at once, you won't have to do it twice.

"Common sense begins with a sense of time. In every life there should be thinking times and doing times.

"When your mind wanders so that your first thought isn't on your job, take a couple of minutes out . . . and find out what you were vaguely thinking about. Then say 'Now that's done!' Expect yourself to attend to business after that, and you will. Momentum in effort is a gift from the great god Keep-at-it."

THE WILLOW TREE

Here's a romantic little yarn that has kind of an odd twist to it.

Seems that back in the days before the American Revolution, a man named Jonathan Arnold, who was the founder of the town of St. Johnsbury in the colony of Vermont, went south to Connecticut to find himself a wife. Well, he found a girl that suited him, and married her, and on the journey back to St. Johnsbury the couple stopped off overnight at the home of a family named Ladd, who lived in Haverhill, Connecticut.

Next morning, before starting out, young Mrs. Arnold picked an armful of pussy willows which she found growing along the Connecticut River, and after she'd gone, Samuel Ladd, the son of the family she'd stopped with, picked up a willow switch she'd dropped by the doorway, and planted it out in front of the Ladd house.

Well, that was all there was to it. The Arnolds rode away to St. Johnsbury and set up housekeeping and were very happy. And then Jonathan Arnold suddenly died, three years later, and within a few months Samuel Ladd was courting the young widow and after a while she accepted him and they were married.

And here's where the odd part comes in. As the newlyweds drove up to the Ladd home, Samuel pointed to the willow switch, now a thriving bush. And he told her the old wives' tale peculiar to that township of Connecticut in the early days: that if a twig was left in a doorway by some bride in passing, some man living in that particular house would be her second husband. In the case of young Widder Arnold, it sure worked out.

GOOD-WILL RESOLUTIONS

Here's a list of Good-will Resolutions which were drawn up back in 1940 for use during Brotherhood Week. And, though Brotherhood Week may be a good many months off, there's no reason why we shouldn't give these good-will resolutions a once over lightly, any old week in the year.

1. I will repudiate the idea that those who disagree with me are not good Americans.

2. I will not allow racial or religious differences to determine my vote.

3. I will appreciate what others than my own group have done to make America great.

4. I will try to understand the background of those of other religious loyalties.

5. I will help to create national respect and trust between members of different religious and racial groups.

6. I will co-operate heartily with those of other faiths in work for the common good.

7. I will always protest when those of other faiths are defamed.

8. I will not be misled by false doctrines of race, nor claim superiority to others on the ground of race alone.

9. I will apply the Golden Rule to those of all races and religions and treat them as I should like to be treated.

10. I will pray for those of other faiths than my own, and prize their prayers for myself.

THE DOLLAR AND THE CENT

A big silver dollar and a little brown cent,
Rolling along together they went.
Rolling along the smooth sidewalk.
When the dollar remarked—for money can talk:
"You poor little cent, you cheap little mite,
I'm bigger than you and I'm twice as bright;
I'm worth your kind a hundredfold,
And written on me in letters bold
Is the motto drawn from the pious creed,
In God We Trust, for all to read."
"Yes, I know," said the cent, "I'm a cheap little mite,
And I know I'm not big, nor worth much, nor bright,
And yet," said the cent, with a meek little sigh,
"You don't go to church as often as I."

TEN BUSINESS COMMANDMENTS

The other day I ran across a set of ten commandments for business men, or business women, that I think kinda covers the ground. You may like this for yourself, or you may want to pass it along to some friend in the business world.

1. Don't wait for the other fellow to come to you. Go to him.

2. In competition with others, always give them the credit of being a little smarter than you are. Then work like the dickens to prove that they aren't.

3. If you have no money and little credit, capitalize on your per-

sonality. Don't be "slick," but remember that sometimes it pays to have nerve.

4. Never admit to anybody—and least of all to yourself—that you are licked.

5. Keep your business troubles to yourself. Nobody likes a calamity howler; besides, he finds scant favor with bankers.

6. Don't be afraid of dreaming too big dreams. It won't hurt you to figure on owning a railroad, even if you have to compromise on owning a trailer.

7. Make friends; but remember that the best of friends will wear out if you use them too frequently.

8. Be square, even to the point of finickiness, and you will have mighty little occasion to complain of a crooked world.

9. Take advice but do your own deciding.

10. Don't toady. The world respects the man who stands up on his hind legs and looks it in the eye.

Now, I don't know who thought up that set of ten commandments for the business man or woman, but it seems pretty sound to me. Of course, you could add a lot of other rules, too, but anyhow that seems a start in the right direction.

WORK NEVER KILLED ANYBODY

Here's a little statement about work which I like real well. It was made a number of years ago by Stewart Browne, at that time the president of the United States Real Estate Owners' Association, and I guess it's safe to assume that Mr. Browne knew what he was talking about. I think it's a real neat little set of remarks on the subject of work in general. So here goes:

Work never killed anybody, nor made any criminals.
Man was made to work.
All his bones and muscles were made to work.
Work produces good health.
Lack of work makes people lazy and lazy people don't enjoy good health.
All the great industrial fortunes have been made by work.

Now, maybe I wouldn't have paid so much attention to that statement; maybe I would have found it kinda grim and humorless, if I hadn't just been dipping into a few real sound books on psychology that point out that laziness and boredom cause more ailments to the human mind and body than just about everything else put together. Enforced, hopeless idleness can break a man's spirit quicker than anything else. The one qualification I'd add to Mr. Browne's statement is that work, to be healthy, must be interesting. Granted that the idle man does not enjoy good health, neither does the workman who takes no interest in his job, who makes one mechanical motion over and over without the faintest idea why he's doing it or how his part fits into the finished product. But there's no better way to stay healthy than to get work that you understand and take an interest in, and in which there's a chance of advancement.

A PRAYER FOR THANKSGIVING

We thank Thee for the joy of common things:
    The laughter of a child, the vagrant grace
Of water, the great wind that beats its wings,
    The sudden light that shines upon a face.

We thank Thee for the heavens that declare
    Thy love, and the abundant earth no less;
We thank Thee for the bread we eat and share
    From hearts that overflow with thankfulness.

We thank Thee that when we grow puffed with pride
    And blurt out wild and foolish blasphemies,
The gentler angels of our nature chide,
    And Thy forgiveness brings us to our knees.

Against the voices counseling despair
    We thank Thee for the clarions of youth,
For humbleness that turns to Thee in prayer,
    For courage that is not afraid of truth.

O Lord, we thank Thee (when no man is sleeping,
    But watches, nor dares he draw quiet breath)
That kenneled and confided to our keeping,
    We guard the dreadful atom brood of death.

We thank Thee that man's spirit need not falter,
  That Faith still fights the good and gallant fight,
That still the torches on the anxious altar
  Of Freedom, though they flicker, burn as bright.

For strength for this day's huge and harsh demanding
  We thank Thee, Lord; for patience yet to find
A brave new hope, a brave new understanding
  In the vast commonwealth of heart and mind.

Lord, from the blind abyss of circumstance
  Whither, by war's grim folly, we were hurled,
We thank Thee for a final golden chance
  To rise again and build a nobler world.

                          Joseph Auslander

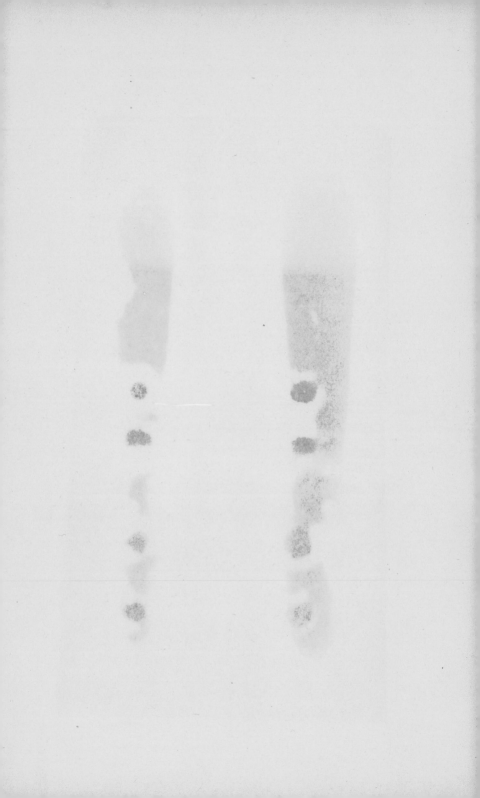

103777

AC
8
.D77

Drake, Galen.
        This is Galen
    Drake.

DATE DUE